Loving Trust

By the same authors

The Handbook of Estate Planning
Incorporating Your Talents
Creating a Loving Trust Practice
A Loving Trust Compendium

ROBERT A. ESPERTI
and
RENNO L. PETERSON

LOVING TRUST

The Right Way to
Provide for Yourself and
Guarantee the Future
of Your Loved Ones

VIKING

VIKING

Published by the Penguin Group
Viking Penguin Inc., 40 West 23rd Street,
New York, New York 10010, U.S.A.
Penguin Books Ltd, 27 Wrights Lane, London W8 5TZ, England
Penguin Books Australia Ltd, Ringwood,
Victoria, Australia
Penguin Books Canada Limited, 2801 John Street,
Markham, Ontario, Canada L3R 1B4
Penguin Books (N.Z.) Ltd, 182–190 Wairau Road,
Auckland 10, New Zealand

Penguin Books Ltd, Registered Offices:
Harmondsworth, Middlesex, England

First published in 1988 by Viking Penguin Inc.
Published simultaneously in Canada

LIBRARY OF CONGRESS CATALOGING IN PUBLICATION DATA
Esperti, Robert A.
Loving trust.
Includes index.
1. Living trusts—United States—Popular works.
2. Estate planning—United States—Popular works.
I. Peterson, Renno L.   II. Title.
KF734.Z9E87   1988   346.7305′2   87-40321
ISBN 0-670-81881-X   347.30652

Printed in the United States of America

Set in Baskerville

For the joys of our lives:
Our wives, Liz and Karen,
and our sons, Rob, James, Andy and Eric,
With Loving Trust

God hath not given us the spirit of fear;
but of power, and of love,
and of a sound mind.
2 Tim. 1:7

Preface
Loving Trust—
For Richer or for Poorer

In sharing our Loving Trust knowledge in the classroom with our professional colleagues—lawyers, accountants, life insurance agents—we have often heard, " 'Loving Trust' is a wonderful concept, but I don't have that many wealthy clients." This response is exasperating, because Loving Trust planning is for almost everyone, rich or not.

If you have life insurance, your family needs Loving Trust protection. If your employer provides you with retirement benefits or disability insurance, or if you own your home or other assets, you and your family need Loving Trust protection.

We all need to be good stewards of whatever we have; that's where Loving Trust planning comes in. It is planning for ourselves and our loved ones that can grow and change with us throughout our lives.

Ninety-seven percent of us will not pay a dime of federal death tax, yet many of us will become disabled, and all of us will die; we will leave loved ones behind. We all want our life insurance and our other possessions—regardless of how modest or grand they may be—to be used to care for our loved ones, just as we would have done if we were there.

In our law practice, we routinely helped our clients with their Loving Trust plans. Our Loving Trust clients came from all walks of life. They were schoolteachers, office workers, salespeople, waiters, and small-business owners; they were executives, tradespeople, professional athletes, retired couples, and tycoons. Our Loving Trust clients were single and married; many were parents and grandparents, others had no children. No matter what their race, economic background, or religion, they all had one common trait: They were people who cared enough about themselves and their loved ones to create Loving Trusts.

If you have little ones, teenagers, or mature children, your Loving Trust will convey your love and guiding hand. If you love your spouse, your Loving Trust will carry your marital vows beyond "Till death us do part." If your dreams include charitable giving, your Loving Trust will help those dreams come true.

Your Loving Trust will allow you to give what you have to whom you want, when and in the way you want; to plan for yourself in your mature years or in case you become infirm; to provide joy to your children and grandchildren alike. It will save legal costs and, if necessary, federal death tax.

We are often asked, "At what age should I start my Loving Trust planning?" Our reply is, "If you have loved ones and insurance or other property, there is no better time than now!"

Acknowledgments

Many people have made this book possible. Our thanks go to:

Our many clients who shared their loving desires in teaching us how to practice with Loving Trust.

Byron Walter, Dick Heiss, and Bates Feuell at the Manufacturer's National Bank of Detroit, and Bernie Hart at the United Bank of Denver, for their guidance.

Frank Elrod, for teaching us that loving and professionalism go hand in hand.

Don Thomas, Jim Buchanan, Bob Meyer, Bill Schmidt, and Arnie Guttenberg, our colleagues who have helped us along the way.

Bob Purcifull, who believed in our dreams.

Otto Belser, Jim Smith, and Jim Groen, for their love and friendship.

Peter Lampack for his patience.

And, to the memory of Arnie Alperstein, a great and loving lawyer.

Contents

PART ONE

Why You Need a Loving Trust

1

Shattering Will-Myths

A financial planner friend of ours believes that the myths surrounding wills ought to be shattered. He asks each of his clients, "Do you have a will?" and if the answer is a proud "yes," his response is a very sympathetic, "I'm sorry." We're sorry, too, because wills are expensive, mostly misleading documents that often create false expectations, which are only discovered at the death of their makers.

Most people have the mistaken belief that by making a will they are prudently fulfilling their duty to those they love. They walk around with a comfortable feeling, believing their loved ones to be safe and secure, assured that if something happens to them all will be taken care of. Nothing could be further from the truth.

We have given presentations to lawyers, accountants, financial planners, and life insurance professionals all over the country. In each of our seminars, we start by shattering the commonly held will-myths. Wills are obsolete. They are antiquated holdovers from a bygone era. They are expensive and often result in thwarting the very purposes for which they were made.

Your Will Doesn't Provide for You

Your will does absolutely nothing for *you*. You have to die to make it live. What good is your will if you become disabled because of accident, illness, or old age? Insurance company underwriters will tell you that you have a greater probability of suffering at least one long-term disability before you die than you do of dying without having an intervening disability. Your will is no good to you or your loved ones if you become disabled.

Your Will Doesn't Provide for Your Loved Ones

Wills are supposed to allow you to leave your property to loved ones efficiently. They seldom do. An overwhelming majority of the wills we see say the same thing. If you are married, it says, "I leave everything I have to my spouse when I die. If my spouse is deceased, then I leave everything to my children, in equal shares." If you are single, your will may leave all your property outright to children, grandchildren, or others.

Leaving property outright to loved ones through a will is like pouring a pitcher of water into cupped palms to take a drink. Most of the water falls on the floor, except for a few drops that you may be able to sip or lick off your fingers. Most of it disappears before it can be properly used.

Your Will Takes Your Family Public

Wills guarantee probate. It never ceases to amaze us how many people think that if they have a will their property will avoid probate when just the opposite is the case.

Probate is a public process. All your family and personal records are available to public scrutiny anytime anyone wants to take a look. What property you own, whom you owe, whom you leave your property to—all are part of the probate court's public record.

Probate is time-consuming and expensive. Lawyers make a lot of money probating will-created estates. They collect their fees from each estate's property and money. Lawyers, by law, are the primary creditors of every estate. They will be paid first. Taxes, other creditors, and your loved ones will be paid—in that order—but only after the lawyer is paid.

You cannot properly provide for your loved ones if you expose them to the probate process.

Your Will May Not Work

The term "simple will" is a misnomer. There is no such thing. Whether a will is one page or one hundred pages, it is fraught with complex legal rules, almost all of which have been around for close to five hundred years.

If you don't sign your will exactly as the rules of your state dictate, it may be worthless. There are many rules and requirements to fulfill in order to make a will valid. Disgruntled and greedy heirs find it easy to go to court to take shots at getting a larger inheritance. These "will contests" are a frequent occurrence in the probate courts. Probate courts are a perfect place for lawsuits. Add an unhappy heir to the complexity of signing a will, and you have all the ingredients for a will contest. Who loses? Your loved ones or those greedy heirs. Who wins? The lawyers do for sure.

If your will can't be found at your death, obviously the entire exercise will have been worthless. If you sign more than one will—duplicate originals—and all of them cannot be found on your death, the exercise again will have been worthless. A good many people think that if one will is good, lots of them are better. Howard Hughes evidently thought that. His estate is still being litigated because of the many wills he allegedly left.

Try moving from one state to another with your will. If you die in your new state without changing your will to fit your new state's law, your loved ones might have significant problems. A will that is valid in one state may not work very well in another.

What are your options if a will is so bad to have? Many of us turn to so-called will substitutes or will alternatives, such as life insurance beneficiary designations, joint tenancy, retirement plan beneficiary designations, and "bare-bones" living trusts. Most alternatives to wills don't work very well either. They suffer from the same congenital defects as a will. They do not take care of you while you are alive. They do not provide for your loved ones. They create lawyer's fees and court costs. They take your family public. They may not work at all! Yet, these will substitutes are used to provide for loved ones as frequently or perhaps even more frequently than simple wills.

In our experience, more people have property in joint tenancy than have wills. Given the significant pitfalls of jointly held property, this poses no small problem.

Working with many clients, giving seminars to fellow professionals, and dealing with media exposure has helped us learn how to spread the word about a better way to plan for loved ones—The Loving Trust.

The best way to expose the myths surrounding wills and most will substitutes is for us to share our experiences, both good and bad, with our audiences; to tell real stories about real people we have worked with. This book will teach you to plan for your loved ones just as we teach the professionals. Our story is not esoteric or complicated. It is based on the simple premise that providing for loved ones is nine parts of love to every one part of legal technicality. We believe that legal technicalities can, and should be, reduced to very simple and understandable concepts.

Dr. Joyce Brothers was on the Johnny Carson show many years ago. That particular night Johnny was being pretty hard on Dr. Brothers because she made difficult concepts seem so simple. After several minutes of enduring Johnny's sharp tongue, Dr. Brothers responded something like this, "Listen, Carson. I've spent years in colleges and universities. I have graduate and doctoral degrees. I have spent years gathering experience in my field. I've done most of this so I can take incredibly complicated material and make it simple enough so people like you can understand it."

The audience applauded, and so did we as viewers. It is to the spirit of making extremely complicated concepts simple that we have devoted our teaching careers. This is a book about basic concepts. Basic concepts can be made to look complicated or simple based upon how well the teacher grasps them and whether or not the teacher wishes the student to attain the teacher's understanding. Beware of those who attempt to make basic premises difficult. They may be camouflaging ulterior motives or a lack of knowledge.

There Is a Better Way

We have reviewed thousands of planning attempts by sincere people who were attempting unsuccessfully to provide for their loved ones. We have experienced firsthand how badly most of these loving attempts have failed. We have observed the abuses of probate, the unexpected and often tragic results of joint tenancy property, and the effect of "bare-bones legal boilerplate." Most of the planning attempts we have reviewed were lifeless and devoid of love.

This book spells out the planning opportunities that we shared with our clients, and those that they shared with us, over the years.

The Loving Trust is our solution to providing for your care and well-being and that of your loved ones. It is our belief that everyone needs, and can easily have, a Loving Trust. The myth that you have to be rich to plan for your loved ones is a cruel deception. A Loving Trust is for everyone.

This book is divided into three parts. In Part One, we are going to show you why wills and other techniques used to provide for loved ones simply do not work very well. We will show you what goes wrong with them, and why. We will teach you about the Loving Trust and show you how it can overcome the problems with wills and traditional will-substitute approaches, such as the typical living trust routinely prepared in most law offices.

Part Two will teach you how to design your Loving Trust to meet your desires for your well-being and that of your loved ones. It will describe in plain language the loving motives we commonly used in our practice. It will give you practical solutions and ideas as to how you can provide for yourself and your loved ones in the way you want, and it will give you a step-by-step checklist format that will allow you to easily design your Loving Trust blueprint.

In Part Three we will show you how you can get your Loving Trust done quickly and inexpensively by almost any lawyer. By using our system, you will be able to find and work with a lawyer without fear or hassle. We will prepare you to deal with your lawyer efficiently so that your Loving Trust meeting time can be kept to just a few hours. We will also show you how to use other people to help you keep your time and expense to an absolute minimum.

A Loving Trust is for all who care about their well-being and that of their loved ones. It is designed to enable you to communicate your ideas with respect to your hopes, fears, dreams, and ambitions for yourself and your loved ones.

2

Trust Betrayed

The life insurance agent who sold you your insurance policies, the real estate agent who sold you your house, the bank officers and clerks who set up your accounts and made loans to you, the clerk in the personnel office where you work who filled in the information with respect to your retirement plans, and the stockbroker who sold you your investments have already provided for the future of your loved ones.

You have never controlled—or even had a chance to control—the bulk of what you own. Worse yet, when you did try to exercise control over your property by writing a will or trust, you probably once again assigned real control to the lawyer who prepared it.

Surprised? Don't be. You are in the same boat as most Americans. In our experience, the property of the majority of people consists of a home, life insurance, retirement benefits, and various types of savings accounts. With each of these types of property, as you will soon see, someone other than the property owner has made the decision about where that property is going to pass.

If, by chance, you were allowed to make that decision, you probably had no idea what the real consequences of your decision would be. It is very likely that you are another innocent victim who believes in people who don't know what they are talking about.

Life Insurance

We recently gave a seminar on the campus of the University of Maryland to a group of top life insurance agents. The session began with a caustic exposé of how most life insurance agents determine where their clients' life insurance proceeds will pass at their deaths. "How can you, without any discussion or thought, unilaterally take control of the largest chunk of cash a person usually leaves to loved ones?" we asked them. "Who gave you the authority to plan for the families of your clients?"

They were shocked. Their indignant response was, "What do you mean? All we do is sell the right product to our clients based on their needs. We don't decide who gets the insurance proceeds. Our clients do." To that our answer was, "Want to bet?"

Do you know where to find the beneficiary designation for each of your life insurance policies? Get your policies out right now and look for your beneficiary choices. See if you can wade through all of the fine print, or even the big print, and determine where your life insurance benefits go on your death.

Do you have a group life insurance policy from work? We challenge you to find the beneficiary designation for that policy. Do you really know who your beneficiaries are? We suspect that you think you know, but are you sure? If you can't find each of your beneficiary designations, you ought to be worried. You may not even *have* a loved one as a beneficiary!

When a life insurance agent sells you a policy, an application has to be filled out and submitted to the home office of the life insurance company. Lost among all of the "vital" application information, you will see a small box entitled "Beneficiaries." It is within that box that you will find—most likely in your life insurance agent's handwriting—who will receive your insurance cash. That is the only place your beneficiaries are designated!

If you are married, you will probably see that the proceeds are payable to your spouse as first or primary beneficiary. It will then name your children, share and share alike, or in equal shares, as second or contingent beneficiaries.

For reasons we shall soon share with you, leaving your insurance proceeds *directly* to loved ones is absolutely *not* the way to leave your life insurance cash.

When we got through with our indictment of how "that little box" is really filled in, our Maryland seminar students were in an uproar. They were the pros of their field, exceptional men and women who took great pride in their professionalism and in their sensitivity to their clients. They did not like being criticized. However, they agreed with us when we told them their clients would probably have a difficult time finding their beneficiaries in all of the policy paperwork. You should have seen their reactions when we told them that they, not their clients or attorneys, were unknowingly providing the planning for most of their clients' estates.

They responded with, "We always ask our clients who they want as their beneficiaries. We never make those decisions for our clients! If the estate is named, it's because the lawyer said to name the estate, or there was no one else to leave it to!" On and on they went; we just listened.

After the initial reaction finally died down, we asked another question, purposefully but politely, ignoring all they had to say in their defense. "How many clients asked you how you thought the beneficiary designation should be filled in?" In most cases, the agents routinely fill in that box without a great deal of thought, discussion, or controversy. They responded, "Most people name their spouse as primary beneficiary and their children as contingent beneficiaries." But, from the looks on our faces, they sensed that their collective answer wasn't as right as they always thought it was. Many of them muttered, "So, what's wrong with naming your surviving spouse and children share and share alike?"

Naming a spouse and children as the beneficiaries of your life insurance policies *appears* to reflect good thinking. It sounds so loving on its face. It reflects a satisfactory discharge of one's duty and seems like the appropriate thing to do.

The fact of the matter is, it is not good. Expecting your life insurance cash to successfully care for your loved ones when naming them as outright beneficiaries is a pipe dream. It is merely wishful thinking and nothing more. Under Murphy's Law, everything that can go wrong, will. When it comes to providing for loved ones, Murphy's Law is always operational.

Too many people plan for the best. Planning for the best is not planning; it's wishful thinking. We have always told our clients, "We must plan for the worst; if we do, no one will ever be unpleasantly surprised. If you plan for the best, you won't need us—or anyone else—to charge you good money to participate in your wishful thinking." Wishful thinking is the quickest way to disaster that we know.

If you leave your life insurance, or anything else for that matter, directly to loved ones, you assume that they will actually receive the use and benefit of what you left to them. There is no guarantee—without using a Loving Trust—that this will occur. A beneficiary designation that directly names a person or group of people (children that share and share alike) results in your losing total control over your property. Worse yet, oftentimes beneficiaries never gain control over their parents' or grandparents' property, and when they do they frequently lose it.

Can you imagine the looks on the faces of the insurance professionals as we made these allegations? We had just shattered a few cornerstones of our group's professional knowledge. They were not happy about it. It was at this point that we reassured them that we would demonstrate what really happens when life insurance is left outright to spouses, children, and estates.

Minor Children as Your Beneficiaries

Minor children cannot own property—at least not in their own names. Property that is left or given to minor children is really held and controlled by someone else for their benefit.

Have you ever attempted to open a savings account for your minor children or grandchildren? If you have, you will remember that the bank or savings officer wouldn't let you put the account just in the name of the child. He or she told you that it would be impossible to do that—that the new account would have to be a custodial account. Its caption would read something like "Eric Johnson, a minor, by Karen Johnson or Louis Johnson," or a variation, like "Karen Johnson or Louis Johnson, custodians for Andrew Johnson, a minor."

"Custodian" is the legal name for the adult person, or institution, that has custody of a minor child's money or property. Minor children cannot withdraw money from their custodial accounts; only their custodians can. Parents are their children's custodians by law and therefore are required to be signatories on their children's accounts. The same is true for all other types of property.

Custodial issues usually do not arise when a child owns toys or other personal property, because they are usually of little value. But try putting real estate in your child's name and then attempt to sell it. There is no way you can accomplish this without your or another legal guardian's signature.

Has your teenage child or grandchild tried to purchase his or her first car directly from the local dealer? If so, the chances are excellent that he or she didn't get very far without your signature.

Severe problems arise when you and your spouse are not around to act as your children's legal custodians. What if you both die in a car accident? What if one of you survives the accident but is in a coma? By law there is always someone around to take care of your children. That someone is the local probate (surrogate, common, or district) court judge representing your local government.

Minor children without parents or with mentally disabled parents are placed under the custody of a probate judge; the judge has total power over them. The judge will name two different sets of court-appointed agents who will act for the children. The first set will be the guardians of the children. Guardians are legally appointed substitute parents. They have no control of the children's money, but they do have the responsibility to care for and raise the children with whatever funds are provided them.

The probate judge will also name custodians for the children who may or may not be the same as the guardians. The custodians will be the financial guardians of the children. They will control the children's purse strings on behalf of that local judge.

The guardians will raise the children. They are the folks who will run beside that first two-wheeler and bandage those scraped knees. The custodians will count the money and account for all of the children's income and expenses. They will hold the purse strings. You can see that the court effectively divides the parental roles into two distinct functions.

The guardians and custodians will be represented by separate lawyers who will act as their legal liaisons with the judge.

How do all of these different players come together on behalf of an orphaned minor? Let's assume that a little boy, Jimmy, needs to have orthodontic work done. Jimmy needs to get braces from the local dentist, and it is going to cost a great deal of money over a long period of time. Once the guardians ascertain Jimmy's need for braces, they will either tell their lawyer who will tell the custodians' lawyer or they will directly tell Jimmy's custodians whose lawyer will in turn tell the guardians' lawyer.

If Jimmy has adequate money, in his custodians' opinion, a recommendation will be made to the judge through the custodians' lawyer to approve the expenditure. The judge will either decide the matter in chambers or in open court. The judge may or may not grant the request. Jimmy's bevy of advisers will, however, take their fees just as the local court will assess its charges.

It is at this point that we must remind you of Murphy's Law. Will Jimmy get his braces? Will the cost of making the decision be greater than that of the orthodontist? Only the judge knows— and he's on vacation. Ah, Murphy's Law!

We are sure that Jimmy's mother and father never intended the courts, court-appointed conservators, guardians and lawyers to become co-beneficiaries of their life insurance program. Did the family life insurance agent or lawyer warn Jimmy's parents of the pitfalls of leaving their life insurance directly to their children, share and share alike? We doubt it. Loving parents, in their right minds, would never knowingly place their children in such a legal quagmire. As we reflect on the situation, Jimmy's parents really never had control. The little beneficiary box on the insurance application controlled their life insurance cash, and it was filled in by an agent they hardly knew, who was just following the "usual procedures."

We each have two boys and have learned that children develop different interests and needs. For example, one son may elect to play football. We know from experience that it costs an arm and a leg to outfit a boy in helmet and pads. If the other son selects soccer, it can save a bank loan. The price of soccer shoes, shorts, and jersey does not approach the cost of the football-playing brother's helmet. The cost of the football uniform can literally be in the hundreds of dollars, while a soccer player's gear will likely be in the tens of dollars.

If you are like most people, you wouldn't give your soccer player son extra money to balance the ledger between the boys because of the comparative costs of outfitting them. Most of us love our children equally, but take care of them based upon their needs. We buy our children the things they need without worrying about an exact monetary division between them. In our seminars, we use a phrase to sum up this concept of equal love, but unequal treatment: "There is nothing so unequal as the equal treatment of unequals."

Over the years we have planned for only two clients who kept, with meticulous detail, a ledger on every cent they spent on behalf of their respective children. John and Wayne were brothers. They emulated their very European parents when it came to balancing their respective children's ledgers at the end of every year.

Under our example, each of their soccer-playing sons would receive a ledger credit. They were astounded when we told them that most parents didn't provide for their children in this manner. But, undaunted, they nevertheless instructed us to draw their Loving Trusts to continue this "common sense" family tradition with respect to their children and grandchildren.

Every person who leaves his or her life insurance cash in equal shares ("share and share alike," "to my children equally," or "per stirpes") to loved ones is mandating a John and Wayne balance-the-ledger master plan for their loved ones.

What has astounded us for years is that we have worked with so many people who believed strongly in loving their children equally—caring for them without this ledger mentality. How parents can so meticulously follow one course of action all of their lives, then suddenly abandon it at death for an opposite course of action can only be attributed to the fact that they do not understand the meanings and results of the legal beneficiary jargon. They, like most of us, never really have control.

If you do not believe in ledger planning, reexamine your insurance policy beneficiary designations. Do they provide for your loved ones just like John and Wayne provided for theirs?

Ledger-mentality beneficiary designations frequently result in inequitable and disastrous consequences for little ones. One such instance involved three children whose parents left them an inheritance that included a substantial sum of life insurance "share and share alike." The local bank trust department was named as the custodian of the children's insurance money. This is not a unique occurrence; bank trust departments are often named as custodians of minor children's funds by probate courts when children are directly left property by their unknowing parents.

In this case, the children were nineteen, twelve, and two years of age at the time of their parents' death. The nineteen-year-old was in college and doing quite well; the twelve-year-old had a learning disability; and the two-year-old was very healthy and had no apparent problems.

Because of medical difficulties and other complications that arose, the twelve-year-old son ran out of money and was made a ward of the state. He was placed in a state home for the mentally retarded. The nineteen-year-old never touched her money. She went through both college and graduate school on academic and service club scholarships. Following graduation she did equally well in a merchandising career that paid her handsomely. Her two-year-old brother, a surprise change-of-life baby, was not left quite as well off. Since he was so young, the bank couldn't spend too much of his money to take care of his basic needs for fear that his money would be depleted too soon. His money had to last until he was twenty-one years old, and with nineteen years to go, it had to be managed tightly and had to be carefully preserved.

Had the parents lived, we suspect that they would have allocated their resources so that the twelve-year-old and two-year-old boys would have been well taken care of. The nineteen-year-old daughter obviously needed less, so less would have been used for her benefit, leaving that much more for her brothers' well-being.

Unfortunately, the parents' life insurance designations created an iron curtain between the children. The boys could not share in their sister's windfall. Her one-third was hers to do with as she pleased. In this case, there was nothing fair about leaving the insurance money "equally" to the children. When the children were placed "in equal shares" in that little box, their parents doubtless gave little thought as to what it would really mean to everyone's well-being and life. Mom and Dad were obviously confused by the jargon, and obviously—for an instant in time—didn't consider the differing and relative needs of their children. They weren't in control; that's for sure!

If you leave minor or disadvantaged children, this sort of thing can easily happen to them. We would agree that it's not likely something will happen to you and your spouse in the near future. But, match an untimely illness or accident with poorly thought-out beneficiary designations, add to that minor or disadvantaged children, and there you—or should we say there your loved ones—are visiting with Mr. Murphy.

Terrible things can happen to your children because you provided for them with legal jargon you did not understand in a little box on an insurance application. The problems with that little box do not end with minor children—they only begin there.

Adult Children as Your Beneficiaries

Many of you are thinking that you don't need to worry about Mr. Murphy and that little insurance application box. Your children are grown, and you are not planning on having more. You are comfortable that there is no reason for you to get excited about equal treatment of unequals or iron curtains. In fact, this is exactly what our insurance professionals brought up to us after we shook them up so badly about directly leaving property to minor children.

Our class needed to feel that at least some of their traditional operating methods did not have Murphy's Law consequences. They were snug in their belief that leaving insurance proceeds directly to healthy adult children reflected sound planning. That was before we told them Luke's story, and then immediately followed it up with Diane's story.

Luke was married and had two children. He was a high school teacher and coach. He had always lived modestly and was happy living within his economic means; he liked his job and enjoyed his family. Luke's grandfather was wealthy. He had always loved Luke, but wisely refrained from interfering in his life by lavishing too much money or too many things on him. He wanted Luke to stand on his own two feet and to be successful as a result of his self-reliance.

Luke's grandfather came to us for planning advice, but his mind was made up before he came. Nothing we said could convince him not to leave everything he owned, including a substantial amount of life insurance, directly to Luke.

When Luke's granddad died, Luke got everything in one lump sum. For the first time in his life, Luke had "real" money. He bought a big car for himself and a sports car for his wife. He bought a huge house in an exclusive area and joined the local country club so he could rub shoulders with others equally well-off.

Luke also got into deals. It became well known around the club that if you needed money to do a deal, Luke would probably be good for it. Luke was a soft touch, and everyone knew it. He no longer had time for teaching high school; the time was quickly taken up with a daily regimen of golf, cards, and a few drinks with the "boys down at the club."

The money left as fast as it came. In less than three years Luke lost everything. All of those surefire deals backfired. Luke was left destitute. He had acquired a taste for gambling and drinking. He lost his money, his wife, and his children. To this day, we believe that Luke's ex-wife is still attempting to collect child support and alimony.

Luke's story is not about a bad person getting his just deserts. It is a story of someone who was overwhelmed by wealth. Luke's grandfather had the wisdom not to spoil Luke while he was alive. Yet, for some inexplicable reason, he felt he could satisfactorily do just the opposite after his death. You cannot take an Eskimo from the North Pole and a Polynesian from the South Seas and, without any warning, change their places in the dead of a northern hemisphere winter. Both will die of exposure, one to the heat, the other to the cold. Drastic change brings on drastic results.

Luke was not prepared for what occurred, and he paid the consequences of his grandfather's lack of judgment. Had Luke been given two or even three chances at wealth, he may well have learned how to handle it. If Luke's granddad had provided that Luke gradually get used to having money, Luke might be happy and prosperous today. He was never given the opportunity to learn. When property is left outright to adult children, there is no room for error. A Loving Trust can provide that room.

Diane's story is different. She was raised in wealth, went to the best schools and had the best training that money could buy. She was levelheaded and not likely to squander wealth.

Her parents died when she was in her early twenties. They left her inheritance to her in trust, with the exception of one large insurance policy that was left to her directly.

Soon after her parents' deaths, Diane married a young entrepreneur who was looking for a fast way to the top. Diane was his ticket. After they were married, her husband, Jeff, decided to build a racquetball facility and health spa. Jeff had nothing. In order to get his loan approved, the bank insisted that Diane co-sign the note, pledging her money as collateral. Diane was a loving and giving wife; she signed the note, trusting that Jeff would not let her down.

Jeff turned out to be both a disloyal husband and a business failure. The project went bankrupt; Jeff left Diane pregnant and with all of his bank debt. Diane quickly lost all of her parents' insurance money to Jeff's creditors. However, the property and money left to her in trust was saved, and as a result, Diane and her baby were not left destitute.

Age does not make a person wise—experience does. And unfortunately experience usually comes from making mistakes. Some mistakes are obviously more costly than others. When loved ones receive property but don't have the knowledge or experience to manage it, the necessary experience may be gained at a cost that is simply too great to bear.

There are many Loving Trust ways to protect adult children

from their inexperience and naïveté. None of these methods entails leaving the outright distributions of life insurance proceeds. We know that Murphy's Law applies to the inexperienced regardless of their age.

For many years we have asked our seminar participants if any of them have children who have learning disabilities or who are disadvantaged in some way. About one in ten participants will answer in the affirmative. In the Maryland seminar, the ratio was a little higher. As soon as we mentioned disadvantaged children, that group of men and women reacted much like any of our other classes: "Oh, no, here we go again. We can see it coming, that little box on the life insurance application is going to make for terrible messes later on!" Most of them were beginning to understand just how important that little box is.

We knew from experience that many of these honorable and excellent insurance professionals had too often filled in that little box without knowing, or even asking, whether a loved one had some form of disability.

There is no greater injustice than leaving life insurance, or any property for that matter, outright to a disadvantaged loved one.

Early in our practice, we ran into a situation where insurance proceeds and other properties were left outright to a disadvantaged child. The "child" was middle-aged, but because of his disability he functioned at approximately a four-year-old mentality. He had been protected and sheltered from the real world all of his life by his parents. Unfortunately, they died within a few months of one another without leaving Loving Trust instructions.

By happenstance, a relative came to us with this man-child's problems. We had to initiate a probate court proceeding that resulted in his being declared mentally incompetent. The court treated him just like it would treat a minor child. A guardian and a custodian were appointed. All of his parents' property went to the custodian to be held on his behalf. The court chose an institution for him, where to the best of our knowledge he still resides. His life is subject, of course, to the court's and Mr. Murphy's approval. Unfortunately, this sad story is not unique; it happens every day.

Oftentimes a child is not sufficiently "disadvantaged" to need court supervision but still needs help with money and finances. Some examples come readily to mind: an emotionally disturbed child; the child who just isn't very intelligent, or a child who is a genius but who never adapted to the real world; and the child who is downright irresponsible.

Unprotected from themselves and the many hucksters of the world, too many "well-heeled orphans" are at the mercy of anyone who has the inclination to prey on them. If you have a child with special needs and problems, would you give him or her a large lump of cash without supervision while you are alive? We believe your response would be, "Absolutely not!" We wonder why so many people do that very thing on their death!

It is a travesty that so many otherwise prudent people attempt to leave their money directly to loved ones. You now know that it often goes to a court and to court-appointed guardians, conservators, and lawyers. Every parent who leaves life insurance proceeds without Loving Trust instructions for the care of his or her loved ones is leaving only half a loaf; the money is there— absent the protection, instructions, and guidelines for its use. The results of leaving half-a-loaf insurance proceeds are not pleasant. These proceeds also end up—all too often—in the hands of creditors, fast-talking strangers, and distant relatives with a good story.

People can inherit money and property when their parents or grandparents die, but they can't inherit any more brains, experience, or emotional stability. A simple and poorly thought-out beneficiary designation simply cannot pass any of these nonmonetary qualities to loved ones. Yet, it never ceases to amaze us that this is precisely the assumption so many people make. As we told our life insurance students, "Your profession is just as guilty of poorly planning for your clients' loved ones as our profession."

Your Spouse as Your Beneficiary

Naming your spouse as the primary beneficiary of your life insurance would seem like the right thing to do. Most people want their spouse to have their life insurance proceeds, and they would like whatever is left to go to their children on their spouses' deaths. We have met very few clients who didn't want exactly this result.

Unfortunately, using a simple beneficiary designation to accomplish loving goals doesn't always work. If you leave your insurance proceeds and other property outright to your spouse, you can hurt rather than help your mate.

Let's assume, however, that everything goes exactly as you planned upon your death. Your spouse is well and receives your insurance proceeds. Your spouse is frugal and is bound and determined to leave all of those life insurance dollars not used during his or her lifetime to the children. Then your spouse remarries.

You can imagine, at this point, all of the clumsy, unfortunate, and catastrophic situations we have seen as a result of nice, but poorly informed, people attempting to cope with their money and a new spouse's demands.

Keep in mind that your spouse can change his or her beneficiary designations at any time. He or she can easily name that new spouse as beneficiary after your death. In fact, under many state laws, if your spouse remarries after your death and doesn't have a signed premarital contract, your "replacement" will have significant rights to your spouse's—or should we say your—property.

We have met too many clients who found themselves in this situation over the years. A typical situation goes something like this: Dad died leaving everything to Mom either by beneficiary designation or by will. Mom, after several lonely years, finally remarried. She didn't change her will, which left everything to the children, just as her new husband didn't change his. Mom died before her new husband. Under her state's law a spouse gets one-half of the estate of the spouse who dies first, unless, either prior to marriage or during marriage, they made a contract agreeing to some other arrangement. There was no contract between our clients' mother and their stepfather.

The stepfather went to court and took his share of the estate as allowed under state law. Our clients wanted us to stop their stepfather from getting "their" money and property. There was nothing we could do. In total violation of their parents' wishes, the stepfather got one-half of their parents' property.

A beneficiary designation that leaves all of your property outright to your spouse means that you have lost control over the proceeds. Using an outright, uncontrolled beneficiary designation is like leaning out of a window on the fifteenth floor of a building and throwing dollar bills out, hoping that one or two of the folks you are attempting to throw them to will somehow catch some of them. A lot can happen to those dollar bills between the time you let go of them and their ultimate arrival.

In more cases than we care to admit, one spouse has had total control of the family purse strings throughout the marriage, and, whether by design or happenstance, the other spouse is in the dark when it comes to the family's finances. The financial spouse handles everything, from investments to balancing the checkbook. The financially unsophisticated spouse generally can't even pretend to play a good game when it comes to money, business, and finance.

Shirley came to us several months after Carl, her husband of thirty-three years, died. She had been referred by an insurance agent. Carl's life insurance was—as with most Americans—his major asset. Shirley was the beneficiary. Carl's insurance was paid to her ten days after Carl's death.

When Shirley came to us, she showed us her joint checking account. Carl was still on the account. There was over $100,000 in cash in it! It wasn't drawing interest; it was just sitting in the account making some bank officers extremely happy.

Shirley had absolutely no idea what to do with that money. Carl, for all of the years of their marriage, had taken care of their finances. Shirley received an allowance that she used to run the household and buy the personal things she needed. If she needed additional funds, she would talk to Carl. "Carl wanted me to do more," she said, "but I never wanted to. I had certain things that I did and enjoyed, and our finances were not among them. It never occurred to me that one day Carl's responsibilities would fall on my shoulders whether I liked it or not."

Shirley was fortunate that Carl's life insurance agent was both professional and caring enough to discern her problem and to offer his help. When we related Shirley's experience to our seminar class at the University of Maryland, they visibly brightened. "See," one of them said, "a beneficiary designation isn't so bad. Shirley got help from her agent; he did his job!"

Helping Shirley was not his job, though. Carl's agent was exceptional. She was very lucky that he pointed her in the right direction. If he hadn't, someone would have pointed her in another direction. Shirley and her money would have soon parted. It is not too difficult for crooks and overzealous business types to take advantage of widows and widowers who have considerable grief and newfound wealth.

There are many people who are willing to marry for money. Leaving life insurance outright to a spouse is like leaving food out on a picnic table; sooner or later, unwanted guests are going to come along to share a free lunch. When you leave large sums of money directly to a naïve spouse, you are inviting others to freeload.

The problems that we have been considering get even worse if your spouse is incapacitated following your death. What happens to your spouse and to your life insurance proceeds if your spouse is in a coma from the same car accident that took your life?

Minor children, disabled children, and disabled adults have one thing in common—they cannot own property! If your spouse is plugged into all kinds of machines in an intensive care unit, loved ones will not be allowed to cash the life insurance check, let alone to spend it taking care of your spouse.

There is always someone around to help. The local probate judge, with all of the judicial machinery provided by the state legislature, is always there. A disabled spouse goes through the same court-oriented legal process as a minor child or any other disabled person. In this situation, the process goes something like this: First there is the court proceeding to declare your spouse incompetent. Then come the guardian and the conservator and the lawyers. The life insurance proceeds are controlled by the court, which makes sure that all of the court-appointed agents are paid. The court makes sure all of the family's creditors are paid, leaving the balance to be used—at the judge's, conservator's, and guardian's discretion—for the benefit of your spouse.

Can matters get worse? If you have minor children, they certainly can! Your children will have to endure the same probate process. The local probate judge is going to be plenty busy naming multiple guardians, conservators, and lawyers and then reviewing all of the red-tape paperwork they generate.

Recently we had reason to be in the Probate Court in Denver, Colorado. The court docket for the week, which is the judge's calendar of what he will be doing, was posted outside the courtroom door on a bulletin board. For five days there was not one death probate—every single trial or hearing scheduled, and there were a lot of them, was for an incompetency hearing for a minor child or disabled adult.

We live in a world where physicians can keep patients alive for a long time using sophisticated medical techniques. The result is that most of us are living longer, even though we may need the help of others to handle our affairs. The probate courts and attorneys are doing a booming business thanks to modern medicine. It's too bad that more of us aren't avoiding them by using a Loving Trust.

Naming Your Estate as Beneficiary of Your Life Insurance

All of the bad, nasty, and evil things that can happen if you name your spouse or children as outright beneficiaries of your life insurance policies are not as bad as the consequences of naming your "estate." At every seminar we give, whether to life insurance agents, lawyers, accountants, financial planners, or the general public, we emphasize this point: "Naming your estate as beneficiary of your life insurance policies is crazy and definitely someone's malpractice."

You should see the panic on the faces in our audience—this is especially true of law and insurance groups—when we attack this practice in "malpractice" terms. Everyone wants to talk at once. "How can you say such a thing?" "You're exaggerating!" "Prove it!" We're used to the reaction, and when the uproar dies down, we patiently go about proving our point.

All insurance policies have what is known as a spendthrift

clause. This clause, which is safeguarded by the laws of all states, protects your insurance proceeds and your beneficiaries from the claims of your creditors. Let's assume you have an insurance policy that pays $100,000 on your death. Let's further assume that you owe various creditors more than $100,000 and don't have a cent to your name. If, on your death, you have named anyone other than your "estate" as a beneficiary of your life insurance, your creditors cannot get the money that you owe them out of your life insurance proceeds. Your life insurance proceeds are absolutely free from the claims of your creditors.

Your life insurance proceeds can only be successfully attacked and seized by your creditors if you leave it to them. You leave your life insurance proceeds to your creditors when you leave it to your "estate"!

Why anyone, especially a professional life insurance agent or lawyer, would take a creditor-free asset and subject it to the claims of creditors is a great mystery to us. When you look at your beneficiary designations, look for "estate" type language in those little boxes. If you see it, immediately call your agent and get it changed! Remember, life insurance proceeds payable to a beneficiary other than your estate avoid probate. Making absolutely sure that you regain control of your insurance program is one of the functions of the Loving Trust.

The "box" controls one of the most significant assets that you own. You did not intend to lose control of your life insurance proceeds, but when your insurance agent filled in that box you probably did just that.

Jointly Held Real Estate

If you are like most people, you lost control of your real estate at your first house closing. Think back to that day; you were probably excited and equally nervous. When you completed signing the reams of closing paperwork, the house was automatically put in both your name and your spouse's name. It was then that you first lost control of your real estate.

We very much doubt that your real estate agent asked you, "Whose name does the deed to your new house go in?" Can you recall your real estate agent asking you this question? If your closing was like most others, the real estate company's secretary simply typed whatever names the agent placed on your purchase offer on the deed to your home.

If perchance your real estate agent asked you how you would like to own your home, you probably answered without much thought or hesitation, "Put it in both of our names." If you weren't asked, it is highly likely that you and your mate were named as the joint purchasers anyway.

Married couples purchasing a home almost universally take ownership as joint tenants. In a few states they own their home as tenants by the entirety. This is a special kind of ownership that's almost identical to joint tenancy. If, for some reason, you recall asking the agent why he or she was putting the deed in joint tenancy, you'll recall that the answer was "You have a good marriage, don't you?" or "We've always done it that way."

"Jointly held" has a nice ring to it. It captures the essence of "the two of us" or "our marital partnership." It is psychologically pleasing. The fact is, both you and your spouse absolutely lose the ability to control your real estate the instant you put both of your names on the deed.

Much has been written to warn the public about the pitfalls and the traps of joint tenancy. *Reader's Digest* has repeatedly written about its Murphy-like traps. Nevertheless, almost all couples keep acquiring their property "jointly." Even most of the professionals we teach, including practicing lawyers, do not have a grasp of how joint tenancy plays into Murphy's hands.

Joint tenancy does *not* mean that each spouse owns one-half of the marriage's property. When each owns half, it is either called tenancy in common or community property, an ownership method unique to eight states (Arizona, California, Idaho, Louisiana, Nevada, New Mexico, Texas, Washington). If you think that you are a half owner with your spouse of your joint property, you are dead wrong!

Imagine two birds sitting on a tree limb. You might say they both own the whole limb since both have an equal right to alight, sit, and take off from any part of it. Now imagine that one of the birds is shot by a boy's pellet gun and falls off the limb, dead. Its mate still sits on the branch. The surviving mate now owns the whole limb. Our lovebirds' situation is the essence of joint tenancy.

The proper title for joint tenancy is JOINT TENANCY, WITH RIGHT OF SURVIVORSHIP. It is the RIGHT OF SURVIVORSHIP—which bird ends up alone on the limb—that really defines how joint tenancy works. The surviving spouse ultimately owns and controls all of the joint property because of the survivorship feature. Joint tenancy is a discreet, but devastating, version of the economic game, "winner takes and controls all."

It is precisely at this point that many of our seminar students respond with, "So what's the big deal? I want my husband (or my wife) to have the house when I die." And we reply, "Sure you do, just like you want your spouse to have life insurance proceeds outright when you die, right?" Joint tenancy is another marvelous testing ground for Murphy's Law.

Residences are only part of the joint tenancy tangle. When you bought your cars, your friendly car salesperson put "joint tenancy" on the title application. With such precedents behind you, and being fast learners, you and your spouse began putting everything in joint tenancy. It was easy to do. It avoided any disputes as to who owned what, because both you and your mate thought you owned everything equally.

You may even recall one of your friends mentioning that joint property avoided probate. Your friend's information was partially correct. Jointly owned property avoids probate when a joint owner dies. That is a fact, or at least half of a fact. When the bird falls off the limb, the courts do not have to decide who owns the property. The law makes it clear that the remaining bird owns the property. Presto! An easy way to avoid the expense, aggravation, and delay of probate—maybe! For now, we'll assume that joint tenancy does avoid probate and all of its related horrors. Now it's again time to test Murphy's Law.

Ginnie and Don owned all their property jointly. It was a second marriage for both of them. Don had three children from his prior marriage. They lived with their mother, who had remarried, and Don really didn't have much contact with any of them. Don's first family was kept mostly out of his thoughts and life. Ginnie had no children from her first marriage, but she and Don had two young children. Ginnie and Don assumed that when one of them died, the other would take care of their children. Neither of them wanted to leave anything to Don's children by his first wife.

Ginnie and Don were flying in a private airplane that crashed on landing. Ginnie died instantly, but Don survived. As the survivor, he automatically received all the property, because it was all in joint tenancy. Don was the bird left on the limb. Don, however, was rushed to a hospital with multiple critical injuries.

All of Ginnie's and Don's affairs came to a halt. Friends of the family contacted a lawyer. He proceeded to get a guardian and a conservator appointed for Don. Next, the court appointed a guardian and a conservator for Don and Ginnie's two children. Luckily, a relative agreed to take both of them; otherwise, they would have been split up or sent to a state facility.

Don died soon thereafter. A probate was opened for him since he was now the sole owner of the joint property. There were no more birds on the limb, so the court had to decide where Don's property would go at his death. Don had no will or trust. Under Don's state's law, his children received equal shares of his property. Don and Ginnie's children each got 20 percent of their parent's property. Don's other children also got 20 percent each.

Don and Ginnie wanted their children to have everything when they were gone. They expected that would be the case. They never knew that their little ones would get only 40 percent of their property. They never intended that Don's older children get anything, much less 60 percent! Why did this happen? Whose fault was it? When it comes to joint property, Mr. Murphy is all smiles.

Jointly owned property between spouses and poorly thought-out beneficiary designations are two sides of the same coin. If it can go wrong it will, and Murphy is doing the flipping! Mountain cabins, lake shore cottages, and seaside retreats owned jointly among brothers, sisters, and their parents or inlaws are fertile breeding grounds for jointly owned catastrophes. These ownership combinations have led to many nasty and expensive lawsuits.

Our clients, Jack and Art, were brothers who were very close to one another. Their pride and joy was a mountain cabin that they had built together over the years. The cabin, which was on beautiful land near Rocky Mountain National Park, was owned by Jack and Art as joint tenants with right of survivorship. Everyone in their families loved that cabin. It represented good times, and Jack and Art wanted it to stay in their families for a long time. Just like everybody else, they assumed that they each owned half of the cabin.

Jack and Art were shocked to hear that they each didn't own half. They were even more shocked when we told them what would happen when the first one of them died.

We explained that the survivor would own the cabin. We also explained that the dead brother's family would have no ownership or right to the cabin, even though he put up half the cost of building it. We stressed that even if the dead brother put up all the money, the cabin would still belong to the surviving brother.

They were silent with disbelief, and we weren't through yet! We stressed that one-half of the value of the cabin would be subject to federal estate tax in the deceased brother's estate. This was the classic double whammy—tax without property! Joint tenancy WITH RIGHT OF SURVIVORSHIP is not designed to be fair.

One of the brothers, after listening to our explanation, then observed, "There's nothing to worry about. Whoever survives will just give half back to the other's family." We answered that his conclusion was a really bad idea. The gift could very well generate state and federal gift taxes in addition to existing death taxes. We also cautioned him that there was absolutely no guarantee that the gift would be made. We posed several additional questions: "What if the living brother was angry with a member of the deceased brother's family and decided to keep it for his family? What if the surviving brother was sick or disabled and couldn't make the gift? What if the surviving brother got greedy?"

We told them that they were certainly welcome to plan for the best, but in our opinion that wouldn't be planning, just wishful thinking. We invited them to ask Murphy if their dreams would come true. We all knew what his answer would be! They certainly got the message that joint tenancy with RIGHT OF SURVIVORSHIP was not a prudent way for them to own their cabin.

Jointly owned property held between elderly parents and

their children is another fertile testing ground for Murphy. A close friend's younger sister took care of their mother after their father died. To facilitate the undertaking, all the mother's property was put in joint tenancy with the sister. This undertaking certainly gave the sister the right to sign everything on behalf of their infirm mother. Their mother had a will leaving 40 percent of her estate to our friend and 60 percent to her sister. The extra 20 percent that was going to the sister was in recognition of the care she was giving Mother.

When our friend's mother died, the sister received all Mother's property. Joint tenancy passed the property to our friend's sister because she was the only bird left sitting on that limb. Mother's will was meaningless because joint property passes automatically to the survivor. It does not pass through the first deceased owner's estate, and therefore it is not subject to the terms of a will.

When our friend asked her sister for her share, the sister responded something like this. "Where were you when I was taking care of Mom? Who spent days and nights, year after year, caring for her? Do you know what I sacrificed? I deserve it all." Once our friend's sister discovered the property was all hers, she conveniently forgot Mother's wishes and the deal she had struck with her sister. Everything went wrong—or right, depending on one's point of view—because joint ownership was used to facilitate taking care of Mother rather than a Loving Trust.

It might hearten you to know that the Internal Revenue Service took away some of the sister's ill-gotten gains. When property is put into joint tenancy and the joint tenants are not husband and wife, a gift is made. The gift is from the original owner to the other joint tenant. In this case, the IRS found out about Mother's joint transfers to her daughter and charged the daughter gift tax and compounded interest for all the years it wasn't paid. The gift tax aspect of joint tenancy is almost always overlooked by everyone except the IRS and Murphy. It is one more reason that joint tenancy is a dangerously poor way to own property.

You lose control of your property when you put it in joint tenancy. It can pass to unintended heirs when you die. While it is used by many as a method to avoid probate, it *never* avoids probate on the surviving tenant's death. It is also often subject to probate expenses on the first death. It can even create death taxes without ownership and gift taxes between everyone except spouses!

With few, if any, exceptions you should not own your property in joint tenancy with anybody! If you do, you should continue reading before making changes in your ownership habits.

Joint Property and Your Bank

Bankers are very smart. They understand what joint tenancy can do for them. They endorse and encourage it because it is good for the bank, not necessarily the borrower.

Even if your realtor counseled you not to purchase your property in joint tenancy, the bank handling your mortgage would have done its best to put your house in joint tenancy anyway. When two names are on a deed, your friendly banker can easily get two names on the mortgage. Two people responsible for the payment of a mortgage are always better than just one, because if there is a default on the payment, the bank can sue two people rather than one.

Bankers also encourage joint tenancy because it saves them time and paperwork. People do not usually object to it, and it is important from the bank's point of view to accustom their customers to two signatures.

We do not have our houses in joint tenancy. Neither do our clients, or at least those who took and remembered our advice. You do not pull a fast one on your bank, or any other creditor for that matter, if you keep your home ownership out of joint tenancy. Rather, you simply avoid all of the joint tenancy problems we have been discussing.

Even though our houses are in one name, the bank has insisted that both spouses sign on the dotted lines of our respective mortgages. Most of our clients and students over the years have been shocked at the notion that the title to a residence or any other property can be in one spouse's name while the mortgage is in both. We continue to tell our students that this is not a problem, and never has been one. If you give your bank a mortgage on your house, you do not give the bank control or ownership, you only give them the house as collateral for your promise to pay back the money you borrowed; if you default on your promise, the bank can sell your house—foreclose on your mortgage—to get the money you still owe them.

You do not have to put your home in joint tenancy in order to get a mortgage on it. Whose name or names you put your residence in is your business. Who signs the mortgage is the bank's business. The bank does not have the right to tell you how to title your real estate. You have no right to tell the bank who is—or is not—going to sign their mortgage. Bankers want to make sure that they can sue as many people as possible if the sale of the property doesn't raise enough money to cover what they are owed. As a result, we rarely see mortgages that are only signed by one spouse.

Bankers have other ways of encouraging their customers to place their property in joint tenancy. Do you remember when you and your spouse opened up your first checking or savings account? You met with their new accounts person, who helped you select the proper account, checkbook cover style, and the color of your checks. That person also gave you an account signature card to sign. That signature card is the legal document that tells the world who is the owner of the account.

Banks have several printed forms of signature cards. When married couples come in, the new accounts person usually automatically presents them with the joint tenancy card. We have often been asked why bankers do this. The response we always give is, "We do not know."

At any rate, you and your spouse signed the account card as joint tenants with right of survivorship. That's the way it's done. You were not presented with alternatives. The new accounts person, like your life insurance agent and your realtor, determined (with Murphy's silent help) how your loved ones would be provided for. You were never given the opportunity to do otherwise.

All the things you buy with the money in your joint accounts are considered to be joint tenancy unless you title that property differently. One hour at a bank clerk's desk has mandated many a joint tenancy marriage. From that point on, almost all of your possessions will be owned in joint property with rights of survivorship. And you never knew the consequences of that innocent account opening. You were in someone else's hands who did not know what he or she was doing.

Are all your bank accounts in both your and your spouse's names? Do you have joint accounts with people other than your spouse? Do you know whether you signed signature cards creating joint tenancy? The only way you will know for sure is to go to the bank and look at those cards. They will tell you how the account is owned.

If the account card does not say how the account is owned but has someone else's signature on it in addition to yours, then only a lawyer can tell you whether your account is in joint tenancy. In some states, property held in more than one name without any other notation as to how the property is owned is presumed to be owned in joint tenancy. Other states presume that the property is in tenancy in common—a form of ownership that works the way most people mistakenly think joint tenancy works.

Tenancy in common between spouses means that each spouse owns half of the property. However, each half cannot be specifically identified. If you own a dog in tenancy in common, you do not specifically own the half that eats or the half that wags. You own half of the whole dog.

If you own a deck of cards tenancy in common, you do not own twenty-six cards; you own half of every card. Should you desire to sell or give your interest to someone else, you can transfer your one-half interest in each and every card. The same thing occurs on your death. If you leave your tenancy in common interest to a deck of cards, your loved ones will own a part of every card in the deck.

With tenancy in common ownership you can direct your property to loved ones rather than rely on where Murphy will pass it. With joint tenancy property the first bird to fall off the limb cannot leave anything, because on death it owned nothing. With tenancy in common property, that bird still owns 50 percent of that limb and can leave it to loved ones in a Loving Trust.

The Personnel Clerk Where You Work

Most of us have a retirement plan and some group life insurance at work. These are employee benefits that offer meaningful security to most employees and their families.

We had group life insurance and a profit-sharing plan in our law firm. They were put in by sophisticated advisers. We had talented insurance agents who placed our insurance with old-line reputable companies. Our bank, one of the largest in town, was the trustee of our profit-sharing plan. The costs of maintaining our benefit package were substantial. Our law firm restricted its practice to tax, business, and estate planning. In those areas, we were sophisticated and knowledgeable in dotting all the i's and crossing the t's.

One day, after each plan had been in force for several years, a memo went out to our bookkeeping department requesting an update on our beneficiary designations. We waited and waited until we received a reply that said, "What beneficiary designations?"

Somewhere in the fine-print documentation of both our plans, it said that the plan's beneficiaries would be designated by the participants. Unfortunately our participants weren't told about their benefit-planning opportunities. A sad, but human commentary on us. We were no worse or better than most businesses at keeping records. It became obvious to us that we were just like our clients: We huffed and puffed about too many little things and forgot to deal with the really important ones. An insurance executive friend of ours calls this all-too-human penchant "majoring in minors."

We thought we had planned for our loved ones, but when it came to our group insurance and profit-sharing money we left the planning to Murphy. Somehow in the daily rush of things, we forgot to hitch the cart to the benefit horse. Our loved ones never had a chance. We are lucky that we discovered our mistake before one of our employees died.

Where would our firm's life insurance and retirement benefits have been paid if we hadn't caught our mistake in time? To the estates of our deceased and disabled employees. Two marvelous fringe benefits that were absolutely probate- and creditor-free would have been paid to our employees' creditors by way of our local probate court.

Let's assume that we hadn't messed up and that we had assiduously distributed beneficiary cards to our employees. Do you think that the results would have been all that much better? In looking back, we don't think they would have been.

We would have had a clerk from our personnel department write a memo telling our employees to fill in the cards and return them to our business office by such and such a date. As a result, a life-and-death, critically important planning consideration would have been relegated to ministerial status and left to the devices of one of our least-skilled employees. We strongly suspect that this is precisely what happens all too often throughout the business sector.

Company-sponsored fringe-benefit proceeds appear to represent the bulk of what most people in the American work force leave to their loved ones. And yet extraordinarily expensive employee benefit packages are not properly going to those loved ones. Why is Murphy put in charge of their distribution? is more than a rhetorical question—it's a national disgrace.

Do you have a group life insurance plan at work? Are you a participant in a pension plan, stock option, thrift, or profit-sharing plan? Who do you think will receive your share if something happens to you? In what manner will they receive it? Do you recall filling in beneficiary cards? Did a personnel clerk fill them in for you? Odds are that you don't have ready answers to most of these questions. If you don't, you'll certainly want to take a break from the daily grind and make some inquiries at the earliest possible moment.

Your Stockbroker

Stocks, bonds, and mutual funds certainly represent assets that are acquired by prudent savers and investors. They go into portfolios that are carefully managed either directly by the investor or through the expertise of a professional money manager. Most investors carefully monitor their investments to assure themselves that their principal is secure and that it is earning them the highest income possible. Most investors scrutinize the credentials of their financial advisers before hiring them, and then continually monitor their investment abilities. In short, those of us who are fortunate enough to put a little away are usually not careless in its management.

But most savers and investors are not so prudent when it comes to making sure that their loved ones will receive those hard-earned and carefully managed assets.

When you open an account with your stockbroker, you go through a process that is very similar to opening a bank account. There are forms to be filled in and documents to be signed. Most of these forms are not for your benefit. They are for the benefit of the IRS and the brokerage house. In the paperwork will be an input form to set up your account on the firm's computer. How that form is filled in will determine how your investments will be handled and distributed in the event of your death or incapacity.

Stockbrokers are in the business of selling securities, just as insurance agents are in the business of selling life insurance. They are not particularly interested in how you designate your beneficiaries. That is your responsibility. When your broker sets up your account, it is likely that he or she will not stress the importance of the account title.

Without belaboring the obvious, you know that married clients are going to fill in joint tenancy account forms and single adults are usually going to have the account put in their own names.

Your broker will not ask you to fill in a beneficiary designation form. In that respect he or she is more akin to your banker than to your insurance agent or personnel clerk. If your account is placed in joint tenancy WITH RIGHT OF SURVIVORSHIP, you are right back with Murphy. If it is placed in your name or in tenancy in common, your interest is going to go through probate.

If your account has more than one name on it but doesn't say anything more, your state law will determine whether you own your interest as a joint tenant or as a tenant in common. In our experience, this rarely occurs with account statements. But if it does, call your lawyer.

On stocks, bonds, and other securities that are in your possession, you need only look to the face of the certificate to find out who owns it. Please remember, if two names appear without any other notation, you need to call your lawyer to ascertain what your interest is.

All your ongoing stock, bond, and mutual-fund purchases will automatically be titled exactly the way you chose in the original paperwork.

The ownership and control over your investment portfolio is subject, just like everything else you acquire, to the "Ten-Second Response Rule": your response to the innocent question, "In whose name do you want it?" You originally sought your broker or investment adviser to facilitate the buying and selling of your securities, not to provide for your disability or your loved ones. And you probably got what you paid for. The system took control of your investments and placed their future—and that of your loved ones—with Murphy and the courts.

We have discussed your life insurance, real estate, bank accounts, retirement plans, and stocks and bonds. These assets represent the property that most of us acquire over our lifetimes. In our analysis we found that each and every one of them was ultimately controlled by the clerical mistakes or ignorance of someone else. If you are like most of us, you have been the system's victim.

Every single tragedy, inadequacy, mistake, and excess that we have discussed so far can be alleviated through the use of a Loving Trust. By finishing this book and following our instructions, you will be able to control everything you own by designing and implementing your Loving Trust to meet your hopes, fears, dreams, and ambitions for your future and that of your loved ones.

3

The Groucho Marx Story

Many of our clients had severe reservations about planning for their loved ones. We're convinced that these clients were subliminally certain that signing a will would result in their death. They associated their wills with death because of the obvious absence of lifetime benefits. They correctly assessed the fact that they had to die to make their wills work.

Good planning is living planning—not death planning! Your living planning starts with providing for you and then your loved ones. It should envision loving care, good and prosperous times, and it should make every attempt to minimize death's aftermath.

Insurance industry statistics generally indicate that people are more likely to become disabled and then die than to keel over dead without warning. We are living longer than ever, but we have not adjusted our planning formulas to provide for the consequences of our longevity.

It is highly unlikely that you or your advisers will plan for your disability. This is a statistical mistake that could have devastating consequences for you and your loved ones. Most professionals equate planning for loved ones with "death" planning and ignore "disability" planning. They rarely think about the likelihood of their clients becoming disabled prior to death or about what will happen to those disability insurance checks. Your will, joint property, life insurance, retirement benefits, and most likely even your disability insurance are not likely to help you if you become disabled!

Groucho Marx is a graphic example of a man who—along with his advisers—ignored living planning for himself and his loved ones. Groucho was infirm in his old age. He spent the last three years of his life in and out of probate court hearings and was totally under the control of the court.

Groucho had a live-in friend named Erin Fleming. Miss Fleming, a constant companion of Groucho's in his later years, went to the probate court in Santa Monica, California, in 1974 to have Groucho declared mentally incompetent. Every state allows a relative or "friend" of a person to go to the courthouse for the purpose of having someone who is no longer capable of caring for him or herself declared incompetent and placed under the "care" of the court.

A court hearing was held, and Groucho was found to be mentally incompetent. In the hearing, Erin asked that she be named as Groucho's guardian and also his custodian. As guardian, she would be Groucho's parent, like a guardian of a minor child. As custodian, she would have control of Groucho's money. Whatever the motive for her action, her success would give her control of Groucho and his money.

Erin was named Groucho's guardian, and the Bank of America and Erin were named as joint custodians. All the court proceedings were covered by the nation's newspapers and magazines. And why not? An incompetency hearing is fully public. It is a living probate. The entire probate record, along with all documents filed with the court, is a matter of public record. Can you imagine the media interest that was created by the anticipation of looking into the inner life of a famous star?

The publicity ebbed and flowed with the testimony in Groucho's final drama. Three years after her partial initial victory, Erin went back to the court, demanding to be named Groucho's sole custodian. The bank protested. Groucho's family joined forces with the bank, taking the position that Erin was not very nice to Groucho and was greedy. Groucho's family and the bank went to court and insisted that Erin be removed as guardian and requested that certain family members be allowed to care for Groucho.

A lengthy and spectacular trial ensued. For months the trial raged. There were allegations of murder plots, sex for hire, and drugs. If the trial dragged at all, one could anticipate that the next witness would testify to even juicier bits of gossip and innuendo.

Movie clips were shown to demonstrate Groucho's state of mind. Filmed interviews were viewed by the jury. A bevy of big-name stars testified as to what Erin and Groucho did and how they did it. Housekeepers, cooks, deliverymen, anyone who had contact with Groucho and Erin—all testified, basking in the media's bright lights. It had all the earmarks of a circus. Groucho held center ring, and the press made sure there was a crowd to watch the performances.

Groucho's feelings and dignity were not important. The spectacle was far greater than its leading man during those final days. Day after day, Groucho was wheeled into the courtroom. The press reported he was in tears some of the time. On other occasions, he was withdrawn and moody. Is it any wonder? The most grisly facts about Groucho and his behavior were amplified in the courtroom. We suspect that Groucho realized that no matter who won, he—and no one else—would be the real loser.

Five days after Groucho's grandson was named as Groucho's new guardian and Erin was removed as conservator, and four or five months after the living probate trial had begun, Groucho died. The saga was over.

Groucho had a will, but it hadn't done him any good. Groucho had a lot of money, but he lost control of it to a bank and to his friend Erin.

The last three years of Groucho's life were controlled by a court that didn't know or love him. Erin and the bank—the probate court's appointed agents—had to answer to the court for all aspects of Groucho's life. All but the most mundane of decisions had to be handled by the judge. Groucho became a matter of public record as he lived in the court's and media's transparent world.

The cost was enormous. Erin had lawyers, the bank had lawyers, and Groucho had money. Erin was looked upon by Groucho's family as an interloper. Erin's every action was carefully scrutinized by their respective lawyers. The lawyers got rich at Groucho's expense.

None of Groucho's advisers had bothered to plan for Groucho's disability. In all respects, except for death, he was a neglected client.

The probate court records showed that compared to most Americans, Groucho had a lot of money. All Groucho's money didn't help him avoid the living probate circus. Having money, power, or resources cannot in and of itself protect one from the probate spectacle. Rich and poor alike need to provide for themselves with Loving Trust planning in order to avoid a Groucho-like circus. If Groucho had had a Loving Trust, his probate extravaganza would have been totally and unequivocally avoided.

What Happens to You, Your Spouse, and Your Children if You Become Disabled?

Many people think of "disability" as the loss of an arm or leg and ignore the very real possibility of a complete breakdown of their mental or physical well-being. When we speak of disability, we mean Groucho's kind of disability, where you can no longer care for yourself, where because of an accident or illness, you do not have either the mental or physical capacity to manage your own affairs.

If you can no longer take care of yourself, you will not be able to endorse your disability checks. You will be incapable of being a good and loving spouse or parent. You will not be able to decide with which relative or in which rest home you would like to live. Someone will have to care and act for you. It is highly unlikely that that "someone" will be a loved one. The odds are great that it will be your local probate court that will cash your checks and spend their proceeds. In this respect Groucho was not unique.

Let's assume that you read about Groucho and said, "That is never going to happen to me!" Let's further assume that you immediately give your spouse and other loved ones your general power of attorney.

If told about your strategy, we would compliment you on a nice try, but tell you that giving out those general power of attorneys wasn't a very good idea. A general power of attorney ends at your disability. It ceases to have any legal effect the minute you or your loved ones need it! A general power of attorney doesn't "generally" work and is also extremely dangerous.

There are few legal instruments potentially as dangerous as a general power of attorney. It comes close to giving the holder a blank check to do almost anything he or she wants with your property. The holder might even attempt to take all your property for his or her own! The holder has the power to generally do whatever he or she wants with your property without answering directly to anyone. If you give a general power of attorney, you have given up substantial control over everything that you own.

Do you remember Murphy? Murphy loves general powers of attorney. People change as circumstances change. Regardless of their new motives, beliefs, aspirations, and "new" relationships with you, their power to take or dispose of your property remains 100 percent within their control. If you have given someone such a power, either get it back or cancel it—in writing—immediately!

Can your life insurance help you or your loved ones in the event of your disability? The proceeds certainly will not be available; you have to die to get those in the hands of your loved ones. Your policy's cash value would certainly be helpful in assisting your family to pay the bills, but unfortunately you'll have to sign the paperwork to get it, and you're disabled. It will take a court order.

Can your joint tenancy property help you or your loved ones in the event of your disability? After all, since there are two names on the property, your other tenant should be able to conduct "business as usual." This is not the case. Joint accounts can be absolutely frozen—by law—if one of the owners is declared legally incapacitated.

Do you remember our bird-on-a-limb analogy? You haven't fallen off the limb yet. Your signature is required, and since you are unable to sign, the law says everyone will have to wait until the court acts on your behalf. As we have told our clients for years, "So much for joint tenancy!"

Can your disability insurance help you or your loved ones in the event of your disability? This would seem to be a foolish question. Disability insurance is purchased to provide for you and your loved ones if you become disabled. Why wouldn't it help? After all, that's why we buy the stuff! It works all right— just like gasoline works when it powers an automobile. The only requirement is that it get into your car's gas tank. If you are incapacitated you will not be able to endorse your disability check if it is made out to you. The court will have to do that for you. Your disability insurance, just like everything else you own, will be subject to the Groucho Marx process. Are you the beneficiary of your disability insurance? If you aren't, you will be the exception that proves the usual rule.

The same problems arise with the disability payments from your retirement plan. Almost everyone is routinely made the beneficiary of his or her plan until he or she dies. Those checks will be coming straight to you even though you are incapacitated.

We have seen desperate spouses resort to desperate measures when faced with their husband's or wife's disability. Ruth came to us in dire straits. Her husband had a stroke and other medical difficulties that left him incapacitated. She and her children struggled to stay free of the probate court. In her zeal she started endorsing her husband's name on his disability checks. Her forgery was picked up by a bank clerk, and she was summoned by the appropriate banking authorities. She readily confessed and came to us for help. We had no alternative but to initiate a living probate for her husband. Luckily, the bank was discreet and did not make an issue of it.

If you become disabled, it is probable that you will hold center ring in a probate circus just like Groucho. Your trial may not be as spectacular, nor your affairs as sordid, but the process will be a facsimile of Groucho's. Your creditors will be notified of the probate hearing, an announcement will appear in your local paper, and all of your colleagues and friends will hear about it. Anyone with the inclination and the motive can go to the court and thumb through your file, picking up interesting tidbits of information with regard to your personal and economic lives.

Just like Groucho, you and your family will pay significant legal fees as an added burden. If you are as rich as Groucho was, the expense will not devastate your savings. If you are not, that could very well happen. Your lawyers may take less from you than Groucho's took from him, but as a percentage of your net worth, they may take much more!

The plans that most of us have made for our disability are woefully inadequate or nonexistent. If you are like most of us, you have two choices: You can trust that somehow you and your family will make it through the living probate circus, or you can plan your way around it by using a Loving Trust.

The Loving Trust is first and foremost designed to take care of you. It is designed to take care of you the way you want, without any interference or "help" from the probate courts. Guardians, conservators, probate lawyers, probate courts, and the fees and publicity surrounding them are totally unnecessary. By law, the Loving Trust eliminates them all!

The Loving Trust can also be used to provide for your loved ones in exactly the manner you deem best. A Loving Trust allows you to plan in advance for sickness, disability, or old age. It is yours to design as you wish for the care and protection of you and your loved ones. It is an inexpensive alternative to Groucho's. It can insure that you will be cared for by those you trust most.

4

First Let's Kill All the Lawyers

This chapter is about money—your money. It tells about how expensive wills are.

Every day, lawyers are advertising their services in your daily newspapers. Most of these ads will list prices for the various services they describe. A typical ad, which we found in our morning newspaper the day this chapter was written, went like this (we changed the name of the law firm):

The Law Firm of Ruff & Ready
Full Legal Services

Divorce (Uncontested) $175.00
Initial Consultation $15.00
Bankruptcy (Personal) $250.00
Simple Will $25.00
Basic Corporation $250.00

Almost every newspaper advertisement for legal services contains the price of a simple will. According to this ad, for only $10.00 more than an initial consultation, you could have your will done. What a great bargain! But have you ever wondered why wills are always such a bargain?

Norman F. Dacey, author of the best seller *How to Avoid Probate!,* has taken the position that wills are cheap because they are loss leaders for most lawyers. A will means that eventually, when the client dies, there will be a probate. That's when lawyers reap the rewards.

In 1966, Dacey's *How to Avoid Probate!* topped the best-seller list for months, selling more than one and a half million copies. Dacey's book consisted of some thirty pages or so of attacks on the legal profession and over five hundred pages of forms to be used for do-it-yourself probate avoidance. Dacey advocated not using a lawyer at all, professing that using his forms was all you needed to avoid probate. Dacey was successfully prosecuted for the unauthorized practice of law, both prior to the publication of his book—when Dacey was on the lecture circuit—and after its publication. He responded by suing lawyers, judges, and prosecutors to no avail.

Dacey was very cautious when he wrote his book, evidently trying to avoid the legal problems that the book created. Most of the comments about lawyers are quotes from other people's speeches, comments, or publications. Dacey tried to avoid the consequences of making a head-on attack on lawyers and judges by letting others make his points for him. Dacey did, however, get in a few shots of his own. To give you a flavor for the tone and content of his book, here are some quotes from the 1983 revised edition:

> It would be wrong, of course, to suggest that there are no honest lawyers, for there are—just as there are four-leaf clovers. Finding either is widely regarded as a stroke of rare good luck.

> If Al Capone could return to Chicago, he wouldn't bother with the beer business—he'd be a "specialist in probate practice."

As you can see, Dacey was less than laudatory about the legal profession as a whole and probate lawyers in particular.

Dacey's examples of abuses of the probate process are numerous and, if true, paint a sad picture of the whole sordid business. His premise—that probate is an antiquated process in which only the lawyers and judges profit—has been validated by the attempted reforms in the probate system that have taken place since *How to Avoid Probate!* was published. Unfortunately, these reforms and Dacey's solutions have not had the far-reaching effect that was hoped for. Most estates are still needlessly probated.

The probate fees that were quoted in Dacey's book ranged from 8½ percent of large estates to almost 60 percent of some smaller ones. Dacey, of course, chose the worst examples he could find, but the examples reflect what can and does happen in the probate process.

Twenty years after Dacey's book burst upon the scene, Barbara R. Stock wrote *It's Easy to Avoid Probate and Guardianships.* Her message was the same as Dacey's; probate is an evil system designed only to make lawyers rich at the expense of the American public. This book is the result of a survey done by Ms. Stock of five hundred probate files. The book relates the results of that survey and an explanation and indictment of the probate process. Like Dacey's book, the better part of Stock's book is devoted to methods for avoiding probate and how those methods work. There are forms for trusts and other probate-avoidance devices. Initially, Stock recommended the limited use of a lawyer. Perhaps it was her thinking that such advice would protect her from the lawsuits and legal problems faced by Dacey in his heyday. However, Stock quickly reversed positions and began a new career as a self-proclaimed expert selling bare-bones boilerplate forms.

Chapter Three of Stock's book is entitled "Probate: A System Designed by Attorneys for the Benefit of Attorneys." It is here, for the most part, that she makes her observations about the legal system and the probate lawyers in it:

> It is to the advantage of the attorneys to maintain an appearance of complexity and to find a way to drag these probate proceedings out.

> Fortunately, doctors are kinder with their scalpels than attorneys . . . at slicing away estate assets.

Stock's message is the same as Dacey's. They both believe that the probate system is fueled by the greed of the legal establishment.

The costs of probate in Stock's survey—taken almost twenty years after Dacey's best-seller went on the market—show a startling similarity to Dacey's conclusions. Her figures show that probate fees average 22 percent on smaller estates and 6.2 percent on larger estates. Stock cited small estates where the probate fees approached 60 percent of the estate, just as Dacey did. It appears that not much has changed over the years.

That brings up some questions. Are more people avoiding probate now than before Dacey wrote his book? Did Stock's sampling adequately reflect what was happening nationwide? Are people still going through probate, despite the hue and cry over the last twenty years?

Howard Hughes, the man with more money than just about anyone else, didn't avoid probate, and goodness knows he had the dollars to hire the best probate avoiders in the world. J. Paul Getty didn't avoid probate, and his estate attorneys' fees were $27 million! How would you like to make that much for a few years of clerical work?

Presidents John F. Kennedy and Lyndon B. Johnson didn't avoid probate! On the other hand, other well-known celebrities like John Lennon and Bing Crosby avoided it by using either a Loving Trust or a bare-bones living trust. We can't ascertain what their documents said because—unlike a will—they were totally private. Our law firm specialized in helping our clients avoid probate, yet other lawyers in our town were totally convinced that the probate process was necessary and that it protected the public.

Who is right and who is wrong?

We believe that both Dacey and Stock are very much right and very much wrong. They are right about probate. It is needlessly expensive, needlessly time-consuming, and needlessly suffered by loved ones. Dacey and Stock make a mistake when they blame lawyerly greed and bad faith as the sole whipping posts for probate abuses. Dacey's and Stock's solutions and approaches to avoiding probate are oftentimes dead wrong. Their attacks on lawyers make good reading; their alternatives are as bad as those they attack! They are practicing bad law without a license.

The Probate Process

Conceptually, probate is not difficult to understand. When you die, your property needs to be distributed to your heirs. You cannot sign deeds, write checks, pay bills, or transact any business. The courts assume these responsibilities. Probate is the process of transferring property to one's heirs. Dying with a will guarantees probate, as does dying without one or without a bona fide will substitute.

Property passing through the probate process acts like water traveling through a leaky pipe. Every few feet some of the water escapes, and at those spots there is always someone to collect the leakage. When it reaches the other end of the pipe—where the heirs collect—there is not always a whole lot left.

The first order of probate business is for the judge to approve or appoint an agent to handle the affairs of the estate. The name for this agent is "executor" or "administrator" or "personal representative," depending on the state and the circumstances. We use the term executor, as it seems familiar to most people. An executor is named in the will of the person who dies. If a person dies without either a will or a bona fide will substitute, the probate judge will pick the executor. Dacey believes that when this occurs the choice will inevitably be a "buddy" of the judge. It is the judge's way of giving a friend some "free" money and is part and parcel of a corrupt probate system.

The executor hires a lawyer to interact with the judge. Sometimes the executor is a lawyer who hires himself as the estate's lawyer. Two different jobs, two different fees. All part of the same leaky pipe.

The second order of probate business is to notify the creditors of the deceased. This entails the often time-consuming task of determining all of the dead person's liabilities.

Creditors are notified either directly by the executor or by advertisements in the local newspapers. The creditors are given a period of time to make claims against the estate. Depending on state law, this can be as short as two or three months or as long as nine months or more. The estate—by law—is required to stay open during this period of time.

All the property in the estate must be appraised. The executor hires an appraiser or appraisers to determine the value of the estate assets, from real estate to cars to furniture and knick-knacks. Everything must be assigned a value. This process is especially important to the lawyer, who often bases his or her fee on the value of the estate. Wealthy probate lawyers are often good friends of their local appraisers.

Estates that have federal estate tax liability have to stay open until the taxes are paid, which is normally nine months. If there is any dispute as to the amount of tax, the estate has to be kept open until the IRS either audits or determines the proper amount.

Anyone who has a beef with the will can bring a lawsuit in the probate court. This is called a will contest. Will contests come in infinite varieties. In many cases, lawsuits seem to be started to intimidate the heirs into staving off unwanted litigation by settling out of court. This is an effective way for the unscrupulous to collect under a will without having much of a case.

After the dust has settled and everybody associated with the probate estate is either paid or paid off, the heirs can receive their shares of whatever is left.

The Costs of Probate

The people who get paid under the probate process itself are the executor, the lawyer, the appraiser, and the court in terms of court fees and costs. It is these costs that both Dacey and Stock say run from 5 percent to 60 percent or more of the value of an estate, before creditors are paid. They average, according to Stock, over 7 percent of the value of the estate, with 60 percent of the total cost going to lawyers and 40 percent going to executors and others.

Probate is expensive. Dacey's and Stock's books are full of examples of how expensive probate really is, and we agree that it is very expensive. They emphasize that the smaller your estate is, the more probate takes from your loved ones; we agree with that, too. Wills are cheap for one reason: there's a great deal of money to be made at the end of the line—exorbitant probate fees paid out of the pockets of your heirs.

Probate Takes Time

According to Stock, the average probate takes sixteen months. The average estate surveyed was valued at $110,000. An estate that size is not particularly complicated. The estates in the survey apparently were not plagued by lawsuits or other problems. They just dragged on. According to Stock, the main "dragger" is the lawyer, who likes to rack up those fees.

In our practice, we were asked with some regularity to review probates that seemed to the heirs to be taking much too long. The longest probate we saw was twenty-eight years in duration. The second longest was twenty-three years. In both cases, we were able to close the estate within months. Someone was sandbagging. What really amazed us was that the heirs would tolerate this for so long. The lawyer and the executor would have to be pretty convincing to be able to pull the wool over someone's eyes for that many years. It is frightening how the legal system can intimidate people to the extent that they really believe probate must take this long.

Probate Is Public

We represented a lot of contractors in our practice. One day, a good contractor client contacted us about one of his competitors who had recently died. Our client, Ed, wanted to buy some equipment from the widow and wanted us to make an offer on his behalf. Ed figured that the equipment he needed was worth about $250,000.

Since we were paid to represent our client to the best of our ability, we recommended that we research the competitor's probate file to get an idea about what he owned and how much it was worth. We sent a paralegal to the probate court, and in a few hours we had the complete probate file. We had his will, a list of all of his assets and liabilities, including litigation his business was in, promissory notes, and mortgages. We had the "private" financial statement of his business.

Our review showed that the estate badly needed cash to pay debts. The widow had petitioned the court for money, stating that she was destitute without aid from the estate. There was no doubt that the estate had to sell assets—and fast—to make ends meet. We told our client to offer fifty cents on the dollar,

$125,000 cash for the equipment. The offer was accepted without negotiation.

Frankly, we are embarrassed to relate this story. It is, in retrospect, a sad commentary on lawyers and the probate system. We can only justify our action by rationalizing that we did our job and did it well. Our job was to do the best for our client, and we did. Incidentally, our client, when he dies, will not go through probate. This little lesson scared him to death.

Probate is public. Anyone can go to the probate court and look up an estate. Would you like to know about a deceased famous man in your town? Go to the probate court. If he didn't avoid probate, you will be able to find out a great deal about him.

You may think that you have nothing to hide when you die. "Who cares if someone sees what I have? I'm not ashamed." It is not a matter of being ashamed; it is a matter of being wise. Some stockbrokers, some lawyers, and some pretty shady salespeople read obituaries and death notices and prey upon the heirs. Widows and children are easy marks for con-men and women. We suspect that the first place these crooks go is to the public probate files to find their marks.

If you play cards, most of the games you play are played with your cards hidden from the other players. You don't expose your hand to your opponents, because doing so gives them the upper hand. There is one game in which one player is required to expose his or her hand, and that game is bridge. The person who has to expose his hand is called, appropriately enough, the dummy. Do you want your family to be the dummy?

First Let's Kill All the Lawyers

"The first thing we do, let's kill all the lawyers" is a commonly quoted Shakespearean line. It is indicative of the feelings expressed by Dacey and Stock and subscribed to by a great proportion of the general populace. Dacey even quotes the Bible to emphasize that lawyers have been the source of mankind's problems almost since the beginning of recorded history.

We are lawyers, members of the fraternity that Dacey and Stock have taken on. One of our ex-partners, Milton E. "Bob" Meyer, Jr., is quoted by Dacey in his book. As a matter of fact,

Bob's writings are probably the source that Dacey used to "reinvent" his solution to probate avoidance. Barbara Stock recommends our *Handbook of Estate Planning* in her book. We have always specialized in probate avoidance.

We share this autobiographical information with you to demonstrate that we are members of both camps—the good guys and the bad guys, depending on what or whom you believe. We work with—and, more importantly, teach—many of those "dirty," "nasty," "greedy," "uncaring" lawyers whom Dacey and Stock talk about. Our firm did a great deal of probate clean-up work, although it was a small part of our overall billings. We know both sides of the probate issue.

Sure, there are corrupt and dishonest lawyers, just as there are less-than-honorable members in every other profession. There are lawyers who do not have professional motives and practice law just to make a buck. However, in our experience, these types of lawyers are in the minority. Honest lawyers are not as rare as four-leaf clovers. They represent the majority. Neither Stock nor Dacey are lawyers. They have only been on one side of the fence. They do not have all of the answers.

We recently gave a seminar to a group of lawyers in Lake of the Ozarks, Missouri, underwritten by a major life insurance company. The seminar was about the Loving Trust. It was supposed to be a relatively technical discussion, with the main thrust being the review of *A Loving Trust Compendium,* our technical practice book for lawyers.

The lawyers in our class were from throughout the country. They ranged from general practitioners who did very little will or trust work, to practitioners who did only simple wills, to planning specialists with many years in the practice. All the lawyers in the room derived some of their income from probate.

The seminar began exactly the way this book did. We attacked wills and probate as outdated. We chastised the lawyers for subjecting their clients to these two superfluous legal dinosaurs. Wow, did we get a reaction.

Our audience apparently believed in wills and probate. If we didn't know better, we'd have assumed that their motivation was solely the money created by probate. We had attacked their professionalism, and they reacted defensively and aggressively.

The more they defended the system and insisted probate was good, the more we responded with our feeling that probate is a cancer, that even a little bit is too much. There was a real confrontation.

The first day of the three-day seminar was to end at five o'clock, but most of the group stayed on for several additional hours to vent their concerns about our critique. That in itself was incredible, because we were at a beautiful resort and most of the lawyers had made plans to enjoy the leisure activities offered. Golf, tennis, and swimming were forgotten as our talks continued.

One of the most vocal critics of our point of view was a Philadelphia lawyer named Dick. Dick is a warm, caring fellow in his late forties who, at that time, believed that probate was a necessary process that was not harmful to his clients. He did not generate a great deal of his revenue from his probate practice because he charged hourly and evidently was very efficient. He did, however, believe in the probate process.

The session ended well into the evening, with no one, especially Dick, having changed his mind. The next two days, however, were magic. As the doubting Thomases learned about the Loving Trust, how it worked and the many positive things it did, they turned around. Dick and his classmates turned out to be big supporters of the Loving Trust.

None of these lawyers appeared to be greedy or dishonest. They were a product of their education. In most law schools there is no course in how trusts are used to help clients. The courses given are on the technical aspects of wills and trusts; they emphasize legalese. The material is purely theoretical; no practical applications or loving plans are alluded to.

Imagine, if you will, a huge gymnasium. It is empty, except for one table that is four feet long and three feet wide. Assuming the gymnasium represents all of the types of law that lawyers practice, the table represents trust law. Trust law is a tiny part of our legal system. There is no time for our law schools to teach aspiring lawyers how to make bare-bones trust plans, much less Loving Trust plans. Most lawyers do not have the opportunity to use even their limited knowledge on a regular basis when it comes to planning for their clients' loved ones.

The Loving Trust is overlooked, not from the bar's greed or avarice, but from a simple lack of knowledge! Lawyers, for the most part, do not understand that probate is bad. They are so close to the process that they cannot see past it. Probate, like shaving every morning, appears to be a necessary evil until lawyers really understand that it can be so easily and skillfully avoided.

We have repeated our Lake of the Ozarks seminar in other places. It wasn't an isolated incident. Our seminar experiences have taught us that lawyers know they are unpopular and that they are losing credibility with the public. They know that there are too many of them; they read their press and are not insensitive or stupid. Most lawyers want to be liked and respected; they want to do a good job, a job that is best for the client, and they want to charge a fair and reasonable price for their services.

Dacey and Stock played the demagogue, secure in their own ignorance, by picking on lawyers. They sought cases of extreme abuse within the process and assumed bad motives or bad law on the part of all lawyers. We know that once most lawyers are educated in the Loving Trust, they are usually more than happy to abandon simple wills and probate and enthusiastically plan for their clients' loved ones. They, like all of us, just need to learn the ropes.

No Solutions at All

Dacey's solution to avoiding probate was to publish an enormous set of forms. Law is complicated. No matter how good the forms, and Dacey's are mediocre at best, it is hard to select the right form for the right job and to fill it in properly. Here are some of the problems that we have seen occur with the Dacey forms:

- The forms are not signed correctly.
- The Dacey trusts are not operable, because nothing is ever put into them.
- They are not written in understandable English, so people have no idea what they are doing.
- There are so many forms, people pick the wrong form for the wrong reason or purpose.

- The forms are so concerned about avoiding probate, they *totally forget to take care of loved ones!*

Like it or not, you need to have a lawyer to help you avoid probate. If you do not, you will be the classic case of the armed citizen who shot himself or herself in the foot. A little knowledge is dangerous. An incorrect Dacey form is as expensive, or more expensive, than a will. When someone messes up a Dacey form, the heirs have to hire a lawyer to clean up the mess. The odds are very high that a Dacey form will be incorrect or that the heirs will not understand what to do with it after the maker dies. A lawyer will then have to be involved, and your loved ones will begin at probate square one. If you attempt to do all your own legal work by using a Dacey form, you will get exactly what you paid for.

The do-it-yourself mentality of the Dacey forms, though, is not their most glaring and harmful consequence. Dacey forgot about loved ones! Out of a book of almost six hundred pages, he devotes a few pages to taking care of spouses, children, and other loved ones. Dacey is so caught up in his probate-avoidance crusade that he blithely dismisses most of the problems of leaving property outright to spouses or children. Dacey suffers from the same ailment he accuses the legal establishment of having: a lack of compassion for people. Dacey's trusts forget love. They are money trusts. They throw out the baby with the bathwater, all in the name of probate avoidance. Avoiding probate is important. Caring for loved ones is more important.

Barbara Stock's motto appears to be that probate avoidance is not everything, it is the only thing. According to Stock, at least 50 percent of all Americans need only put all their property into joint tenancy to avoid probate and all the problems associated with it. How wrong she is. We have already addressed how joint property is the worst possible probate-avoidance method. It offers loss of control, the real possibility of unintended heirs; it creates gift taxes among nonspouses; it is great for creditors; and it creates death tax problems. Joint tenancy has been around for a long time, and probate fees and lawyer fees have not gone down. Joint tenancy won't prevent probate when the last joint tenant dies. It never prevents probate on disability. As for saving fees, in some states lawyers can and do charge a probate fee on joint property.

Like Dacey, Stock forgets about loved ones. In her opinion, a trust or other probate-avoiding device that is over a few pages long is totally unnecessary, except for rich Americans. What bunk! You spend your whole life building up what you have. Countless hours are spent carefully nurturing your property, keeping taxes down, saving, agonizing over how to live comfortably. It seems kind of sad that all that work, time, and effort can be reduced to a few pages.

Stock is right when she claims that it is easy to avoid probate. The hard part is to pass on your wisdom, your hopes, your dreams, and your aspirations to those you love. Stock thinks that passing love is reserved for the rich. Only they can afford to have elaborate trusts that avoid probate, avoid taxes, and provide for loved ones. How wrong she is.

Our solution to probate avoidance and to providing for loved ones is over a thousand years old—it is the revocable living trust, filled with your loving instructions—it is the Loving Trust.

5

The Loving Trust

We are often asked: "What does a trust look like?" "How does it operate?" "Where do you find one?"

Many people think a trust is a sophisticated legal device used only by the superrich; this is a misconception. Trusts are for people who care and who have some property or life insurance that they want to pass to loved ones. Generally, trusts are written instructions that allow their makers to give what they have to whom they want, in the way and when they want. A trust has a maker and beneficiaries who will receive property according to the maker's instructions; it also has a trustee who will follow those instructions.

Wills can create trusts. These are called death (testamentary) trusts. Trusts are also created in simple contracts (indentures) called living trusts. The instructions "I want my brother to use my property to take care of my two children until they reach the age of twenty-one" could be found in a will, and if so, would create a death trust. If they are written down outside of a will, they would create a living trust. When the maker reserves the right to change the trust at any time and for any reason, it is called a revocable living trust. When a maker wants to make an absolute gift to the trust beneficiaries—a gift with strings attached—the trust is irrevocable; the maker cannot change the trust instructions once the trust is signed.

A death trust comes into existence only upon the death of its maker. It must go through probate to get assets in it. Unlike

58

a death trust, a living trust can avoid probate, and it can be used to take care of its maker. Living-trust property can be immediately put in the care of a trustee, or it can be delivered at some later date. A living-trust maker can be both a trustee and a beneficiary of his or her trust.

Unfortunately, most living trusts that we have reviewed are not very thorough or explicit. They do not give the trustee meaningful instructions as to what the maker desires. These "bare-bones boilerplate" living trusts don't do much planning for either the maker or loved ones, but they can avoid probate if properly set up.

The Loving Trust gives more—much more—for much less. It does so because it can:

- Provide for you.
- Provide for your loved ones.
- Keep your affairs and those of your loved ones private.
- Avoid probate.
- Work in every state.
- Avoid complex will rules.

A Loving Trust can do everything a will can do and much more. A will merely disposes of property when you die. A Loving Trust does that, too. A will can create death trusts for your loved ones, but these trusts will be subject to the control of the probate court and the probate process. A Loving Trust can create those same trusts, free from the supervision and control of the probate court and the probate process. A will can be used to minimize federal estate taxes. So can a Loving Trust. A will cannot take care of you; a Loving Trust can. A will most likely does not control all of your property. A Loving Trust is specifically designed to control all of your property. A will is cheap on the front end and extraordinarily expensive on the back end. A Loving Trust has no hidden rear-end charges and involves a reasonable front-end preparation fee.

A Loving Trust can properly embrace all the work done by your life insurance agent, your realtor, your bank's clerks, the clerk where you work, and your stockbroker. A Loving Trust assures that your property will be used for you and your loved ones. It places control where it belongs—with you. It is not a pitcher that pours its water into open fingers. A Loving Trust allows you to control your destiny as well as that of your loved ones. It takes the control of your life away from well-meaning but unknowledgeable advisers and clerks.

A Loving Trust is a <u>revocable</u> living trust that far surpasses the "bare-bones" living trusts suggested by Dacey and Stock. Used solely for the purpose of avoiding probate, their living trusts are terse sets of instructions that set out where property will pass on death. Bare-bones living trusts only do part of the job; they are the zombies of the trust world, only half-alive. Their emphasis is on one benefit, probate avoidance, and that is all.

Loving Trusts are fleshed-out living trusts that are brought fully to life with loving directions. They not only avoid probate but also allow you to provide for your loved ones in the manner that you choose. Loving Trusts allow your hopes, dreams, and aspirations to survive you.

Bare-bones living trusts are commonly used as a panacea for will planning. Perhaps we should say that they are commonly misused, because most living trusts we have reviewed simply do not do what their makers expect them to do.

The Chairman of the Board of a major national bank asked us to review his living trust to make sure it met his objectives. When we are asked to review existing plans, our first step is to take a page from a legal pad and fold it in half from top to bottom. We ask our clients what they think their current will or trust says. We ask them to be very specific, detailing what they think will happen to them, their spouses, and children upon their death or disability. We write their perceptions down on the left half of the page. Next, we review their will or trust and write down what it really says on the right half. We then compare the two halves to see if there is a match.

When the chairman saw the left half juxtaposed against the right half, he was astounded. What he thought his trust said and what it really said were miles, or even light-years, apart. He thought there were all sorts of provisions for him and his loved ones. There were very few, and the few there were did not say what he thought they should say.

This experience was not new to us. It repeats itself almost every time we go through this exercise. Usually the client believes that he or she has conveyed to the lawyer the essence of what is needed on death or disability. The lawyer fits the client's requests into his or her own preconceived notions of what is called for, and a miscommunication results. The reasons for such miscommunications are many. The client is usually at fault for not communicating clear planning objectives. The lawyer is usually at fault for being a poor listener and questioner, forcing the client's wishes into very restrictive legal forms. Both are guilty in that neither spent the time to educate the other. The client does not educate the lawyer as to the client's real motives. The lawyer fails to educate the client as to all of the legal options available to meet the client's motives.

Most clients end up with bare-bones legal work. The client's loved ones suffer, and so does the image of the legal profession.

In our lectures to lawyers, the most disturbing point, at least to them, is when we speak about bare-bones legal work, whether it be bare-bones (simple) wills, or bare-bones (simple) living trusts. It's as if these lawyers finally realize what has been wrong all these years, why clients have been so reluctant to do any planning, and why heirs are usually so unhappy.

Lawyers have been selling death. Death does not sell or make people happy. Bare-bones legal work does not sell, nor does it make people happy. Love sells. Love makes people happy. Providing for clients and for their loved ones makes all the difference in the world between happy clients and dissatisfied ones. No plan is good without LOVE! And no other method of providing for you and your loved ones is as effective or as satisfying as a Loving Trust.

A Loving Trust is a revocable living trust fleshed out and made truly alive by adding big doses of love. To understand how one works, you need to understand what a trust is. Explaining a trust intimidates most professionals. They want to make it a great deal more complicated than it really is. We believe that a trust's terms are similar to the instructions parents leave with their childrens' baby-sitter. This analogy has helped many of our clients and students to visualize just what a trust is and how it operates.

The Baby-sitter Story

Both of us have two boys. We love our boys, but once in a while we like to leave home and spend time alone with our wives. When we leave, we have a baby-sitter take care of our boys. Our wives are loving and caring. They want to make sure that the baby-sitters are fully apprised as to what they need to do.

If we are going to leave for a weekend, the baby-sitter receives about twenty minutes of verbal instruction. He or she is left wih a notepad of several pages detailing all that needs to be done for the boys. Any contingency that our wives (and we) can think of is added to the instructions. Little gummed stickers are stuck all over the house with notes on them, both for the boys and the baby-sitter. We will be close to a phone, and, of course, we will call at least two times a day to clarify our instructions. You can't be too careful when it comes to caring for those you love.

Does this sound familiar? We think it does, because when we share this story in our seminars, the students always start smiling, nodding, and laughing.

A Loving Trust is your set of baby-sitter instructions for the care of your loved ones. Like those instructions, it provides for your loved ones' basic needs and care, as well as for their special needs and circumstances. The difference between the two is that with a Loving Trust you will ultimately not be near a telephone to clarify or add to your instructions.

If you have a will or a trust, now is the time to look at it. If it is not handy, try to remember what is in it. When we review wills and trusts, there are usually, at most, one or two paragraphs about how children are to be cared for. There may be a few more for a spouse, but not many. Most of the language in a will or a trust is merely bare-bones boilerplate legalese, containing no instructions to speak of, but plenty of other very cold and sterile verbiage that no one with less than a law degree can understand.

A will or a trust is supposed to contain explicit instructions on how you want your loved ones cared for with your property. It is our experience that almost all wills and trusts do just the opposite.

Sad, isn't it? Most of our baby-sitter instructions for our loved ones are far more complete than our instructions for our final trip. Why is this the case? Because we somehow believe that short is better; that a legal document that is longer than a few pages is no good. Bare-bones legal work is supposed to tell a trustee baby-sitter what we want to have happen to our property and how we want to take care of our loved ones. But, by definition, it cannot succeed. Little can be accomplished in one or two paragraphs.

A Loving Trust is a complete set of legal baby-sitter instructions. The baby-sitter is called a trustee. As your baby-sitter follows your instructions, so must your trustee. Your instructions will be for yourself if you are disabled and for your spouse, children, or other people you love and wish to care for when you are gone. Those who receive the benefits of your Loving Trust instructions are called beneficiaries. When you make your Loving Trust, you are called a trustor, grantor, or settlor. They all mean the same thing: maker of a trust.

Your Loving Trust contains your instructions. By the law of every state, your trustee must follow your Loving Trust's instructions to the letter for the benefit of your beneficiaries. That is what a Loving Trust is all about.

For those of you who have heard of a revocable living trust, the Loving Trust should sound familiar. A Loving Trust is the next step beyond the ordinary bare-bones living trust. In our experience, most bare-bones living trusts are used exactly as Norman F. Dacey or Barbara Stock say they ought to be used—merely to avoid probate, no more, no less. They are living trusts without love.

The Loving Trust embodies far more than just probate avoidance. It emphasizes caring for loved ones and follows your instructions rather than bare-bones legal forms. It is a living trust format infused with your loving directions.

Lawyers can easily draft living trusts if they have the knowledge and the desire to do so. Most lawyers have access to good legal forms, books, and word processors. But, being able to draft a Loving Trust is only one of the necessary ingredients. Someone has to take the time to listen to your instructions, to anticipate the worst and head off Murphy's Law. Someone has to flesh out those general instructions with loving detail to make sure your trustees do just what you would do if you were there.

Picture in your mind the following scenario. You see a tall, elderly man; he is very skinny, almost a skeleton. His skull-like head is covered with a top hat. He is wearing an old-fashioned frock coat that ends just below his knees. In his hands is a snap-open coin purse. It is old and threadbare. It is so old that a tiny moth flies out when he opens it.

He reaches his long, bony fingers into the coin purse and pulls out a bright, shiny nickel. In front of him is a poorly dressed widow. At her side are several obviously destitute children, looking very morose and exceedingly hungry. He smiles with a macabre grimace and hands the widow and children the nickel. It is their trust allowance for the week.

To many people this scene captures the essence of a bare-bones trust—an old, conservative banker, handing out nickels to widows and starving children. It's no wonder that when the word "trust" is mentioned, there is a silent—or sometimes not so silent—groan and a shudder of fear.

Loving Trusts can and do present a picture exactly the opposite of the traditional banker and the widow with her starving children. They offer a portrait of a smiling and happy widow or widower with well-fed kids being taken care of with love from their parents' or spouse's Loving Trust.

A Loving Trust offers much more than a will. It offers you much more control than your advisers have ever previously given you. It offers you more than a bare-bones living trust. A Loving Trust offers much more than all those alternatives and does so at far less cost to you or your loved ones.

6

Our Loving Trust

Our Loving Trusts:

- Allow us to control our property while we are alive.
- Provide for us, our spouses, and our children, without any court supervision, if we become sick, injured, or disabled.
- Provide for our loved ones in exactly the way we want after we die.
- Make absolutely sure we don't take our families public and make a lot of strangers richer at our expense or the expense of our loved ones.

You can have your own Loving Trust and achieve the same results as we have with ours. It is not difficult to design and build a Loving Trust once you know how. We would like to show you an example of what a Loving Trust is by sharing a summary of our Loving Trusts with you. Our actual trust documents have a bit more legalese in them than our translation, but our translation will do them justice. We used this plain English translation technique when we went through our clients' trusts with them. There is no reason to explain a Loving Trust in more complicated language.

Both of us are very happily married and have been married only once. We both have two boys who are about three years apart. As you can guess, our Loving Trusts are pretty similar, but there are differences. The Loving Trust translation that follows will blend a little of each of our actual Loving Trusts together. For purposes of avoiding confusion, the names are fictional. The Loving Trust is not.

Creating a Loving Trust begins with desires and motives. You must determine what your motives are before creating a Loving Trust. Our primary motive is to be assured that we will be well taken care of if we become sick or disabled. We do not want to end up like Groucho. We want to reduce our federal estate tax, while taking care of our wives, children, and grandchildren (neither of us has grandchildren now, but we hope to have some someday). We want our wives to be able to use all our property for themselves and for our children and grandchildren. Half of our property is our wives' to do with as they please. When our wives die, we want to make sure that at least half of our property goes to our children and grandchildren.

We want our wives to have complete control over our property, but we do not want to leave it outright to them. We want our spouses to have the assistance and expertise of our friends and colleagues in administering our trusts and investing their assets. We do not want our children or grandchildren to have their trust property outright at our spouses' death. We would like to ease our children into their inheritances by providing them with two distributions.

As you read through our Loving Trust synopsis, it is likely that you will encounter paragraphs that you will not understand or that will be foreign to your experience and thinking. Do not despair. At this time we simply want to give you an understanding of what a Loving Trust covers. Once you have finished reading through Part Two, we would like you to read our Loving Trust again. We think you will find that your understanding of its terms will be significantly increased.

With these basic motives in mind, here is our Loving Trust:

Introduction

My name is Rob Epson, and this is my trust. My wife's name is Lisa. My wife, Lisa, and I are the trustees of my trust. We have two children, Billy, ten, and Don, seven. Any other children we may have or adopt, I want automatically added to my trust.

My Rights

This is my trust. While I am alive I have total control over it. I can put property in it, and I can take property out of it. I will also control the income it creates. I can change my trust for any reason at any time. If I don't want my trust anymore, I can also cancel or revoke it at any time.

I Wish to Provide for Myself

If I become disabled, my trustees shall care for me according to my instructions. After I am taken care of, my trustees may use my property to care for my wife and children.

Distribution of My Personal Property

I give my personal property to my loved ones according to the written instructions on the attached memorandum. Whatever I have not listed shall go to my wife, or to my children if she is not alive. If my children fight over my personal property, my trustees are to sell it and divide the proceeds.

How I Want My Property Allocated

I want to reduce federal estate tax, give my wife whatever she needs, and make sure that at least one-half of my property goes to my children on her death.

I want my property divided into two parts. One shall be called my Wife's Pocketbook Trust. The other shall be called my Family Trust.

I want my trustees to save federal estate tax by properly allocating my property between my Pocketbook and Family Trusts. If my Trustees need to create two Pocketbook Trusts to achieve this goal, they are to do so.

How to Provide for My Wife

My wife's share of my property shall go to a Pocketbook Trust. It is hers. She can have any or all of it anytime she wants. If she is sick or disabled, then my trustees are to care for her in whatever she needs. She can leave her trust property to anyone she wants. If she neglects to do so, it shall automatically go to my children's trust.

If I need two Pocketbook Trusts, my wife will receive all the income and get whatever she needs from the property in her second trust.

How to Provide for My Family

My Family Trust shall be for my wife, my children, and my grandchildren. My trustees shall take care of my loved ones based on their needs, but shall always give first priority to my wife.

How to Provide for My Minor Children

My Common Trust for my sons and grandchildren will begin when my wife dies. It will have the property my wife didn't give away and my remaining Family Trust property.

It will remain in effect until my youngest son is twenty-three years of age, or finishes college, whichever happens first. Until this happens, my trustees are to take care of my sons in whatever they need. My trustees do not have to use the property in my Common Trust equally for each son. They are to care for each of my sons based on their respective needs.

My trustees may use my property to assist my sons' guardians in caring for them. They must be sure that the funds are used with my sons' welfare in mind; they are not to give the guardians a windfall.

If one of my sons would like extra money for a business, a profession, a wedding, a house, or any other extraordinary need, my trustees are to ask themselves two questions:

1. Is the extraordinary need valid?
2. If it is, will giving him the funds be financially harmful to my other son's basic financial needs?

If these tests are passed, my trustees shall give my son the money for this extraordinary need as an advancement against his ultimate inheritance. When his inheritance is ultimately paid out, they are to deduct the advancement.

If one of my sons dies while this trust is in existence, and he has children, they will then be beneficiaries of this trust.

When my youngest son reaches the age of twenty-three, or completes college, my trustees shall divide the Common Trust property into a separate trust for each of my sons.

How to Distribute My Sons' Property

My trustees shall take care of my boys in everything they need from their respective Separate Trusts.

I love my boys and want to give them two opportunities to receive their inheritances. When my son is twenty-five, my trustees shall give him half of his trust property. He can have the other half when he reaches thirty. If he is already over twenty-five when his trust is created, my trustees shall immediately give him half. He can have the other half in five years. In the meantime, my trustees shall provide for each of my sons from their respective trusts.

What Happens to My Property on the Premature Death of a Son

If one of my sons dies, he may leave his trust property to whomever he wants. If he fails to do so, it will stay in trust for his children. If he has no children, then his trust property will pass to his brother's trust.

How to Ultimately Distribute My Property

If I have no surviving family members, half of my property shall be distributed equally between my relatives and my wife's relatives. The other half shall be distributed to the United Way.

My Trustees and How They Can Be Terminated

My wife and I are the initial trustees of my trust. Either of us can resign at any time, as can any other trustee. I can fire a trustee at any time for any reason.

After I die, or become disabled, my wife can fire a trustee for any reason. After my wife dies, a majority of my children can also fire a trustee for any reason.

After I die, or become disabled, Jack Cravets and Jean Douglas shall be added as co-trustees, along with my wife. If any of these trustees resigns, or is fired, then he or she will be replaced by the following people in the order as shown:

> Pete Johnson
> Kiley P. Thornton
> Paula Hoffman

If these trustees aren't available, then First National Bank shall serve as a co-trustee.

My Trustees' Powers

I give my trustees every power that I would have in administering my property for my loved ones.

Our actual trusts are several pages long because, like our baby-sitter instructions, we want to be sure that our instructions are clear and detailed. We won't have an opportunity to correct any mistakes once we are gone. The length and the detail are what distinguish our Loving Trust from a bare-bones living trust. We love our wives and children, and we have much to say as to how they should be cared for.

Some of what we said in our trust synopsis, even though it was stated in simple language, may be confusing or unclear. That's all right. The following chapters will bring all of it into perspective for you. For now, we want you to get a feel for what a Loving Trust does and how it is put together.

The most important aspects of our Loving Trust for you to remember are these:

- A Loving Trust contains your instructions about how you wish you and your loved ones to be cared for.
- A Loving Trust names trustees to operate your trust. You are a trustee while you are alive and well, but other trustees will take over when you become disabled or die.
- Your instructions can be as detailed or as terse as you want. You can do whatever you want with your Loving Trust, as long as it is not illegal or against public policy.
- Your Loving Trust will create a number of separate trusts for your loved ones that will have specific instructions for their care.

To help you better visualize what a Loving Trust is, we have included a diagram of Our Loving Trust (see insert following page 211). When you fill in the diagrams provided for your Loving Trust at the end of Part Two, refer to our diagram. It will help you to better understand how a Loving Trust really works.

7

LeRoy's Story

Shortly after one of our seminars, LeRoy, a financial planning participant from Abilene, Texas, called us. The first exasperated words out of his mouth were, "Do y'all know of any lawyers in this part of Texas that can do one of these trusts?" We didn't and felt bad about it. LeRoy had left the seminar extremely excited about Loving Trusts, but quickly became subdued when he couldn't find a local lawyer to do his Loving Trust.

The most common question we are asked, whether by seminar participants or talk-show callers, is how to find a lawyer willing to do a Loving Trust. There has definitely been a shortage of legal talent out there willing or able to prepare a Loving Trust. We share LeRoy's frustration; not being able to refer other advisers and nonprofessionals to lawyers skilled in Loving Trust techniques has been a great frustration to us.

We want everyone to have a Loving Trust. They can be effectively used in every single state. We are confident that if we just get the word out, they will be broadly taken advantage of by both professionals and the public.

There is no way we personally can do everyone's Loving Trust. We tried that and made little headway; the more we did, the greater we found the demand to be. We have done thousands of them over the years. There are select lawyers and firms of lawyers who do them all over the country, and, fortunately, these Loving Trust lawyers are increasing in numbers.

It has long been our goal to educate the public and professionals alike in order to start a Loving Trust momentum. To do this, we have to convince the American public that the Loving Trust is the best method for providing for loved ones; we must also build a force of competent lawyers to do the work. With the knowledge in this book and the directions we provide, you should be able quickly and confidently to get your Loving Trust accomplished. Keep in mind, however, that you should not be a planning Lone Ranger.

We read a recent best-selling health book about how the food you eat can affect your health, and how, through vitamin supplements, diet, and experimentation, you can strengthen your immune system and feel better. The how-to part of this book was virtually impossible for us to utilize. Changing foods all the time, trying to maintain records, and all of the other methods of self-diagnosis were not practical. Finding the correct vitamins and their proper dosages proved to be expensive and even more difficult for us to do. We finally concluded that the only way we could do what the book suggested was to see the doctor who wrote it. He claimed to have tests that would find our food allergies. He could prescribe and dispense the correct vitamins as well as their dosages.

The book gave us false expectations of what we could do. In the end, we had to go see the "guru" to get the job done. Only the doctor could really apply the principles in the book. Other people may be missing out on the benefits of the doctor's program because, unlike us, they cannot travel to see the doctor. This is a classic Catch-22 where the doctor wins through royalties and the rest of us lose through false expectations.

Parts Two and Three of this book are designed to help avoid this syndrome. Part Two will allow you to design, step-by-step, your own blueprints for your Loving Trust. Through our instructions and checklists, you will have a pathway to accomplishing your Loving Trust. By examining your every motive, you will be able to build a series of subtrusts, created especially for each of your loved ones, that will make up your Loving Trust. You will be your own Loving Trust architect. Your plans or personal blueprints need only be given to a lawyer to be put into legal language.

Part Three will show you how to find a lawyer to write your

Loving Trust. It will also show you how to use the checklist in Part Two to significantly reduce the time and dollar costs of setting up a Loving Trust. We will instruct you on how to work with your lawyer to create a final product that will be tailored to you and your loved ones. We will also show you how to get your property into your trust in order to make it fully operational. This, too, can be done at a low time and dollar cost by using our techniques. In addition, Part Three will show you how you can use advisers to keep your costs to an absolute minimum.

PART TWO

How to Design Your Loving Trust

8

What Do You Want to Do?

All of us have certain feelings and ideas about how we want to be cared for and about how we would like to provide for our loved ones. But, oftentimes, our feelings and ideas are nebulous and hard to express. It sometimes takes the help of others for us to define and articulate our feelings so that they can be understood. The next nine chapters are structured to help you come to grips with your desires and motives for the care and well-being of yourself and your loved ones.

In our law practice we were able to assist thousands of clients in planning for their loved ones. To our amazement, most of our clients expressed remarkably similar feelings and planning motives for their loved ones. In Part Two, we offer you a variety of practical and loving planning solutions based on those desires and motives that we have repeatedly identified over our planning careers. We are confident that you can accomplish significant Loving Trust planning by selecting the particular desires and motives that best fit you and your loved ones. Chapter by chapter, we'll give you the opportunity to create your own Loving Trust planning solutions by building on those that we have so often successfully utilized.

The building blocks of your Loving Trust are the subtrusts that are created within it. Every Loving Trust has various subtrusts that lie dormant until some event activates them. Throughout Part Two you will be your own Loving Trust architect. You will select subtrusts that fit your situation and motives that reflect your desires. An architect adds room after room and detail after detail to the blueprints of his or her client's dream home; you will likewise be creating your Loving Trust blueprints for the care and well-being of your loved ones.

You do not have to read all of Part Two. You *do* need to read those chapters that pertain to your loving needs and desires. Once you have done that, you only need to select the motive or motives in each chapter that meet your desires. We strongly suggest that you place a check mark next to the motives you select on the checklist that concludes each chapter; doing so will help you to keep track of your choices.

Upon completing Part Two you can fill in *My Checklist for Designing My Loving Trust.* By simply transferring each of your chapter-by-chapter choices to this master checklist, you will have completed your Loving Trust master blueprint. And you will be able to see a picture of what your Loving Trust looks like— how all the various subtrusts work together—by filling in the diagrams we have drawn for you at the end of Part Two.

We have found that being able to look at a picture of your Loving Trust will allow you to get a better idea of its structure and how it operates. Your diagram should give you a broad overview of its design and should facilitate your understanding of how all its subtrusts interact for the well-being of your loved ones.

In Part Two, we refer to "my property" or "my trust" as we take you through the planning alternatives. If you are married, you may be confused or concerned when we say this, particularly if you view your marital property as "ours" because you own it in joint tenancy with your spouse. "How do I convince my spouse that I should take 'our' property and put it in my Loving Trust?" is a question that invariably is asked when we share the benefits of Loving Trust planning with our clients. Most married couples own their property jointly. As joint tenants with right of survivorship, they believe that they own this property equally and that they each can dispose of their "mythical" one-half. Once we explain how joint property really works, most couples find it difficult to conceptualize how they should own their property for Loving Trust planning purposes; they have a terrible time coming up with an alternative to their joint tenancy habit.

We almost always receive questions like: "Does all 'our' property have to be put in my husband's name?" "Wouldn't it be better if it was all put in my name?" "Isn't there some way we can still somehow own our property together and still have a Loving Trust?"

You can only plan for those assets you own. If you are married and wish to control your marital assets, you could take "your" joint tenancy property and put all of it in your name only. Of course, you would have to get your spouse's permission; a necessary condition that is rarely achieved.

Based on your spouse's feelings, you may opt to put all your marital joint property in your spouse's name as the sole owner, although we doubt if many of our readers would go along with this alternative either.

In our experience, it is far more likely that you and your spouse will select one of two ownership planning approaches:

- Change your jointly held property into tenancy in common property.
- Place property approximating one-half of the total joint property in your name alone, and place the other half in your spouse's name.

If you decide to own your property in tenancy in common, you would own half and your spouse would own half of each marital asset held in tenancy in common. You could sell your half, give it away, or transfer it to your own Loving Trust; your spouse could do likewise with his or her half. This is a convenient way to own property. For example, the deed to your home would have both your names on it along with the magic legal words ". . . as tenants in common" instead of ". . . as joint tenants." Since most couples that we have done Loving Trusts for think that their joint tenancy property works just like tenancy in common property, tenancy in common is not a radical departure from their perceived status quo.

If you live in Arizona, California, Idaho, Louisiana, Nevada,

New Mexico, Texas, or Washington, your marital property is already owned equally with your spouse—you can plan your half, and your spouse can do likewise—under your state's community property laws. For planning purposes, community property functions precisely like tenancy in common.

Regardless of where you live, if you elect to place half of your marital assets in your name and half in your spouse's name, you each would own, control, and plan those assets titled in your name. Many of our clients have elected to place specific assets in one or the other's name; this was particularly true when one or the other of them brought substantial assets into the marriage.

As an example of this method of eliminating joint tenancy property, you may have your home in your name and your spouse may have a second residence or other property in his or her name.

Some of our clients put some of their property in individual names and other property in tenancy in common, blending the two alternatives together. No matter how you and your spouse choose to title your marital property, the important thing to remember is this: Joint tenancy property *cannot be planned*. This is true regardless of whether you want to use a Loving Trust, a bare-bones boilerplate living trust, or a simple will.

"Should my spouse and I each have our own Loving Trusts?" "Can't we just have one Loving Trust for the two of us?" "Which is better, separate Loving Trusts or one Loving Trust for both of us?" These are other questions that we are almost always asked.

You most certainly can have your own Loving Trust, and your spouse can do likewise. Or, if you and your spouse prefer, you can have a single Loving Trust that will deal with each of your respective wishes and property; we refer to this approach as a "joint" Loving Trust.

It is important that you do not confuse a joint Loving Trust with jointly owned property; a joint Loving Trust is a single Loving Trust document that will manifest both your and your spouse's respective wishes as to your respective property. A joint Loving Trust is nothing more than one document with two parts to it: "his" wishes and "her" wishes and "his" property and "her" property.

A joint Loving Trust is most always used in community property states; for specific tax purposes—all beneficial—it should always be used by California couples. In our experience, a joint Loving Trust is not used as much in the forty-two non-community-property states as it is in the eight community property states.

One non-community-property state in which joint Loving Trusts are frequently used is Pennsylvania. Pennsylvania imposes, quite illogically, a 6 percent inheritance tax on property passing from one spouse to another through a will or a trust, but provides an exemption for such property if it is held as tenants by the entireties. To avoid this inheritance tax problem, a joint Loving Trust is often used.

In response to the question "Which way is better?" there is generally no right answer. In our experience, the work and costs involved with either approach are about the same. Each spouse has his or her own property and his or her desires with regard to loved ones in either alternative.

Proponents of the joint trust approach say that it takes a shorter trust to accomplish the desires of the planning couple and that it is easier to operate and maintain. Proponents of the "each spouse should have his or her own trust" approach believe that their way is less complicated and cumbersome, because each spouse's wishes and property can be dealt with more efficiently in his or her own Loving Trust document. We have no preference; in most cases, both ways work equally well.

For your convenience we have designed *My Checklist for Designing My Loving Trust* in Part Two to reflect *your* desires and *your* planning alternatives. If you are married, your spouse should also check those alternatives that best fit his or her objectives. Once you have both selected your respective planning desires, you both can decide—with the help of your Loving Trust lawyer—whether you would prefer individual Loving Trusts or a single joint one.

Part Two is the loving portion of your Loving Trust. It is here that you need to spend your planning time. It is here that you will have the opportunity to examine how you feel about your well-being and the needs and requirements of your spouse, children, grandchildren, parents, and other loved ones. It is this process of self-examination and the thought behind it that is so often neglected in a lawyer's office and in boilerplate how-to-do-it books.

You are the architect of your Loving Trust; your lawyer is the contractor who will build it. Your Loving Trust is a legal document. There will be many technical or legal phrases in it. We call these phrases "legalese" or "boilerplate"—standard and repetitive legal language. Just like a construction contractor must follow the appropriate engineering and building-code requirements, so must your lawyer follow the appropriate legal requirements.

A Loving Trust's basic principles are based on hundreds of years of law and judicial experience. Every Loving Trust needs to be written with the appropriate legal boilerplate. That's where your lawyer comes in. You design it, and he or she builds it to your specifications. Between your knowledge of your loved ones and the planning they require and your lawyer's expertise in legalese, you can readily and inexpensively bring your Loving Trust into existence.

9

How to Provide for Yourself

When we introduced the concept of a Loving Trust to our clients, many of them became very concerned over what would happen if they signed one. "Will I have to pay fees to a battery of lawyers, accountants, and trustees beginning on the day I sign? Will I lose control of my property? Will I create problems with the IRS? What if I change my mind? Will it change the way I do business?" In essence, they were asking what would happen to their lives if they signed a Loving Trust. Our answer was always the same: "Nothing will happen to change your life if you have a Loving Trust. A Loving Trust is simply your set of instructions that automatically kick in on your disability or death."

If you are like most of our clients, the odds are pretty good that you have never planned for your disability. We understand when people tell us that it doesn't seem practical to plan for themselves. Most of us have the attitude that no matter how bad things are for others, those things could never happen to us. As a result, we are usually taken by complete surprise when those things do indeed happen to us.

At one time, we too had "it will never happen to us" attitudes. Our attitudes quickly changed when experience taught us that many of our clients became sick, injured, or were otherwise incapacitated prior to their deaths. On numerous occasions we had to go to hospital rooms to have Loving Trusts signed. On other occasions we were too late; there was nothing we could do.

When emergencies occur, planning mistakes and miscalculations can be made. Not enough thought goes into emergency planning; loved ones are often inadvertently hurt because of hasty planning.

The motives that we have found most important to our clients over the years in planning for their possible disabilities have related to the priority of care in a "Me" subtrust. Almost all our clients have felt that they should be taken care of first; that their own well-being should be the top priority of their "Me" Trust. They also wanted their dependents—spouses, children, parents, etc.—cared for.

Here are the five motives we commonly see in a "Me" Trust:

9–1 Take care of me and nobody else.

9–2 Take care of my needs first and then my spouse's needs.

9–3 Take care of my needs first, then my spouse's, and then my children's or dependents', in that order.

9–4 Take care of me, my spouse, and my children based solely on our needs, without any priorities among us.

9–5 Take care of me and my children based solely on our needs, without any priorities among us.

9–1 *Take Care of Me and Nobody Else*
If you are single and have no dependents, this alternative is for you. You have undoubtedly relied upon yourself for your well-being and wish to continue that self-reliance by establishing your "Me" Trust with yourself as its sole beneficiary.

You may want to use this alternative if you are elderly or partially disabled and are being cared for by a relative or close friend. It should be used in lieu of a general power of attorney or putting your property in joint tenancy with a trusted family member or friend. By using this alternative, you can allow the same person or persons you would give your power of attorney to or who would be your joint tenant to care for you by naming them trustees of your "Me" Trust. As your trustees, they would take care of you within the limits imposed by your instructions, without a general power of attorney, joint property, or any other cumbersome device to allow them to help care for you.

9–2 *Take Care of My Needs First and Then My Spouse's Needs*

If your spouse is economically dependent on you, you will undoubtedly want to provide for your spouse's care as well as your own. This alternative provides that both of you are to be taken care of from your trust property, but that your needs are to be taken care of on a priority basis.

Children and other dependents are not relevant in this alternative. Your children may be grown or you may have no children. This alternative assures you that both you and your spouse—and this is true if your spouse is disabled as well—will be taken care of subsequent to your disability.

9–3 *Take Care of My Needs First, Then My Spouse's, and Then My Children's or Dependents', in That Order*

This alternative is the same as alternative 9–2, except that your children or other dependents are added as beneficiaries. This alternative is used when you are married and have minor children or disadvantaged adult children dependent on you. It can be easily modified to include an aged parent or other persons economically dependent on you. The priority in which your trustees are to exercise their care still retains you as your trust's primary beneficiary; your spouse, children, and other dependents follow in that order.

9–4 *Take Care of Me, My Spouse, and My Children Based Solely on Our Needs, Without Any Priorities Among Us*

We include this alternative to show you that you do not have to make yourself the primary beneficiary of your "Me" Trust. This alternative allows your trustees to look at the economic needs of all your beneficiaries and to care for you and them based solely upon your respective needs.

This mandates that your trustees ask two questions before distributing your trust money. "Is there enough money and property to care for you, your spouse, and your children?" If there is, then your trustees can proceed to care for all of you without determining whose needs are greater. If your trust funds are limited, the second question is, "Who is most in need of those funds?" Your trustees will determine a priority among your beneficiaries based on their respective needs and the funds available at that time.

This alternative gives your trustees the discretion to make the best decision based upon the circumstances at that time. Your trustees are charged with exercising the same judgement and making the ultimate decisions that you would make if you were healthy.

This alternative was almost always used by our clients with good marriages or those with close family ties. It was, by far, the most preferred "Me" alternative.

9–5 *Take Care of Me and My Children Based Solely on Our Needs, Without Any Priorities Among Us*

This alternative is specifically designed for the single parent. Like alternative 9–4, it states that your trust funds will be used to take care of you and your children based solely on your respective needs at that time. It was almost always selected by our single-parent clients.

There are six alternatives for a "Me" Trust that follow, including the five discussed here plus an alternative that you can use to create your own motive. Please check the alternatives that most nearly coincide with your desires and motives.

( ) 9–1 Take care of me and nobody else.

(✓) 9–2 Take care of my needs first and then my spouse's needs.

( ) 9–3 Take care of my needs first, then my spouse's, and then my children's or dependents', in that order.

( ) 9–4 Take care of me, my spouse, and my children based solely on our needs, without any priorities among us.

( ) 9–5 Take care of me and my children based solely on our needs, without any priorities among us.

( ) 9–6 My own motive:

_____

_____

_____

_____

10

How to Provide for Your Spouse

You may provide for your spouse by designing your Loving Trust so that, at your death, it creates a special subtrust for him or her that we call a "Pocketbook" Trust. A Pocketbook Trust is used to control and protect the property that you want to pass to your spouse on your death; that is its only purpose. It should always be used instead of leaving property outright or directly to a spouse.

The sole beneficiary of your Pocketbook subtrust will be your spouse. The degree of your spouse's control over the property in this trust will be dictated solely by your motives. For example, your Pocketbook Trust can be very liberal. It can give your spouse the right to take and spend any or all of your trust property at any time for any reason. Or it can be very restrictive, severely limiting the benefits your spouse receives.

There are no provisions in a Pocketbook Trust to care for your children, grandchildren, or any beneficiaries other than your spouse. The property in this kind of trust is *solely* for your spouse's benefit. If your trust is liberal and allows your spouse to take funds out when your spouse so chooses, he or she can use them for the benefit of anyone, including children, grandchildren, or others. Your husband or wife can use the funds for others only after those funds are taken out of the trust.

In our seminars, there is usually a woman in the audience who has a purse at her side. We ask her if we can have her purse, and after much prodding, more often than not, she reluctantly obliges. We then tell her that we are planning on opening it in order to share its contents with the rest of the class. As you can imagine, she is appalled at the thought and quickly asks for—or snatches—her purse back. No one can blame her for wanting to keep the contents of her purse private.

Purses and wallets—pocketbooks—were invented to hold personal belongings. They are convenient and private. Their owner may carry and store personal property without worrying that it will be exposed, helter-skelter, to the prying eyes of sometimes not-so-innocent bystanders.

Now you can understand why we call such a trust a Pocketbook Trust rather than a <u>Marital Trust</u>—its proper technical name.

A Pocketbook Trust springs into existence on your death. The money and property you leave in a Pocketbook Trust are for the benefit of your spouse but are limited by your instructions. These instructions can be liberal or restrictive, depending on your motive.

A Pocketbook Trust is used to keep the affairs of your spouse private. Because it is a subtrust of your Loving Trust, it totally avoids probate at your death. It avoids a living probate if your spouse is disabled or incapacitated. It avoids probate on your spouse's death. It works like your "Me" Trust, but simply has a different beneficiary and a different set of instructions to take care of your spouse after your death. Please remember that you will design it according to your desires and motivations.

The funds in your spouse's Pocketbook Trust may even be protected from your spouse's creditors. We know of a case where a widow was left a substantial amount of money and property in such a trust. Even though the widow's husband named a bank as trustee, the trust had very liberal provisions for her use and enjoyment of her husband's property. She had the right to all of the income—the money her trust made— and access to the principal of her trust at any time and for any reason. She even had the right to leave the money and property in her trust to anyone she wanted on her death. As you can see, she had full control over the trust and everything in it!

This widow's son was a budding entrepreneur who wanted to be a developer. To get financing for one of his building projects, he asked his mother to sign a promissory note along with him. She did. Soon thereafter her son went bankrupt. The son's creditor sued his mother to collect on the note, won the lawsuit, and then proceeded to try to collect on the note by going after the property in Mom's trust. The creditor's theory was that, since Mom could take money and property out of her trust at any time, the creditor should be able to force her to take the property out and pay him off.

The trustee of Mom's trust refused to allow the creditor to collect from the trust. The creditor sued the bank as trustee and, when the appeals were over and the case decided, the court held that the creditor could not collect from Mom's trust.

Mom's trust had a spendthrift clause—we call it an immunity clause—that prevents creditors from taking trust assets. A spendthrift clause is an instruction to the trustees that the trust property is free from the claims of the beneficiaries' creditors and that the trustees *should never* pay those creditors. Since Mom had received her husband's property in trust, the spendthrift clause protected the trust property from the claims of Mom's creditors.

An immunity clause is allowed by all states and has long been considered a legitimate safeguard that trust makers can take advantage of for the protection of their loved ones. It is absolutely mandatory that your lawyer put an immunity or spendthrift clause in your Loving Trust for the protection of your loved ones.

We cannot guarantee that an immunity clause will work in every situation or that other courts will follow this same legal reasoning or result. We do know, however, that immunity clauses have worked for centuries, and we see no reason or likelihood that their effectiveness will be diminished.

If you have already made a leap in logic and concluded that you could set up a trust for yourself that would, of course, include an immunity clause so that you could avoid the claims of your creditors, you will be disappointed to know that your logic has been rejected by the courts. An immunity clause works only for loved ones other than the trust maker!

Perhaps the widow in our story would have liked to have said no to her son but was afraid to confront him. Under our Loving

Trust techniques, she could keep her Pocketbook Trust private, even from her son! She could deny his request by saying that it wouldn't be allowed by the terms of the trust or that the other trustees would not approve it. She would, in effect, be using its confidentiality to protect herself from her own children.

Most of our clients immediately understood the beauty of a Pocketbook Trust when it came to controlling their property after their death. They did not, however, so readily understand why they needed one if they loved their spouses and wanted them to have everything on their death. We were perplexed by this until we finally understood that most of our clients incorrectly associated the word "trust" with negative motives, feelings, or results. This is why we always took time with our clients to review the advantages of Pocketbook Trusts over leaving property outright to spouses. We told them that a Pocketbook Trust:

- Avoids a living and a death probate for your spouse.
- Keeps both your affairs and your spouse's affairs totally private.
- Allows your spouse to lean on and get assistance from your trustees.
- Keeps your spouse's creditors—not *your* creditors—from taking what you left.
- Gives your spouse the ability to say no to friends, relatives, and others who are requesting loans or investment opportunities, by blaming the "no" on the terms of the trust or the trustees.
- Can do all of this without restricting your spouse's rights to the use and enjoyment of your property.

Leaving All Your Property to Your Spouse in a Pocketbook Trust

The five most common motives in this area are:

10–1 I want my spouse to have total control over my property.

10–2 I want my spouse totally taken care of, but I want to limit my spouse's right to leave my property on his or her death.

10–3 I want my spouse totally taken care of, but I will decide where my property goes on my spouse's death.

10–4 My spouse can have only the income my Pocketbook Trust earns and nothing more; I will say where my property goes on his or her death.

10–5 My spouse will get only whatever my state's laws require that I must leave him or her.

10–1 *I Want My Spouse to Have Total Control Over My Property*

If your motive is to give your spouse maximum use and control over your property, this is the alternative for you.

With this alternative, your spouse gets all the income produced by the property in the trust. Your spouse may also use the trust property—the principal—at anytime and for any reason. There are absolutely no restrictions on the use of the trust property. In addition, if your spouse is disabled, the trustees will care for your spouse's needs, even though your spouse may be unable to ask for assistance. This will avoid the need for court-appointed agents and all of the expense and problems associated with court intervention.

When your spouse dies, the trust property will pass pursuant to your spouse's desires. Here you have purposefully relinquished control to your spouse. However, if your spouse does not specifically create a trust or a will to leave the property, it will automatically pass to those loved ones you have chosen in your Loving Trust.

Where both spouses are committed to each other and to leaving property to their mutual children or others, this alternative is very useful. Your spouse does not have to direct where the trust assets will pass on his or her death; they will automatically pass under other terms of your Loving Trust.

This alternative gives your spouse total control by:

- Giving your spouse all the trust income.
- Giving your spouse access to all the trust property whenever and in whatever amounts your spouse desires.
- Instructing your trustees to totally care for your spouse

during any period when he or she is disabled or incapacitated.

- Allowing your spouse to leave the trust assets to anyone he or she wants.

This alternative—more than any other—is an "I love and trust in your judgment" trust. It is used for privacy and to avoid probate, the unscrupulous, and creditors. It does not restrict your spouse in any manner. It is designed to assist rather than hinder your mate.

10–2 *I Want My Spouse Totally Taken Care Of, But I Want to Limit My Spouse's Right to Leave My Property on His or Her Death*

If your motive is to give your spouse maximum benefits from your Pocketbook Trust without giving your spouse maximum control over where your property ultimately goes, this alternative may interest you.

In this alternative, your spouse receives all the income from the trust. Your spouse may also receive principal, *but only when your spouse needs it.* Principal can only be used for your spouse when the trustees determine that it is needed for his or her health, education, maintenance, or support. (These are IRS words that, when used in conjunction with one another, mean that the trust property can be used for almost any conceivable need).

In this alternative, the trustees are instructed to look to any property or other sources of income your spouse has outside of the trust before parting with trust funds. Trust funds will be used only if no other source of property or income is available to your spouse.

When our secretary reviewed this paragraph, she said, "It sound like lots of red tape is involved in order for one's spouse to get the money." We replied that she was right, that "need," not "desire," was the requirement here, and that the trustees had to find "need" before parting with the trust funds.

Very often, this alternative is used if a spouse has substantial property of his or her own. It is also commonly used in community property states (Arizona, California, Idaho, Louisiana, Nevada, New Mexico, Texas, Washington) because in those states one's spouse already has half of the marriage property in his or her name as a matter of state law.

This alternative allows your spouse to decide who, among a group of beneficiaries, will ultimately receive the trust property. For example, you might leave instructions that upon your spouse's death you want the remaining trust property to pass to your children and grandchildren. Since you cannot predict the future and have considerable confidence in your spouse's judgment, you give him or her the right to decide which children or grandchildren get what. It may be that one of your children has married into a wealthy family and is very comfortable, while one of your grandchildren has a severe health problem and needs money. Your spouse can evaluate the circumstances and allocate the property according to his or her assessment at that later time.

Your spouse can divide all the trust property in any manner, including disinheriting any—but not all—of the members of that group. For example, if your group consisted of your children and grandchildren, your spouse would have to name at least one of them as the beneficiary of the trust funds.

This alternative is often used when spouses are loved, but when their ability to care for themselves is lacking or suspect. We have seen many breadwinner spouses leave such a plan for spouses who have not shown the slightest inclination for understanding investments, basic money management, or business.

10–3 *I Want My Spouse Totally Taken Care Of, But I Will Decide Where My Property Goes on My Spouse's Death*

If you wish to provide for your spouse without giving your spouse any control over your property, this alternative may interest you.

This alternative is identical to alternative 10–2 with the exception that you determine where the remaining trust property passes on your spouse's death. The decision is entirely yours. Your spouse has no control whatsoever over the ultimate disposition of your property when he or she dies. This alternative is often used by trust makers who have children by a prior marriage and who want to be assured that their property will go to their own children rather than their spouse's family. You would clearly favor using it if your spouse had different ideas than you about who should ultimately get your property.

10–4 *My Spouse Can Have Only the Income My Pocketbook Trust Earns and Nothing More; I Will Say Where My Property Goes on His or Her Death*

You should select this alternative if you want your spouse to have only the income your property produces and to never have—under any circumstances—the ability to touch your trust property.

In this alternative the trustees are required to pay the trust's annual income to your spouse for the rest of his or her life. Upon your spouse's death, the trust property will pass pursuant to your instructions. Your spouse could never use any of your trust principal under this alternative.

This alternative is most often used in pure federal estate tax planning situations where a spouse is independently wealthy and would never foreseeably have any need for your principal. By giving your spouse the right to the trust income, all federal estate tax on your property is forestalled until your spouse's subsequent death.

10–5 *My Spouse Will Get Only Whatever My State's Laws Require That I Must Leave Him or Her*

Many states require that upon the death of a spouse, a certain minimum amount of the deceased spouse's property be given to the surviving spouse. In our *Handbook of Estate Planning*, we devote an entire chapter to spousal rights under state law.

It is our belief that even when one attempts to leave his or her spouse the absolute minimum allowed by law, he or she should still leave it in a Pocketbook Trust. This is not as altruistic as it sounds. By leaving property in trust, you can control where it will ultimately go if your spouse either neglects or refuses to take the necessary actions to dispose of it under the terms of his or her own will or trust.

This alternative is designed exactly like alternative 10–1. It gives your spouse complete control over the property in his or her trust. What distinguishes it is that it's funded with the minimum amount necessary to comply with your state's laws.

If this alternative interests you, be sure to ask your lawyer whether under your state's law a Loving Trust will allow you to totally bypass your spouse in order to leave your property entirely to other people or charities. In a handful of states, a Loving Trust can be used to get around state will laws requiring that spouses be left certain minimum amounts. In these states, a husband or wife who uses a trust can leave all of his or her property directly to children or others.

If either the amount of property going into the trust or its terms gives your spouse less than he or she would otherwise be entitled to under your state law, your spouse can ignore your trust and take his or her state-mandated legal share.

Some of our clients have responded with, "So what do I have to lose by disinheriting my spouse?" "If he or she doesn't fight it, I've won!" "If he or she doesn't fight it, I'm right back where I would have been if I gave him or her the minimum required under my state's law."

The answer to this argument is that your spouse gets to pick exactly what assets he or she wants when gathering his or her state-given share. In our experience, your spouse will pick the wheat and leave your children or other loved ones with the chaff! Spouses fighting for their rights will always select and take the best property.

There are six alternatives for a Pocketbook Trust in the following checklist. These include the five discussed here, plus an alternative that you can use to create your own motive. Check the alternative that most nearly coincides with your desires and motives.

( ) 10–1 I want my spouse to have total control over my property.

( ) 10–2 I want my spouse totally taken care of, but I want to limit my spouse's right to leave my property on his or her death.

(✓) 10–3   I want my spouse totally taken care of, but I will decide where my property goes on my spouse's death.

(   ) 10–4   My spouse can have only the income my Pocketbook Trust earns and nothing more; I will say where my property goes on his or her death.

(   ) 10–5   My spouse will get only whatever my state's laws require that I must leave him or her.

(   ) 10–6   My own motive:

_____

_____

_____

_____

11

How to Provide for Your Family

A Family Trust is a subtrust of your Loving Trust that is specifically created on your death for the benefit of loved ones other than just your spouse. Your Family Trust can name just your children as its beneficiaries. It can name your children and your spouse as its beneficiaries. It can name a parent or other loved one as sole beneficiary. It can name any number or combination of beneficiaries you wish.

We often ask our students to think of a Family Trust by picturing a dining-room table packed high with food. Around the table sits a family consisting of a widow, her children, and her deceased husband's elderly parents. The menu has been decided, the food has been prepared according to the deceased husband's instructions, and the meal is being served by a local catering service. The servers are to distribute and apportion the food among each of the family members pursuant to the instructions of the deceased husband.

We further ask our students to pretend that they are planning that dinner. We then ask them to create as many different sets of serving combinations as they can think of. The results of this exercise always amuse us. It doesn't matter whether we are teaching attorneys, accountants, insurance agents, or financial planners. Each profession can get equally bizarre in the serving instructions they contrive in responding to our request. We bring the exercise to a close with: "Replace the food with financial assets and the caterers with trustees, and you've got a

98

classic Family Trust planning situation. The variety of your catering instructions represents the variety of the planning instructions available to you in providing for your loved ones with a Family Trust."

You may ask us, "Why would I want to create a Family Trust?" You would generally do so if you wanted to provide for your children, grandchildren, parents, or other loved ones while your spouse is living.

A Family Trust is not just for loved ones other than your spouse. It can, and most often does, provide for the well-being of one's spouse as well. Your spouse can even be named as the primary beneficiary of your Family Trust.

It is at this point that many of our students express confusion. We tell them to remember the dining-room table analogy and to relax because, as we explain more about a Family Trust, it will become readily apparent how and why they are successfully used by so many different people.

Why Family Trusts Are Used

Family Trusts are generally used for one or more of five reasons. They are used when:

You Wish to Save Your Family Federal Estate Tax

A Family Trust can save a family a great deal of federal estate taxes. Every dollar that is put in a Family Trust is free of federal estate tax up to a maximum of $600,000. Let's assume that you leave $600,000 directly to your spouse, and that your spouse has more than $600,000 of his or her own funds. When your spouse leaves your combined funds to your children, the tax on your $600,000 will be a whopping $235,000! If you leave your $600,000 in a Family Trust for the benefit of your spouse and children, there would be absolutely no federal estate tax.

We discuss the tax ramifications of your Family Trust in Chapter Sixteen, "How to Save Federal Death Tax." If the value of your and your spouse's assets—including life insurance proceeds and retirement benefits—is approaching or is greater than $600,000, you should carefully read Chapter Sixteen, "How to Save Federal Death Tax."

It Is Important to You That Your Family Members
Are Provided For

This desire is usually present when a person loves his or her spouse and family, but does not believe that the spouse loves or will take care of other family members.

We often see this situation in second marriages. Imagine that you have children by a first marriage and that your spouse also has children by a first marriage. If you leave all your property to your spouse, you can pretty well anticipate that he or she will use it to provide for his or her children's well-being rather than that of your children. This dilemma is easily circumvented with a Family Trust that provides instructions for the care of your children.

This need also frequently comes up with respect to the desire many people have to provide for their extended family members, such as parents or brothers and sisters. Imagine that your spouse dislikes your parents; that their meager savings and social security income is augmented to a large extent by your economic assistance. You are fearful that, should you leave all your property to your spouse, he or she will cut off your parents' much-needed economic assistance. This dilemma is circumvented by leaving appropriate funds in your Family Trust with specific instructions as to how your parents are to be cared for following your death.

You Want Your Family Trust to Pass to Your Children

This desire usually reflects one's concern that his or her spouse just might leave his or her inheritance to a new spouse or to some unworthy person or cause.

This situation almost always surfaces in second marriages. Imagine that your spouse has children of his or her own, or that he or she has no children but is not particularly fond of your family. You would be understandably concerned that your spouse would leave your inheritance to his or her family rather than to your loved ones. Your dilemma could be easily solved with a Family Trust that specifically provides that, after your spouse's death, its funds be distributed, pursuant to your instructions, to the loved ones you specify.

It also frequently occurs when one is concerned about a spouse's emotional stability or his or her ability to make prudent decisions. Imagine that your marriage is a good one—the first for you and your spouse—and that your spouse is an excellent parent to your children. But let's further imagine that your spouse is extraordinarily emotional and easily taken in by the guile of others. You would be understandably concerned that if you left all your property to your spouse, he or she could easily leave it to a new spouse or to someone else who entered his or her life. Your dilemma could be easily solved with a Family Trust that provides instructions to the contrary.

You Wish to Leave Your Property to Other Loved Ones

This desire is usually present when one's spouse is independently wealthy or when—for whatever reason—one chooses to leave property to loved ones other than a spouse.

Imagine that your spouse has received a substantial inheritance from his or her parents and that, though your children are all young adults who are making good on your expectations, they would welcome any available economic assistance to improve their lifestyles. It would certainly be reasonable for you to leave the amount you determine appropriate directly for your children's benefit in your Family Trust.

The need to provide for loved ones other than a spouse frequently occurs when one's love of others is greater than one's marital love. This situation can frequently surface in other than romantic scenarios. Imagine that the child you were always closest to was severely injured in an automobile accident that left him or her a quadriplegic, and that your spouse was more concerned about his or her golf game than the well-being of your child. Given this circumstance, it would certainly be understandable for you to want your Family Trust funds to care for your child rather than your spouse.

We often see marriages where convenience has replaced love as the motive for staying together. Imagine that your marriage is such a marriage and that you are particularly close to your children or to your brothers and sisters. It would certainly be understandable if you wished to leave a substantial sum to family members other than your spouse through your Family Trust.

You Wish to Reduce Your Loved Ones' Income Tax Burden

Let's assume that you love your spouse and wish to leave everything to him or her on your death. Let's further assume that you have nothing in common with any of the situations we have illustrated as to why people utilize a Family Trust, but that you are keenly interested in reducing your spouse's income tax burden following your death. A Family Trust could certainly meet your objective.

A Family Trust's ability to reduce income taxes can be easily illustrated. Let's pretend that your spouse is in a high income tax bracket, say 28 percent, and that your children do not pay income tax—a typical planning situation. If you leave all your property outright to your spouse or in a Pocketbook Trust, 28 percent of every dollar your money makes will go to Uncle Sam. Only seventy-two cents of every dollar your money earns can be used to pay for your children's health, support, maintenance, and education.

If you create a Family Trust that allows your trustees to provide for your children, income tax can be saved. Under the Tax Reform Act of 1986, a child can receive $1,000 of tax-free income. Children fourteen years of age or older will be taxed on their trust income at their own bracket. This means that they could be paying income tax in the 15 percent bracket on a great deal of their trust income rather than at the 28 percent bracket, a saving of 13 percent.

A Family Trust can be created as your only Loving subtrust, or it can be created at the same time and in addition to the Pocketbook Trust for your spouse. For our purposes, your Family Trust, like your spouse's Pocketbook Trust, lasts only until your spouse dies. On your spouse's death a new subtrust is created called a Common Trust for your children and grandchildren.

How You Should Allocate Your Property Between Your
Pocketbook and Family Trusts

When you establish your Pocketbook and Family Trusts, you must make the decision as to how much of your property will be allocated between the two trusts. If saving federal estate tax is one of your motives for designing and creating your Loving

Trust, Chapter Sixteen, "How to Save Federal Death Tax," will help you determine how you should allocate your property in conjunction with federal estate tax planning.

If your estate is valued at less than $600,000—as are the majority of all Americans' estates—the only restraint on how you divide your property between the two trusts will be your spouse's right under your state law to a certain percentage or dollar amount of your property. Put another way, the minimum amount that you can allocate to your Pocketbook Trust is the amount that your state's law requires you to leave your spouse. Most states' laws require that surviving spouses get a portion of their deceased spouse's property. To find out what the law is in your state, you will have to ask your lawyer or refer to the appendix in *The Handbook of Estate Planning*, which briefly explains each state's law concerning spousal rights. Once you know the "magic" minimum, you can thereafter allocate as much as you like to your Family Trust.

As you think about how you would like to allocate your property between your Pocketbook and Family Trusts, keep in mind one very helpful concept. In our judgment it is not wise to allocate your property between the two using actual dollar amounts. For example, let's assume that you have $100,000 and your intention is to leave one-fourth of it to your spouse. Do not say "$25,000 to my spouse in my Pocketbook Trust and the balance to the Family Trust." The value of your property may be less than $25,000 when you die, which would mean that your children will not receive any of your property. Or the value could increase greatly, leaving your spouse with relatively little to provide for his or her needs. With inflation, deflation, and all the other changes that occur, using a dollar figure can be very dangerous.

Always choose a percentage of your property that you wish allocated between your Pocketbook and Family Trusts. Use half-and-half, or one-third/two-thirds, or sixty/forty; use any percentage you think appropriate. This will always give you a result that will allocate your property the way you want without all the problems associated with naming a fixed dollar amount.

As you review and decide upon which Family Trust alternative best fits your motives, keep in mind the precise allocation that you want to make. Also keep in mind that your allocation decision may change based upon your desires and the loving alternative you ultimately select. Following are those *non-tax* allocation alternatives we have seen commonly used:

11-1 I want all my property to pass to my spouse in my Pocketbook Trust.

11-2 I want my spouse to receive whatever he or she is entitled to under state law with the balance passing to my Family Trust.

11-3 I want my property equally divided between my Pocketbook and Family Trusts.

11-4 I want _____ percent to pass to my Pocketbook Trust and _____ percent to my Family Trust.

11-5 I want all my property to pass to my spouse in my Family Trust.

Using a Sole Family Trust
In some situations, a Family Trust is used without a Pocketbook Trust. If you live in a community property state (Arizona, California, Idaho, Louisiana, Nevada, New Mexico, Texas, or Washington), one-half of your marital property is yours to do with as you want at your death. The other half belongs to your spouse. You may also have what is referred to as "sole and separate property," property that is solely yours. It is not legally considered to be part of the marriage property.

Since your community property spouse will also have half of the marital property, you may want all your property to pass to your Family Trust based upon any one or more of the desires that we have already discussed. Under this circumstance a Pocketbook Trust may not be needed.

However, you should not necessarily elect to use a sole Family Trust if the combined value of your half of the marital property and the value of your sole and separate property is more than $600,000. If it is, and one of your motives is to reduce federal estate tax, read Chapter Sixteen, "How to Save Federal Death

Tax." After you do, it is likely that you will be adding a Pocketbook Trust to your Loving Trust.

Motives

You can design your Family Trust in order to provide liberally for your spouse, or you can design it so that your spouse is not even a beneficiary. Between these two extremes you can design your Family Trust in any manner you like. Some of the more common Family Trust alternatives that we have seen repeatedly used over the years are:

11–7   I want primarily to care for my spouse by providing him or her with as many benefits and as much control as possible.

11–8   I want to provide for my spouse and my children based upon their respective needs, while giving priority to the needs of my spouse. I want my children and grandchildren to get what is left after my spouse's death.

11–9   I want to provide for the respective needs of my spouse and my children, but if my spouse remarries, I want to provide only for my children.

11–10 The same as alternative 11–9, except that I want my spouse taken care of during any period of time that he or she is single.

11–11 I want to provide for the respective needs of my spouse, my children, and other loved ones and will set forth my priorities.

11–12 I want to provide for loved ones other than my spouse.

11–7 *I Want Primarily to Care for My Spouse by Providing Him or Her with as Many Benefits and as Much Control as Possible*

This alternative is often selected by happily married couples whose only motives are to reduce federal estate taxes and provide complete control and benefit to the surviving spouse, while providing secondary care for other family members. Use of this alternative assumes complete confidence in one's spouse.

If this alternative fits your desires, you would name your spouse as a co-trustee of your trust. You would also give him or her the power to fire co-trustees at any time and for any reason, so long as a replacement is named pursuant to your instructions. The provisions of your Family Trust would give your spouse:

- All the income the trust earns.
- The greater of $5,000 or 5 percent of the funds each year as a matter of right without having to show any need.
- The opportunity to have his or her every need for health, support, maintenance, or education paid for by the trustees on a first priority basis.
- The right to leave whatever is left in the trust at his or her death to family members in whatever amounts or percentages the spouse chooses.

The secondary provisions of your Family Trust will provide for the health, support, maintenance, and education of your children.

It is readily apparent that should you select this alternative, you would be giving your spouse awesome power and control over your Family Trust. As a co-trustee your spouse would have the power to make every decision with respect to the investment of and the withdrawal from the trust funds. Should your spouse and his or her co-trustees disagree about any decision, your spouse could simply fire that trustee, and a replacement that you have previously named in your Loving Trust will take over.

The income from the trust will all be paid to your spouse, and will therefore be taxed in your spouse's personal income tax bracket. This might be considered poor income tax planning. However, that criticism would be of no consequence to you since income tax planning is not one of the motives associated with this alternative.

The bizarre configuration of $5,000 or 5 percent was not selected on an arbitrary basis. It represents a right expressly authorized by the Internal Revenue Code; that is the only reason it exists. You would obviously take advantage of this right, since your motive in using this alternative is to provide your spouse with the absolute maximum bundle of rights possible, while still avoiding federal estate tax on the Family Trust funds.

Your spouse's right to be cared for with respect to his or her every need for health, support, maintenance, and education is of critical importance in meeting your liberal requirements. These words come right out of the Internal Revenue Code; they mean literally everything. Since your spouse is both a trustee and the primary beneficiary of the trust, he or she should have absolutely no difficulty removing funds at whim.

Your spouse's power to control the Family Trust funds continues even subsequent to his or her death as a result of the fourth benefit this alternative bestows. You can give your spouse the right to leave the balance of the trust to any person or persons in any amounts or percentages that he or she selects— the only qualification being that you set the parameters as to the group your spouse can select from. In this alternative, the group is your children and grandchildren. It could just as easily be your spouse's family or any other group.

11–8 *I Want to Provide for My Spouse and My Children Based Upon Their Respective Needs, While Giving Priority to the Needs of My Spouse. I Want My Children and Grandchildren to Get What Is Left After My Spouse's Death*

This alternative is generally used by happily married couples who are interested in maintaining the pre-death status quo and who are also interested in reducing their family's income taxes. It is commonly selected by those people who love their spouses and who have children or grandchildren who are dependent upon them or their spouses. This alternative was the one most frequently selected by our clientele over the years.

If it fits your desires, you would most likely wish to name your spouse as a co-trustee of the trust. You would also give him or her the power to fire a co-trustee at any time and for any reason, so long as a replacement is named. The provisions of your trust would be:

- I want my trustees to take care of my spouse and children in their every need for health, support, maintenance, and education from the income and principal of my trust.

- In caring for my loved ones, I want my trustees, at all times, to give primary consideration to the needs of my spouse.
- Whatever is left in my Family Trust on my spouse's death shall immediately be used for the care of my children and grandchildren, pursuant to further subtrusts that I will create in my Loving Trust.

The key to this alternative is its flexibility. It allows your spouse to use all the Family Trust funds—both income and principal—to care on a "needs basis" for your beneficiaries. It also makes manifestly clear that your number one priority is your spouse's welfare.

This type of Family Trust is often called a "spray" or "sprinkle" trust. It gets its name from the fact that it operates just like a nozzle on your garden hose. Income and principal can be directed at one beneficiary, in the same way you can adjust the garden hose nozzle to a hard, accurate jet of water. Income and principal can also be diffused among many beneficiaries, just as the nozzle can be adjusted to give a broad, soft spray of water for a garden full of tender flowers.

A sprinkle or spray trust can offer significant income tax advantages. Spraying income over a lot of income tax brackets creates less income tax in most cases than directing income into one bracket.

There is also a gift tax problem that can be circumvented with this alternative. The gift tax problem can be easily illustrated:

Assume that Mr. Jones left a Family Trust that gave his spouse all its income each year and provided that the principal could be made available only to Mrs. Jones. Further assume that Mrs. Jones wanted to make gifts to her children of her surplus funds after she paid her income taxes.

Her lawyer would tell her that any gift she made in excess of $10,000 would be subject to federal gift tax laws. If Mrs. Jones took principal from the Family

Trust and then attempted to give it to her children,
her lawyer would tell her the same thing.

Contrast Mrs. Jones' plight with your spouse's under this
alternative. Your spouse as a co-trustee would have the right
to care directly for the needs of your Family Trust's beneficiaries
without having first to pay the money to himself or herself.
Since your trustee-spouse could pay the money directly from
the Family Trust to your beneficiaries there would be no gift
and, therefore, no federal gift tax.

A major difference between this alternative and our first
alternative is that your spouse will not have the right to leave
any of the Family Trust property to whom he or she wants on
death. This alternative locks in trust funds for the benefit of
your children and grandchildren.

A vast majority of our clients took particular delight in this
provision. It appeared that they thought it both fair and appropriate. Their thinking went something like this: My spouse
has his or her own funds (independent monies, community
property share, or a Pocketbook Trust) and can leave them to
anyone he or she desires. My Family Trust represents my share
of our marriage and I want its funds ultimately to go to my
loved ones.

11–9 *I Want to Provide for the Respective Needs of My Spouse and
My Children, But if My Spouse Remarries, I Want to Provide Only
for My Children*
This alternative is identical to our previous alternative with
one exception. It gives a spouse benefits from the Family Trust
only so long as that spouse remains single. If he or she should
remarry, this alternative automatically and permanently re-
moves that spouse as a Family Trust beneficiary. A spouse cannot return as a beneficiary even if he or she is later widowed
or divorced.

This alternative is often selected by the same people who
selected alternative 11–8, but who are sensitive to the potential
conflict-of-interest dilemma their spouses may find themselves
in following remarriage.

We can best illustrate this dilemma by sharing a conversation that occurred many years ago in our offices:

> Martha came to us for advice with respect to a trust dilemma. Her first husband left property to her and their children in a Family Trust. As primary beneficiary she could have whatever she needed whenever she needed it. She loved her second husband very much, and wanted to be loyal to him. Unfortunately, he was an extremely poor provider. They quickly went through her independent money, and he was constantly harassing her to invade the funds of the Family Trust for their mutual benefit.
>
> Our client was beside herself. She wanted to be loyal to her second husband and acquiesce to his demands. On the other hand, she did not want to disinherit her children by bleeding the Family Trust. If she refused to invade the Family Trust she was fearful that her second husband would perceive that she was disloyal and divorce her. If she invaded it, she was fearful that there would be nothing left for her children.
>
> Martha was in tears during most of the interview. Unfortunately, we could not offer her any advice or direction that would alleviate her burden. She had to make a decision, and she couldn't win regardless of how she made it.

This alternative is specifically designed to circumvent Martha's dilemma. It allows your spouse to continue to care for your children as a co-trustee of the trust. It also gives your spouse the ammunition to tell that subsequent spouse that he or she cannot touch a penny of the Family Trust as a result of remarrying. It takes the heat off your spouse while allowing your spouse to continue caring for your children.

11–10 *The Same as Alternative 11–9, Except That I Want My Spouse Taken Care Of During Any Period of Time That He or She Is Single*

This alternative is exactly like alternative 11–9, except that if your spouse is no longer married, then your spouse again becomes a beneficiary of the Family Trust.

This alternative is used by people who are concerned about their spouse's well-being following a divorce from or death of a subsequent spouse. It manifests much love and concern for one's spouse.

If you used this alternative for your spouse, he or she would always be a beneficiary of your Family Trust during any period of time that he or she was single. Your spouse could marry and divorce several times or lose subsequent mates to death and still be a beneficiary of your Family Trust during interim unmarried periods.

11–11 *I Want to Provide for the Respective Needs of My Spouse, My Children, and Other Loved Ones and Will Set Forth My Priorities*

This alternative is used in those situations where a person is very much concerned about the well-being of loved ones in addition to members of his or her immediate family.

It is commonly used by people who view that they are responsible for aged parents, disadvantaged brothers or sisters, or needy nieces and nephews. It is used to include close family friends as additional Family Trust beneficiaries.

If this alternative fits your desires, you would name loved ones in addition to your spouse, children, and grandchildren as beneficiaries of your Family Trust. You will create a nightmare for your trustees unless you provide them with a list of which beneficiaries are to be given first nod with respect to the income and principal of your Family Trust.

Let's assume that you have named your spouse, children, grandchildren, parents, and your spouse's parents as your Family Trust beneficiaries. Let's further assume that each has substantial needs for the same trust fund dollar. You must provide your trustees with what we refer to as a priority list, in effect saying: "Here's the way I would spend my money caring for my loved ones." In our example, you might say: "I want primary consideration given to the needs of my spouse and thereafter to my children, grandchildren, parents, and finally my spouse's parents, in that order."

We point this out to you because in our experience it is a frequent problem and concern in the trust world. There are often times when there are simply not enough funds available to adequately provide for the needs of all of a trust's beneficiaries. This situation always causes significant consternation among the trustees and can frequently result in threat of litigation and actual courtroom battles. Your loved ones will avoid all of this and your desires will be effected if you will take the time to set forth your priorities.

11–12 *I Want to Provide for Loved Ones Other Than My Spouse*

You may want to create a Family Trust where your spouse is not a beneficiary. This alternative is designed exactly like the spray or sprinkle trust found in alternative 11–8 with the exception that your spouse is not a beneficiary.

This alternative is frequently used when your spouse is independently wealthy or in second-marriage situations where it is critical that your children are exclusively provided for by a Family Trust.

A key decision that has to be made is whether you would be comfortable having your spouse as a co-trustee of your Family Trust. If you choose not to name your spouse as a co-trustee, your spouse would not have any control over the trust funds. If it is your desire to place your spouse in a trustee's role, then your spouse will be able to exercise control over the Family Trust by exercising his or her judgment in implementing your instructions.

We have never seen a consensus among our clients as to when one should and should not name a spouse as a trustee under this motive. It is our experience that every situation is unique. However, it is our strong belief that you should not name your spouse as a trustee when using this alternative unless you have extraordinarily strong and good reasons to the contrary. People who are disinherited are often full of bitterness and rancor.

The Family Trust alternatives that we have discussed are listed below. Please take a moment to check the alternatives that most closely meet your desires and motives.

How to Allocate Between
My Pocketbook and Family Trusts

( ) 11–1   I want all my property to pass to my spouse in my Pocketbook Trust.

( ) 11–2   I want my spouse to receive whatever he or she is entitled to under state law with the balance passing to my Family Trust.

( ) 11–3   I want my property equally divided between my Pocketbook and Family Trusts.

(✓) 11–4   I want _____ percent to pass to my Pocketbook Trust and _____ percent to my Family Trust.

( ) 11–5   I want all my property to pass to my spouse in my Family Trust.

( ) 11–6   My own alternative:

_____
_____
_____
_____
_____
_____
_____

How I Want My Beneficiaries
Provided for from My Family Trust

( ) 11–7   I want primarily to care for my spouse by providing him or her with as many benefits and as much control as possible.

( ) 11–8   I want to provide for my spouse and my children based upon their respective needs, while giving priority to the needs of my spouse. I want my children and grandchildren to get what is left after my spouse's death.

( ) 11–9   I want to provide for the respective needs of my spouse and my children, but if my spouse remarries, I want to provide only for my children.

( ) 11–10   The same as alternative 11–9, except that I want my spouse taken care of during any period of time that he or she is single.

(✓) 11–11   I want to provide for the respective needs of my spouse, my children, and other loved ones, and will set forth my priorities.

( ) 11–12   I want to provide for loved ones other than my spouse.

( ) 11–13   My own motive:

_____

_____

_____

_____

12

How to Provide for Your Minor Children

A major planning problem that we have frequently encountered relates to what we called "ledger mentality" in Chapter Two. You'll recall our story about John and Wayne and how they had a penchant for keeping a ledger on every penny spent on behalf of each of their children, periodically making the appropriate adjustments so that the sums spent on each were exactly the same. In our experience, most people do not subscribe to this approach to parenting, yet that is precisely how they care for their children and grandchildren on death.

Life insurance and employee benefit designations that leave property "share and share alike," "equally," or "per stirpes" mandate exact ledger equality regardless of the needs and relative economic circumstances of the children. Simple-will or bare-bones living-trust planning that leaves property in this fashion also creates ironlike inflexibility and oftentimes has disastrous results.

Your Loving Trust has a special subtrust—called a Common Trust—that comes into existence for your children after both your and your spouse's death. It is specifically designed to make sure that your children are cared for based on their needs rather than through some arbitrary division or amount arithmetically created by an insensitive adviser. It fully complies with the concept that you love your children equally but wish to care for them based on their needs, that there is nothing so unequal as the equal treatment of unequals. It only terminates when your youngest child has attained some age or requirement that meets with your desires.

In our seminars, we refer to the Common Trust as a "Chicken or Vegetable Soup Pot Trust." Can you recall your mom's soup specialty? If it was like our moms', it had just about everything in the pantry and refrigerator in it. When it was ladled out, the hungrier children at the table got more than those who were not as hungry. Some got more meat, because that was their favorite; some got more vegetables or rice or noodles. If a particular brother or sister had a penchant for a particular ingredient, that ingredient was always found in abundance in his or her bowl. Mom controlled and monitored the whole process to make sure that everyone was nourished and as happy as possible, and she ultimately decided who got what.

A Common Trust is designed to act like Mom's soup pot. Its trustees replace Mom's function and decide who gets what based upon the relative needs and desires of the children. Just as Mom ladled out the soup, your trustees distribute your property to your children based upon each child's needs as they compare to the needs of the other children with respect to the available trust resources.

We may love our children the same, but we do not treat them the same. The cornerstone of your Common Trust is this: When it comes to minor children, need is more important than equality. Your Common Trust's purpose is to provide for all your children's needs from a common source just as if mother or father were living and doing just that.

Allow us to contrive an extreme example that illustrates the need for a Common Trust:

> Assume that you have two children, a twenty-four-year-old electrical engineer and a five-year-old aspiring ballerina. Further assume that your entire estate—including life insurance—is $100,000. We doubt that you would leave $50,000 to each child knowing that your son is making a fine living and that your ballerina has sixteen years to go to reach adulthood or to complete college.

Since truth can be stranger than fiction, let's take a look at a more typical situation that frequently occurs in the probate courts across the country when a Common Trust is not used:

> Parents of three children, aged seven, thirteen, and eighteen, died in an accident. The parents left a will that created a separate death trust for each child. The parents' property was divided equally among the three separate trusts. The seven-year-old was injured in the same accident that killed her mother and father. Medical bills mounted quickly and by the time she reached eleven years of age, her trust property was completely gone. Her two sisters' trusts had substantial amounts of money and property in them. Unfortunately, none of the property in these trusts could be used for the seven-year-old. She became a ward of the state, even though her two sisters had a great deal of property.

Because the parents chose to immediately establish separate trusts for their children, they created an iron curtain between the children. Had these parents been given the opportunity to create a Common Trust, they would have undoubtedly jumped at the chance. They would have been able to keep all of their property in a Common Trust until the youngest child reached a certain age or achieved a certain level of education. Then, and only then, would whatever property that was left be divided among their children, either outright or to their respective separate trusts. If these parents had utilized a Common Trust, all of their children would have been able to share in their property based on actual need, rather than on an arbitrary percentage or arithmetical division.

Had our storybook parents not been killed, we are sure they would have spent their money caring for their truly needy child. They would not have said, "No more for you, you've used your one-third. You're on your own." The question again surfaces, "Why should we do on death something we would never consider doing in life?"

To be effective, we believe a Common Trust needs to have certain critical provisions that are often overlooked.

Need Is More Important Than Equality

The first and foremost provision of an effective Common Trust is an instruction to the trustees that each child is to be cared for based upon his or her needs as measured against the other children's current and anticipated needs and the amount of trust resources available. It is important that you instruct your trustees that it is permissible to spend more on one child if that is what needs to be done. Make sure that your Common Trust is a soup-pot trust. That's what it is all about.

Assist Your Guardians

Instruct your trustees to use the trust funds to assist the guardians of your children in caring for and raising them. Let's face it, if you and your spouse die and leave your children in your sister and brother-in-law's care, they are going to have their hands full, not to mention their house, their car, and their lives. Allow your trustees to use your trust money and property to help your guardians.

It is entirely foreseeable that the guardians of your loved ones may need to put an addition on their home to properly house your children. They may need a station wagon or van to replace their two-door sedan or sports car. They may need to change or add a great many things in order to make their lives, and the lives of your children, comfortable as a result of adding your family to theirs. Most of our clients have expressed their sensitivity to this requirement and have instructed us to "Be sure and provide that our children's guardians are provided with whatever they reasonably need to care for our little ones."

Allow for Advances

Clients who have children with a significant age disparity are caught on the horns of a major planning dilemma. If they immediately distribute their property equally to their children, they are ledger planning. If they leave it all in a Common Trust until their youngest child attains a certain age, they may be punishing their older children with respect to their economic needs for such things as establishing a business or profession, purchasing a home, paying for their weddings, etc.

This dilemma is solved with instructions that we refer to as "extraordinary advancement" language. In our Loving Trusts, our trustees are allowed to advance money or property to an older child for extraordinary needs or opportunities. However, there are conditions that must be met before such an advance is made. Our trustees have to determine if the particular child's need is a good one. Does he need funds to purchase a home? Does he need such a home? Is it appropriate for his and his family's needs? Is it fairly priced? If your trustees' investigations support the need for such an extraordinary request, they must make an additional determination before providing the requisite funds.

They must further ask, "Is there enough money in the soup pot to satisfy this need or request, while still leaving enough for the anticipated care of his younger brother?" Put another way, "If the money is given to my older son to purchase a new home, could that advancement in any way adversely affect my younger son's rights to funds for the basics: health, support, maintenance, and education?" This is a tough question to answer, but it needs to be answered before the trustees can make an advancement. If there is any doubt in our trustees' minds, they should not make the advancement.

You should provide your trustees with instructions that they are always to be mindful that the Common Trust is for all your children; that one child's special business or nonessential social needs are not to be satisfied when there are younger children with basic needs (such as food, clothing, education, etc.).

An advancement is not a gift that would deprive your other children of their ultimate share of your property. Many of our business-oriented clients referred to this advancement procedure as an interest-free loan to an older child that will automatically be paid back when the Common Trust splits into Separate Trusts or outright shares for all the children.

A few real examples should bring this concept to life for you:

> In the midsixties we worked on a trust that did not provide for advancements from its Common Trust. Its beneficiaries were a young man named Tom, who was twenty-six years of age, and a daughter named Sue, who was nineteen years of age. Tom was a suc-

cessful young executive and Sue was a high-achieving college sophomore.

Tom went to his deceased parents' trustees with the request that they advance him funds to purchase a fast-food franchise. There were considerable funds in the trust, and its terms stated that it would terminate in two years when his sister reached age twenty-one. Unfortunately, however, its terms did not provide advancement language. The trustees felt bad because their investigation concluded that his proposed venture was both sound and very exciting. But their hands were tied; he would have to wait two years for such funds. Two years later he had the funds, but the business opportunity had passed him by.

If our young entrepreneur's parents had provided advancement instructions, he could have made a good career and business investment without hurting his sister's financial rights in any way.

Let's assume that there was $500,000 in the Common Trust and Tom's request for $100,000 was honored by the trustees; that when his sister, Sue, turned twenty-one there was $400,000 in the Common Trust. Given our advancement language, Sue would have received $250,000 and Tom would have received $150,000.

Let's assume the same situation, only let's change the facts a little. Assume that the trust contained advancement language, and that it had only $200,000 in it; that Sue was only fourteen, a freshman in high school, and she had a learning disability. Would the trustees make the advancement? Put yourself in the trustees' shoes. Tom would be asking for half of the Common Trust funds. Sue would need expensive tutors and it would be seven years until she reached age twenty-one. Would the remaining $100,000 be enough to provide for her health, support, maintenance, and education? If we were the trustees, we would not advance the funds. Would you?

Advancement language is designed to enable your trustees to do what you would do under the same set of circumstances. That is its only purpose.

Providing for the Death of a Beneficiary

Your Common Trust must also provide a method for distributing its property in the event one of your children dies before the Common Trust terminates. Our Loving Trust instructions make it clear that if one of our children dies while the Common Trust is in existence and that child has children (our grandchildren), then our son's inheritance will be preserved—in trust—for our grandchildren. For example, if you have three children and the oldest dies leaving two children of his or her own, then when the Common Trust is divided, that dead child's share will be split equally among your grandchildren. During the time the Common Trust is still in existence, however, the grandchildren will be cared for from the chicken-soup pot just as if they were your children.

If one of our sons dies and leaves no children, then his share will pass equally to our other children when the Common Trust is divided up. We feel, and so have the vast majority of our clients, that this is the fairest way to handle a deceased child's inheritance with respect to the Common Trust. You may choose to handle it differently. If you do, simply state to whom and how you want the funds to pass.

Define When the Common Trust Will End

The final provision needed in an effective Common Trust is at what time, or upon what event, it will end and the property in it be divided.

We have found that almost all our clients have liked the instructions that we include in our Loving Trusts for needs versus equality, assistance for guardians, advancements, and the death of beneficiaries. They have had different opinions, however, as to when their Common Trust should end and its funds split into Separate Trusts for each of their children.

Some of the alternatives that we have seen repeatedly used over the years are:

12–1 All my children are adults. I do not want a Common Trust.

12–2 I want my Common Trust to end when my youngest child is twenty-one years of age.

12–3 I want my Common Trust to end when my youngest child is twenty-three or completes college, whichever happens first.

12–4 I want my Common Trust to end when my youngest child is _____ years of age.

12–1 *All My Children Are Adults. I Do Not Want a Common Trust*

A Common Trust is almost always used when one leaves minor children. If you have only adult children, you would generally skip this trust and move on to Separate Trusts for your children as described in Chapter Thirteen, "How to Distribute Your Children's Property."

12–2 *I Want My Common Trust to End When My Youngest Child Is Twenty-one Years of Age*

Twenty-one has historically been the popular age for children to be considered adults and on their own. This alternative calls for the Common Trust to terminate when your youngest child attains that magic age of majority.

The variations that can be used in this alternative are endless. Any age can be substituted for twenty-one.

A few of our clients have opted to utilize the Common Trust far past the time when their youngest child has attained the age of twenty-one. In such cases, we have reminded them that the age chosen is only used to terminate the Common Trust and divide it equally among their children's Separate Trusts. However, a very small percentage of our clientele became so intrigued with this concept that they designed their Loving Trust to keep their Common Trust in existence for the entire lifetimes of all of their children. When asked for our thoughts on the subject, we always shared our Loving Trust planning for our children, but quickly continued, "It's your Loving Trust, and you can do whatever you want. It is entirely up to you. We encourage you to do what you feel is best for you and your children."

12–3 *I Want My Common Trust to End When My Youngest Child Is Twenty-three or Completes College, Whichever Happens First*

We would like to give our children the opportunity to receive a college education. That is why our Common Trust stays in force until our youngest son reaches age twenty-three or completes college, whichever occurs first. Our reasoning is simple. If we live as long as we think we will, we are going to make sure that each of our sons has every chance to go to college. If we die before each of our sons has this opportunity, we want to make sure that each has the opportunity of finishing his undergraduate college education before our Common Trust terminates and is divided into Separate Trusts for each of our sons.

In discussing this alternative with our clients, we have stressed that if a child does not finish his or her undergraduate college education by a certain age it would be wise to terminate the Common Trust before the "professional student" drains away his or her siblings' inheritance. The age you use depends upon your particular perceptions and desires. You may like the concept but think that twenty-three is too old or too young. You can certainly substitute any age that you think appropriate. Some of our clients have even instructed us to substitute graduate or professional school graduation requirements as their Common Trust termination provision.

We do not particularly care what colleges our children attend, but we do care that they attend an accredited university. This is why we set forth certain minimum standards in our Common Trust before authorizing our trustees to expend funds for educational purposes. We have carefully written our Loving Trusts to reflect what we would do if we were around to make the decisions on how our money was being spent on our children's education.

12–4 *I Want My Common Trust to End When My Youngest Child Is ___ Years of Age.*

This is identical to alternative 12–2, except that it allows you to pick the age that your youngest child must attain for your Common Trust to terminate.

The Common Trust alternatives that we have discussed are listed below, including an alternative that you can use to create your own motive. Take a moment to check the alternatives that most clearly meet your desires and motives.

( )	12–1	All my children are adults. I do not want a Common Trust.
( )	12–2	I want my Common Trust to end when my youngest child is twenty-one years of age.
( )	12–3	I want my Common Trust to end when my youngest child is twenty-three or completes college, whichever happens first.
( )	12–4	I want my Common Trust to end when my youngest child is _____ years of age.
( )	12–5	My own motive:
		_____
		_____
		_____
		_____

13

How to Distribute
Your Children's Property

You can immediately divide your property among your children upon your death or you can leave it in a Common Trust that will divide it among your children at a later time. Either way, you will eventually be dividing your property among your children. The question that remains to be answered is, how do your children receive their shares? You could certainly leave them their inheritance outright. We discussed this bare-bones planning approach in Chapter Two. A better alternative is to leave each of your children with a Separate Trust that will provide instructions for his or her individual care and for the orderly distribution of your funds pursuant to your desires and motives.

A Separate Trust, as its name implies, is a subtrust of your Loving Trust that is funded and designed to take care of a specific beneficiary. Separate Trusts for your children can be created immediately upon your death or upon the deaths of you and your spouse. They can also be created upon the termination of your Common Trust.

This chapter will outline and discuss several methods of distributing property to a child from his or her Separate Trust. The methods we share with you are those that have been most commonly selected by our clients over the years.

Just as a properly designed Common Trust should have certain instructions in it, a Separate Trust should contain instructions as to how your trustees should administer it prior to distributing its funds. We will discuss the basic operating instructions that each of your children's Separate Trusts should contain before providing you with your distribution alternatives.

Advance Distributions

While each of your children's inheritance is in his or her Separate Trust, your trustees will almost always be instructed to make distributions to your son or daughter for his or her every need. You will recall that the legal words that convey this instruction come right out of the Internal Revenue Code regulations. They are "education," "health," "maintenance," and "support." By instructing your trustees to so care for your children, you can be assured that they will be well taken care of.

You can amplify your instructions to your trustees by instructing them to meet your children's extraordinary needs. For example, we instruct our trustees to assist each of our children in starting a business or profession, purchasing a home, meeting the expenses of a wedding, or any other extraordinary need that may surface.

Your child's Separate Trust need not be like a bank vault or safe-deposit box that is meant to be kept perpetually locked with its contents rendered unavailable. It can be designed to be a living and compassionate vehicle that fully implements your instructions for the care and financial well-being of each of your children. It can be structured as a buffer between your children and the cruel reality of an aggressively competitive marketplace.

Your Separate Trust instructions are meant to help, teach, and encourage your children in the ways of money and spending. Like us, most of our clients have instructed their trustees to be liberal in caring for the needs of their children, emphasizing that the preservation of the trust funds is not as important as taking care of the children's needs. We have always viewed our Loving Trusts as people-oriented trusts that conjure up visions of Thanksgiving dinner, roaring fireplaces, and joyful family reunions rather than stingy, cold, and heartless devices that only say no to the children.

We have encountered a minority of clients who, for whatever

reasons, did not subscribe to our liberal Separate Trust philosophy. These clients had desires that were the opposite of ours. They wanted to be assured that their trust instructions were restrictively conservative. Their desires were more like J. Paul Getty's than ours. They wanted to preserve their children's trust funds and only wanted to provide for advancements on a most rigorous and exacting basis.

In your Loving Trust you can select one of the approaches that is most conducive to your thoughts about and feelings for your children.

13–1 I want my trustees to liberally provide for each of my children.

13–2 I want my trustees to provide only for the health, education, support, and maintenance of each of my children.

The Premature Death of One of Your Children

A standard instruction found in our Separate Trusts deals with the premature death of a child. If one of our sons dies before taking all the property from his Separate Trust, we provide that the funds should go to whomever he wants—that is, if he took the time and attention to leave a will or a trust of his own.

It is our desire that our sons leave whatever was left for them to anyone they want, including family, friends, or charity. It is our feeling that if our sons care enough for someone to take the time to plan for him or her, his wishes should be respected. On the other hand, if he doesn't take the time to make a will or trust of his own, we provide that the balance of his Separate Trust share will pass equally to his children, our grandchildren, or, if he doesn't have children, then it will pass to his brother's trust.

Over the years, we have found that roughly 50 percent of our clients have liked this Separate Trust feature. The remaining half did not want to give a child the power to direct where unused trust funds would be distributed. It was the feeling of these clients that it was their money and they would determine where it went on a child's premature death. The bulk of these clients directed that it went to their deceased child's children. If there were no grandchildren, they wanted the funds to pass equally to their other children. A small percentage of our clients chose to leave the funds to their deceased child's spouse or to some other person or charity.

You can select the approach that most clearly meets your desires and motives from the two that follow:

13–4 I want my child's trust property to pass pursuant to my child's directions.

13–5 I want my child's trust property to pass to my child's children or, if none, to my other children.

Distribution Alternatives

Like a Common Trust, a Separate Trust can have a limitless variety of distribution alternatives. Your Loving Trust can provide for a single distribution from each of your children's Separate Trusts or for multiple distributions. It can provide for distributions at different ages or on special occasions. It can provide unique distribution provisions that differ from one child to another; each of your children do not have to be planned for in exactly the same way—unless they are exactly the same and you wish to treat them just that way.

Some children have the ability to handle financial affairs better than others. There is no rule stating that children, grandchildren, or other loved ones need to have exactly the same Separate Trust instructions and provisions. Children often have different needs that require different planning approaches. Your Loving Trust allows you to comfortably meet those needs and to be secure in the knowledge that your love and caring will survive you.

Following are eight alternatives that were commonly selected by our clientele. We hope that one or more of them will match your desires and motives. At the very least, their broad spectrum will enable you to create your own Separate Trust distribution instructions.

Most of the Separate Trust alternatives refer to mandatory

distributions by the trustees. However, Loving Trusts usually have a paragraph that instructs the trustees to keep a child's funds in trust if he or she is disabled or chooses to leave them there to be taken at a later date.

13–7   I want my property distributed to my children immediately.

13–8   I want my children to have immediately whatever they want from their Separate Trusts.

13–9   Make two distributions to my child, one-half at a minimum age, the remainder at another stated age.

13–10 Make two distributions to my child, the first at a minimum age, or immediately if that age has been met, the second to occur five years from the date of the first distribution.

13–11 Make four distributions to my child, the first to occur at a minimum age, or immediately if that age has been met, the second through the fourth to occur every five years.

13–12 Make multiple unequal distributions, the first to occur at a minimum age, or immediately if that age has been met, the others at stated ages.

13–13 Make no mandatory lifetime distributions to my child, but take care of my child in whatever way he or she needs, whenever he or she needs it from the trust funds.

13–14 Make entirely different distribution patterns for each of my children.

13–7 *I Want my Property Distributed to My Children Immediately*
Despite our admonitions to the contrary, we have had clients who have insisted that their property be immediately distributed outright to their children. This alternative is almost always chosen when there are adult children who have proven themselves responsible.

If your children are adults and you have absolutely no concern about their financial ability, this alternative may be for you. However, we must ask you to carefully reflect on your position. Do you remember the problems we addressed with regard to disability? Assume that your daughter has a heart attack and is unable to care for herself. If you left her inheritance directly to her, she would be unable to utilize your funds without court intervention. She would be in the same predicament as Groucho.

A well-designed Loving Trust would have a provision for just this situation. It would tell your trustees to take special care of your disabled daughter and to hold off making any outright distributions to her until such time as she is able to care for herself. In effect, it would give your trustees the option to continue her Separate Trust for her benefit.

Another concern we would like to share before you select this alternative centers on our earlier discussion of immunity or spendthrift clauses. You will recall that life insurance proceeds are generally immune from the claims of creditors because of this clause. So, too, are funds left in properly designed Loving Trusts. If you leave your property to your children in a Separate Trust, it is probable, under your state laws, that your children's creditors will not be able to take your trust funds to satisfy any indebtedness owed to them by your children.

We are generally opposed to outright distributions. However, if that is your desire, this is the alternative for you.

13–8 *I Want My Children to Have Immediately Whatever They Want from Their Separate Trusts*

This alternative is what we have offered our clients in lieu of an outright distribution or division. It is designed to accommodate those parents who have adult children who have proven themselves to be mature when it comes to financial matters.

If you leave your property outright to such children, you will expose their funds to both their creditors and the probate court in the event of a disability. These are risks that do not have to be taken.

If instead you leave your child's inherited property in a Separate Trust with instructions that provide that he or she is to receive whatever trust funds he or she requests at any time, you will have circumvented these problems.

Your child's Separate Trust will function just like the liberal Pocketbook Trust we discussed in Chapter Ten. It will keep his or her inheritance confidential, avoid a living probate, and, most likely, avoid the claims of creditors.

We heartily recommend this alternative to anyone who is seriously considering the first alternative. It provides significant benefits.

13–9 *Make Two Distributions to My Child, One-half at a Minimum Age, the Remainder at Another Stated Age*

This alternative delays any mandatory distribution to your children until each child reaches a certain minimum age. When the required age is reached, one-half of your child's Separate Trust is his or hers to use without having to show or prove need. When your child reaches the next stated age, the remainder of his or her Separate Trust will likewise be distributed.

If your child has already reached the second stated age by the time of your death, he or she would receive all of his or her inheritance in one distribution. For example:

> After my Common Trust ends, each of my children shall receive an equal share of my property to be held in a Separate Trust.
>
> When each of my children reaches age twenty-five or, upon the creation of this Separate Trust, if any child of mine is already twenty-five, then pay out one-half of my child's trust property to him or her. When my child is thirty or, on the creation of this Separate Trust, if my child is already thirty or older, then pay out the balance of the trust property.

Under this example, if at the time that the Separate Trusts are created, one of your children is twenty-three, then all of that child's property will remain in his or her Separate Trust. The trustees will care for the child out of his or her Separate Trust for health, education, maintenance, and support. The trustees will be liberal, if you choose, and will allow advancements for the extraordinary purposes you have set forth in your instructions. When your child is twenty-five, he or she will be entitled to receive one-half of your trust property; the other half will be distributed to your son or daughter at thirty.

What if your child is twenty-six at your death? If that is the case, one-half of your child's Separate Trust property will immediately be distributed; the other half will stay in trust until he or she is thirty.

What if your child is thirty-one on your death? If your child is thirty or older when the Separate Trust is formed, then he or she will receive an immediate distribution of the entire trust property.

The assumption implicit in the selection of this alternative is that if children are under twenty-five they are not experienced enough to be trusted with their inheritance. If they are over twenty-five, but under thirty, they should be given a chance to flex their financial muscles with half of their inheritance. If they are thirty years of age or older, they should be trusted with their entire inheritance.

There is nothing special about these ages. They are an example of what can be done under this alternative. If you like how this alternative is designed, but are not happy with the ages, you can replace them with others that better fit your desires.

13–10 *Make Two Distributions to My Child, the First at a Minimum Age, or Immediately if That Age Has Been Met, the Second to Occur Five Years from the Date of the First Distribution*

For some reason, a substantial percentage of our clients felt that two distributions five years apart seemed to be the ideal method for distributing property to their children. Here, emphasis is placed on the minimum age that triggers the first distribution.

A Separate Trust designed under this alternative would have instructions something like this:

> After the Common Trust ends, each of my children
> shall receive an equal share of my property to be held
> in a Separate Trust.

Pay one-half of each child's Separate Trust to him or her at age twenty-five. If my son or daughter is over twenty-five when this Separate Trust is formed, distribute one-half of its funds immediately. Distribute the other half five years from that date.

A child who is under the age of twenty-five when his or her Separate Trust is created will not receive an immediate distribution. The trustees will care for the child based upon need until the child reaches twenty-five, when one-half will be distributed. The other half will remain in trust and will always be available to the child, based on the trustees' judgments and your instructions, until it is distributed five years later.

What if a child is over twenty-five when the Separate Trust is formed? There will still be two distributions five years apart. A child who is thirty-one when the Separate Trust is formed will receive one-half of the trust property immediately. The other half will remain in the Separate Trust until the child reaches thirty-six.

The unique quality of this alternative is that regardless of your children's ages at your and your spouse's deaths, they will always receive their shares in two distributions five years apart. It specifically addresses the adage that "Age does not a wise person make, experience does."

13–11 *Make Four Distributions to My Child, the First to Occur at a Minimum Age, or Immediately if That Age Has Been Met, the Second Through the Fourth to Occur Every Five Years*

This alternative is similar to alternative 13–10. However, here four distributions are called for rather than just two.

An example of how this Alternative is typically designed is:

After my Common Trust ends, each of my children shall receive an equal share of my property to be held in a Separate Trust.

Pay one-fourth of the Separate Trust funds to my child when he or she is thirty. If my child is over thirty when this Separate Trust is formed, pay out one-fourth immediately. Pay out the balance in three additional equal distributions, each distribution being five years apart.

If your child is twenty-two when the Separate Trust is created, there would be no immediate distribution. The trustees would provide for your child from the trust funds pursuant to your instructions. Your son or daughter would receive one-fourth of the trust property at thirty. At thirty-five, forty, and forty-five, three additional equal distributions would be made. If your child is over twenty-five at the time the Separate Trust is created, say thirty-two, then one-fourth would be paid immediately and the other three installments would be paid at thirty-seven, forty-two, and forty-seven.

In our experience, four distributions would be the upper distribution extreme. There is a drawback in using too many installments. They can become cumbersome and make some children unnecessarily and overly dependent on your trustees' judgments. This does not mean that you can't select a hundred distributions in designing your Separate Trusts, but you should have good reasons for doing so.

13–12 *Make Multiple Unequal Distributions, the First to Occur at a Minimum Age, or Immediately if That Age Has Been Met, the Others at Stated Ages*

Distributions from the Separate Trust do not have to be equal in amounts, nor do they have to be five years apart. If you wish to give a child multiple distributions in different amounts, you can certainly do so. Any distribution can be delayed for as long as you choose.

Following are instructions that illustrate this approach:

After the Common Trust ends, each of my children shall receive an equal share of my property to be held in a Separate Trust.

Pay one-fourth of the Separate Trust to my child when he or she is thirty-five. If my child is over thirty-five when the Separate Trust is created, pay out one-fourth immediately. When my child is fifty, pay out

another fourth. When my child is sixty, pay out the
balance of the Separate Trust.

This alternative can be adapted to meet a variety of motives.
Sometimes it is used to make uneven distributions at set inter-
vals. For example, the clause may be written to state that if your
child is over thirty-five when the Separate Trust is created, then
one-third of the trust property is paid immediately. The remainder is paid fifteen years later.

This alternative is also used to make as many distributions
as you desire; it is not limited to two. It is also used to make
other types of uneven distributions, such as three distributions
of 20 percent, 30 percent, and 50 percent. This alternative can
accommodate almost any motive or desire you may have with
respect to designing uneven distributions from your children's
Separate Trusts.

13–13 *Make No Mandatory Lifetime Distributions to My Child, But
Take Care Of My Child in Whatever Way He or She Needs, Whenever
He or She Needs It from the Trust Funds*

For some children, especially the disadvantaged, it is better
to keep your property in trust for them all their lives. They will
never be able to adequately manage money or property. Your
trustees will always have to supervise their financial affairs pursuant to your instructions. Other children simply cannot handle
finances or wealth. Many parents have shared with us that they
have a child who has a proven inability to manage his or her
financial affairs.

We have most frequently seen this alternative used to protect
a child from his or herself or from others where there is:

- A learning disability.
- A drinking, drug, or gambling problem.
- A spouse who is irresponsible or who is perceived to have
  married for money.
- No motivation for the child to achieve and succeed on his
  or her own.
- An irresponsible, spendthrift child who has no regard for
  responsible financial behavior.

- Fear that the child will give his or her inheritance to a cult or sect with little regard for his or her own well-being.

The list is endless. If you have a parental situation where you are fearful of putting significant sums of income or property in the hands of a child, this might be the alternative for you.

You would select this alternative if you wish to protect and provide for a particular child for his or her lifetime. You would instruct your trustees to provide for whatever your child needs for his or her education, health, maintenance, and support. You would further instruct your trustees to examine your child's other sources of income and to determine whether or not that income needed to be supplemented from the child's Separate Trust funds.

You can certainly include instructions directing your trustees to give assistance to your child in order to start a business or profession, purchase a home, or any other extraordinary opportunity. Or, if you choose, you could instruct your trustees to provide only the bare necessities for your child's well-being.

Most of our clients who have utilized this alternative have designed it to help and protect their children. They did not design it as a parsimonious vehicle to deprive a child of his or her inheritance.

This Separate Trust alternative generally passes the trust funds directly to grandchildren, other children, or wherever else you wish the funds to go upon your child's death. Its very structure dictates that you do not give your child the right to dispose of the trust funds on his or her death.

13–14 *Make Entirely Different Distribution Patterns for Each of My Children*

It is not necessary, or in some cases even desirable, to treat all your children the same when distributing property from their respective Separate Trusts. One of your children may be totally self-sufficient and need no guidance. Another may be just the opposite. You may have different hopes and fears with respect to each of your children. If so, you might wish to address and manifest those hopes and fears by designing different provisions in each of your children's Separate Trusts.

We had a client who immigrated to this country shortly after the Second World War. He was a very successful self-made man who held strong views. "You know," he said to us, "I believe with all my heart that men and women should be treated for what they are, not for what gender they happen to be. I am a real believer in equal rights for all. It's just too bad that it's not that way. Women are not equal with men. They get taken advantage of, and I want to make sure my girls are protected. My boys need protection, but not as much as my girls. My boys are not subject to as much discrimination."

He had us draft his Separate Trusts differently for his sons and his daughters. His design went something like this:

> My sons shall receive two distributions from their Separate Trusts. One-half of the trust property will be distributed when a son is twenty-five or when his Separate Trust is created, whichever is later. The balance will be distributed five years after the first distribution.
>
> Each of my daughters shall receive one-fourth of their property when they reach twenty-five or at the creation of the Separate Trusts, whichever is later. Five years after that distribution, a second distribution will be made of one-third of the remaining trust balance. All of the other trust property will remain in trust for the life of each of my daughters to care for their every need. When a daughter of mine dies, her trust property shall pass to her children.

You may not agree with what this client did, but you have to agree that he was able to set forth his views and make them work in his trust. It was his feeling that women needed more protection than men. Right or not, it was his trust and his property. His Separate Trusts manifested his concerns and fears and addressed them in a constructive and loving manner.

We used this example to demonstrate what you can do with your property if you have particularly strong desires or motives that differ from child to child. If you do, you can fully express all your desires in your Loving Trust.

The Separate Trust alternatives that we have discussed are listed below. Please check the alternatives that most closely meet your desires and motives.

Advancement Distributions

( ) 13–1   I want my trustees to liberally provide for each of my children.

( ) 13–2   I want my trustees to provide only for the health, education, support, and maintenance of each of my children.

( ) 13–3   My own motive:

_____

_____

_____

_____

Premature Death of a Child

( ) 13–4   I want my child's trust property to pass pursuant to my child's directions.

( ) 13–5   I want my child's trust property to pass to my child's children or, if none, to my other children.

( ) 13–6   My own motive:

_____

_____

_____

_____

Distribution Alternatives

( ) 13–7   I want my property distributed to my children immediately.

( ) 13–8   I want my children to have immediately whatever they want from their Separate Trusts.

( ) 13–9   Make two distributions to my child, one-half at a minimum age, the remainder at another stated age.

( ) 13–10   Make two distributions to my child, the first at a minimum age, or immediately if that age has been met, the second to occur five years from the date of the first distribution.

( ) 13–11   Make four distributions to my child, the first to occur at a minimum age, or immediately if that age has been met, the second through the fourth to occur every five years.

( ) 13–12   Make multiple unequal distributions, the first to occur at a minimum age, or immediately if that age has been met, the others at stated ages.

( ) 13–13   Make no mandatory lifetime distributions to my child, but take care of my child in whatever he or she needs, whenever he or she needs it from the trust funds.

( ) 13–14   Make entirely different distribution patterns for each of my children.

( ) 13–15   My own motive:

_____

_____

_____

_____

14

How to Ultimately Distribute Your Property

Lawyers refer to planning for the ultimate distribution of your property as the "ultimate remainder," a term that sounds somewhat depressing. To many it conjures a picture of Armageddon. That picture is accurate, because that is exactly what ultimate remainder means—Armageddon. We knew a family, a husband, wife, and two children, who left on a trip in their new camper and never came back. They were killed instantly in a tragic and senseless car accident. One moment they were alive and happy, the next, dead.

Losing a family in a single accident is horrifying to think about. But when providing for loved ones, it has to be addressed. What would happen to your property if the worst happened and your entire family was killed in a single catastrophic accident? Your Loving Trust should be designed to answer this question. The ultimate remainder is used to pass your property to distant family, friends, or charity if your immediate family doesn't survive you.

When you die without a will or a bona fide will substitute, your state's law determines who will receive your property. This law, called the law of descent and distribution, also applies if your whole family is killed, unless you provide for an ultimate remainder in your Loving Trust.

Most states' laws mandate that the next set of living relatives on your family tree will get your property. For example, if your parents are living and you, your spouse, and children all die in a single accident, your parents would receive your property. If your parents are deceased, but you have brothers or sisters, then they will receive your property. Each state has a complex system of determining who is the next relative, or generation of relatives, on the family tree to receive your property.

As you can imagine, the laws of determining heirship can get quite complicated. In law school, we learned about the "Doctrine of the Laughing Heir." It comes from the mental picture that is formed when a poor, working person is informed that a distant relative has died. This heir has never heard of or met the now-deceased relative. At first, the reaction is one of sadness. When that poor heir finds out that there is a sizable inheritance and he is the only legal heir, out comes a whoop of joy as he laughs all the way to the bank.

When we mentioned ultimate remainders to our clients, we elicited some fairly strange reactions. Most people began to fantasize, and even agonize, over what should be done. We have had clients delay signing their Loving Trusts for months while they contemplated an ultimate remainder.

Ultimate remainders are important. They are a facet of your Loving Trust that allows you to control your property even in the worst scenario imaginable. However, the odds of ultimate remainders ever having to be used, at least for most families, are incredibly small. Nevertheless, in good planning everything is possible, and it is necessary that you squarely face this possibility and attempt to resolve it in your own mind.

Determining an ultimate remainder is not so important that it should cause you to delay completion of your entire Loving Trust. A Loving Trust can be changed at any time with little trouble or expense. If you cannot decide what to do with respect to your ultimate heirs, select one of the following ultimate remainder alternatives and sign it. It is better for you to have your plan in force for you and your immediate loved ones while you are deciding on the specifics of your ultimate remainder than it is to do nothing while you are thinking about a contingency that will most likely never occur.

Over the years we have found that ultimate remainders fall into one of four categories. We have turned these categories into four different Loving Trust alternatives:

14-1 I want one-half of my property to pass to my heirs and one-half of my property to pass to my spouse's heirs under my state's laws.

14-2 I want all my property to pass to my heirs under my state's laws.

14-3 I want my property to pass to certain individuals.

14-4 I want all my property to go to charity.

14-1 *I Want One-half of My Property to Pass to My Heirs and One-half of My Property to Pass to My Spouse's Heirs Under My State's Laws*

This alternative is used when one spouse owns most of a family's property in his or her name. If the whole family were to die in one accident and no ultimate remainder was in effect, then by law all the property would pass only to the owner's relatives. Many people do not like this result. They would rather have their property pass equally to their family and their spouse's family.

Use of this alternative reflects the attitude that even though one spouse is the owner of the marriage's property, the property is treated as if it were owned equally by each spouse. It is by far the most common ultimate remainder alternative that we see used. Most of our clients have had little or no concern about using state law to determine who will ultimately receive their property.

14-2 *I Want All My Property to Pass to My Heirs Under My State's Laws*

This ultimate remainder follows the laws of your state. It simply reaffirms that you wish your property to pass to your heirs as they are determined under state law. This alternative is commonly used if you are single. If none of your Loving Trust beneficiaries is alive at your death, then state law will determine who on your family tree will receive your property.

You may want to use this alternative if you are married and you and your spouse each have property in your own names. Your spouse will leave his or her property to his or her heirs and you will do likewise with yours.

14.3 *I Want My Property to Pass to Certain Individuals*

Rather than rely on your state to determine who your ultimate remainder heirs will be, you may wish to specifically designate them.

Of all the ultimate remainder alternatives, this one presents the most potential for problems. What if the ultimate remainder beneficiaries you name are not alive when you and your immediate family die?

There are two methods of solving this problem. The first is to state that if an ultimate beneficiary dies, the property that would otherwise go to him or her would pass to his or her heirs under state law. This approach assumes that you want your property to follow that beneficiary's family lines.

The second approach is to name several contingent beneficiaries. If a beneficiary is not living when the ultimate remainder is needed, then the other named beneficiaries would share your property equally. Of course, if you ran out of these beneficiaries, your property would pass by your state's laws anyway.

You can see why some people get carried away with ultimate remainder clauses. The "what if" game can be played forever, and a solution never reached. On this one, we urge you to play the odds. Name whom you want to name as your ultimate remainder beneficiaries, decide on backup beneficiaries, and use your state's laws.

14.4 *I Want All My Property to Go to Charity*

You may decide that if your immediate family cannot have your property, it should go to a charity or charities. Many of our clients have come to this conclusion. You only need to list the charities that you would like to see receive your property and to specify what percentage each will get. It is better to do this on a percentage basis than to use dollar amounts. Using dollar amounts can create confusion and controversy, especially if the dollar amounts you specify are greater than the value of your property. Percentages are more flexible and infinitely safer.

Designing how you wish to leave your property to charity can be a gratifying experience. If you are interested in making gifts to charity in your Loving Trust, please read our book *The*

Handbook of Estate Planning. It will give you a better idea as to how charitable giving is done in trusts.

There are five alternatives for an ultimate remainder in the following checklist. These include the four we have discussed, plus an alternative that you can use to create your own motive. Please check the alternatives that most nearly coincide with your desires and motives.

( ) 14-1   I want one-half of my property to pass to my heirs and one-half of my property to pass to my spouse's heirs under my state's laws.

( ) 14-2   I want all my property to pass to my heirs under my state's laws.

( ) 14-3   I want my property to pass to certain individuals.

( ) 14-4   I want all my property to go to charity.

( ) 14-5   My own motive:

_____

_____

_____

_____

15

How to Select Your Trustees

"**W**hat do my trustees do?" and "How do I select my trustees?" are two questions that we are frequently asked when we lecture on Loving Trusts. This doesn't surprise us because choosing trustees has traditionally been viewed as one of the most difficult tasks a person must undertake when establishing any type of trust. While choosing your trustees is certainly important and will involve some serious deliberation, we suspect that many lawyers, bankers, and other professionals have so muddied the trustee waters that choosing a trustee is often viewed as a much harder process than it really needs to be. With the answers to these two questions, we believe that you should be capable of selecting your Loving Trust trustees with a minimum of anxiety and deliberation.

What Do My Trustees Do?

Very simply, your trustees will follow your instructions in administering your Loving Trust property for the benefit of your loved ones.

Follow Your Instructions

Your trustees must be able to understand your instructions. Your Loving Trust will be only as effective as the breadth and clarity of the instructions you leave and the wisdom that you have employed in selecting your trustees. If your instructions are sparse and ambiguous, your trustees will have to care and provide for your loved ones by relying on their mores and judgments in lieu of yours. Sparse, incomplete, or ambiguous trust instructions will place significant pressure on your trustees. They will either have to substitute their philosophy for yours, or be so careful in not violating what they guess your loving intent to be that they become unresponsive and, as a result, do little to care for your loved ones.

A "bare-bones" trust puts both your trustees and your beneficiaries in an extremely bad position. Your trustees will not be comfortable because they will not have a well-defined path to follow, and they will be justifiably concerned about their liability for making incorrect judgments. Your beneficiaries will suffer as a result of the incorrect or unmade decisions of their underdirected "bare-bones" trustees.

We do not believe that you would entrust your loved ones to a baby-sitter without giving that sitter thorough instructions. Regardless of the competence of the baby-sitter, you will not want his or her notions of how to care and provide for others to override yours when it comes to your children. The same is true for your trustees. No matter how good your trustees are, leaving them with incomplete instructions will force them to make decisions that you might not make.

All those charlatans who preach that the only good trust is a short or bare-bones trust are either ill informed or uncaring.

Most of us spend our entire lives providing for loved ones and accumulating property to promote their comfort and well-being. We sacrifice daily pleasures in order to purchase disability and life insurance. We have a great deal to say when asked about how we discharge our spousal and parental duties. Given a choice, we would not want our loving care and guidance to end abruptly with our death or disability.

You should design your Loving Trust with the same thoroughness with which you run your household. If concise instructions accomplish your goals, then by all means use them. But if you opt for brevity only to reduce the length of your Loving Trust, you will shortchange your loved ones. Do not let anyone intimidate you with respect to the length of your trust instructions. As long as they are clear and complete, you will not have to apologize to anyone. Bare-bones planning will make

Murphys out of your trustees and a shambles of your loving intentions.

Many people have a great concern, bordering on outright fear, that their trustees will not do what they are supposed to do. We are often asked, "How do I know that my trustees will do any of the things I've instructed them to do?"

A trustee's actions are very highly regulated by the laws of all states and the decisions of their courts. There is an important rule of law that states, "There is no duty known to the law greater than that duty which a trustee owes to the beneficiary of a trust." This is an extraordinarily powerful and far-reaching statement of the law with respect to your trustees' duty to follow your instructions in caring for your loved ones.

Your trustees have an absolute legal obligation to care for your Loving Trust beneficiaries with the highest standards of prudence and care mandated by our entire legal system. They can be brought to task and sued for not following your instructions. The law makes it clear that they are on the hottest of all legal hot seats if they do not act prudently within the instructions you have provided.

Administer Your Loving Trust

While you are alive and well, your Loving Trust property will be under your direct control. There will be absolutely no constraints on you or your Loving Trust property. You will continue—just as you always have—paying your bills, collecting your income, buying and selling things, filing your tax returns, and performing all of the innumerable functions that are part of living in our society.

Upon your death or disability, someone has to take over all these tasks. If you do not have a Loving Trust, the probate court will assume them. If you have a Loving Trust, your trustees will do so according to your instructions. They will perform all the tasks that are required to care for you, your loved ones, and your property.

How much administration your Loving Trust needs will depend on the extent and mix of your trust property and the completeness of your instructions. Your trustees will have to keep records of all their transactions, as well as file all necessary income tax returns. They will be accountable to your beneficiaries for all their actions.

The longest chapter in our Loving Trust is devoted to giving our trustees the power to accomplish and implement our instructions. Most bare-bones trust planning skimps or totally ignores these critically important trustees' powers. If your trust does not give your trustees the power or legal authority to accomplish your instructions, then your trustees will have to go to the probate court and get the judge's approval before doing so.

When we were children, our parents would frequently send us to the store to purchase cigarettes for them. The storekeeper would not sell them to us unless we produced a note from our parents saying that it was all right. Think of the storekeeper as the law and the child's notes as the trustee's power portion of your Loving Trust. The trustee's power portion of your Loving Trust gives your trustee the power to do whatever is necessary to administer your Loving Trust pursuant to your instructions.

Every state has laws that automatically grant authority to trustees. These laws attempt to be complete, but in our experience, they are often silent with respect to specific situations. When that happens, your trustees will have to seek the judge's direction. A well-designed Loving Trust gives its trustees the power to do everything necessary in order to accomplish its maker's instructions.

We wholeheartedly believe that your Loving Trust would be bare-bones without this important language. Please insist on it when working with your lawyer.

How Do I Select My Trustees?

Your Loving Trust must always have at least one trustee to operate it. No trust, not even a Loving Trust, has an autopilot that keeps it on course when there is no one to run it. No matter how many years your Loving Trust lasts, it will always have to have at least one trustee who is following and implementing your instructions.

Trustees are named in one of two ways. You can name them or a local judge can name them. If you choose the former, you would name your initial trustees in your Loving Trust; you would also provide for their replacement in the event of death, disability, or resignation by prenaming whom you would like their replacements or successors to be. Your replacement trustees are referred to as successor trustees.

If you fail to name a trustee, or if for some reason the trustees you do name are unable or unwilling to serve, a local judge will name a trustee for you. When confronted with this situation, the judge almost always names a bank trust department. Our law will not allow a trust to fail because it doesn't have a trustee.

Your trustee selection process should take into consideration different circumstances as you name your trustees. Who should be your trustees when you are alive and well? Do you want different trustees administering your Loving Trust on your disability? What individuals, banks, or trust companies should be your trustees after your death? In the case of individuals, how do you wish to replace them if they die, become disabled, or choose not to serve?

You May Be Your Own Trustee

All our clients wanted to be an initial trustee of their Loving Trust. We recommend that you choose to do so in designing your Loving Trust. Many people hold the incorrect view that when they establish a trust they must name an independent trustee to operate it. Many hold the equally incorrect opinion that their trustee must be a bank that will immediately charge a fee for being a trustee in name only.

You may choose to retain a bank or other professional trustee while you are alive. However, if you do, they will charge you a fee if there is property in your trust. You do not have to name an institutional trustee as one of your initial trustees! Professional trustees are usually named as initial trustees only when there is significant property that the maker wants to have professionally managed.

As an initial trustee of your Loving Trust, your duties will be minimal. We will explain how you accomplish the few tasks you will have to perform with regard to your trust in Chapter Twenty-two, "How to Get Property into Your Loving Trust."

You do not have to be anxious about the trusteeship of your Loving Trust while you are alive and able to act as your own trustee. It is when you cannot act as a trustee or take care of yourself that your choice of trustees becomes critical.

No trustee will ever be as good at the job as you are. As long as you are healthy and lucid, you should be your own trustee.

You Need a Co-trustee

We recommend that you name an additional co-trustee of your Loving Trust. If you become disabled or die and do not have a co-trustee, there will be no one to take over the trust reins. If that is the case, a local judge will need to get involved in order to pass the reins. Imagine the following:

> You are a spectator at a track meet. A major relay event is about to take place. The gun goes off and the race is on. Your team does well, as each of your first two runners leads his opponent and makes a smooth hand-off of the baton to his teammate. Your third runner expands the lead, but as he attempts to hand the baton to the anchorman he clumsily drops it. Your team's hopes of victory end with the falling baton.

Now, imagine that you are your trust team's lead relay runner. As the initial trustee and lead runner you do well and hold your own, taking care of yourself and your trust property. Suddenly you become disabled or die. It's time to hand the baton to the next runner or trustee. But there's no one there. The baton drops to the earth and will stay there until a local judge picks it up and hands it to a successor trustee named by the court.

Let's assume that you named your spouse as one of your initial co-trustees. While you are alive and healthy, he or she is a trustee in name only. Now let's assume that you become disabled. Your spouse, as your co-trustee, becomes an active trustee. The baton does not drop to the earth.

Your co-trustee spouse will continue to administer your trust following your disability. He or she will hand the baton to your successor trustee if that is what your instructions provide. If your instructions provide for a successor co-trustee, your spouse will offer the baton to and share it with your replacement co-trustee.

If you are single, the same continuity problem presents itself, except that you will not have the convenience of naming a spouse as your co-trustee. You will have to name another family member, good friend, or perhaps one of your professional advisers as your initial co-trustee.

If your Loving Trust has at least one other co-trustee, you will not have to be concerned that the probate court will get involved in order for your "trustee baton" to be passed on. If your Loving Trust has two or more trustees, you can be assured that it will be continuously administered without any outside or public intervention.

If you decide that you wish to act as your Loving Trust's sole trustee, you can certainly do so. The only danger is that if you become disabled or die, there will be a period during which your Loving Trust has no trustee. Until someone notifies your Loving Trust's new trustee that you are disabled or dead, your trust is not going to be administered for anyone's benefit.

You may have some concern or fear that if you initially name a co-trustee, you may lose some control over your property. If you properly design your Loving Trust, this will not be the case. Your trustees work for you at all times. While you are alive and healthy they must do what you tell them—not more, not less! After your disability or death, the only thing that changes is that they will receive your orders through your Loving Trust instructions rather than directly from you.

You may terminate a co-trustee at any time and for any reason. While you are alive and well, you can maintain complete control of your Loving Trust. Naming another trustee does not deprive you of any control. As the maker of your Loving Trust, you may hire and fire trustees at will. You can delegate as little or as much authority as you want to another trustee. You can structure your Loving Trust so that your co-trustee can only pass the baton to successor trustees on your death or disability.

If you are happily married, it is common practice for you and your spouse to act as co-trustees of your Loving Trust. We would certainly recommend that you do so. You should not be concerned that by doing so you will create problems for yourself later on if you have domestic difficulties or go through a divorce. You may terminate your spouse as a trustee at any time, for any reason. During the time your spouse is a co-trustee, he or she does not control your property. Your mate follows your lead and instructions and, as a trustee, awaits your disability or death to pick up the baton and follow your trust instructions.

Both you and your spouse will remain as trustees until subsequent events trigger a change. You will remain a trustee until you become disabled, die, or simply resign. Your spouse will remain a trustee until he or she becomes disabled, dies, resigns, or is terminated.

You need to select your initial co-trustee. You will also need to name who you want to be your successor trustees upon your disability or death and the termination, resignation, disability, or death of one or more of your trustees.

The Characteristics of a Good Trustee

You want to make sure that your successor trustees have the capability of administering your Loving Trust instructions with skill and empathy for your loved ones. Finding a trustee with these characteristics is very difficult and, in most cases, impossible. This is why we almost always recommend that our clients name multiple co-trustees. You can select your trustees so as to blend their talents and virtues in order to create a collective "super-trustee."

"Many hands make light work" and "Two heads are better than one" are adages that apply to trustee selection. When it comes to trustee selection, too many cooks don't spoil the broth, they make for a more efficient kitchen.

In selecting your trustee team you should be looking for individuals or institutions that will:

- Be knowledgeable with respect to beneficiaries.
- Have a liking or empathy for your loved ones.
- Know how to manage and invest your funds.
- Understand your thinking.
- Be collectible for any mistakes that are made.

If you understand the relative advantages and disadvantages of institutional and individual trustees, the difficulty of your selection task should be greatly reduced.

Using a Bank or Other Trust Department as a Trustee

There is a lot to be said for naming an institutional or professional trustee. Bank trust departments and local trust companies are organized to provide trust services to you and your loved ones for a fee. They have staffs of highly trained and qualified trust specialists who work with trust documents and beneficiaries daily. Professional trustees are thorough and will make objective decisions based on the facts as they see and interpret them. They are usually not influenced by emotional issues that could taint their objectivity.

Institutional trustees are geared to administer trusts. With banks of computers and sophisticated equipment, they keep fabulous records and create and maintain all the accounting information that anyone could reasonably want.

Because institutional trustees are corporations, they cannot die or become disabled. The fact that they will outlive the trusts they administer has been reassuring to many of our clients.

Many of our clients and seminar students have been concerned about the viability of their local banks. While bank failures occur, banks are legally structured and regulated in such a way that their trust customers do not have to fear that their assets will be taken to satisfy claims of the bank's creditors or stockholders. The trust assets of a financial institution are segregated from the assets and liabilities of the institution itself. That means that creditors of the financial institution cannot seize trust assets to satisfy debts.

The main advantage we see in naming a financial institution as one of your trustees is based on a concept that we call "collectibility." Because all trustees are liable to their trust beneficiaries for their mistakes, it is important that they can back up their liability with cash or other assets. If your trustees make a mistake, they are liable for the damages sustained by your trust and its beneficiaries.

If your trustees make a major blunder and lose your trust funds, they would be absolutely responsible for making good their mistake and making your trust whole. But, if they have no money or assets of their own, they obviously cannot make good on their mistake. You won't be able to take "blood from a turnip" just because that turnip is a trustee.

Financial institutions usually have lots of money and other assets. They have the ability to make good on their errors. That is why we frequently recommend that our clients use them as co-trustees in building their trustee team.

There are also disadvantages associated with naming a professional trustee. They may be so objective that they take all the love out of your Loving Trust. While their employees most likely will know you, in all likelihood, they will not know your loved ones. And it's unlikely that they will know you and your thought processes well enough to "read between the lines" in your Loving Trust to further infuse it with empathy. We are not suggesting that their employees are not caring or capable of emotion. They are simply paid professionals who will predictably "follow the book" in discharging their institutional trustee duties.

There are a few other disadvantages of using a professional trustee. For one thing, there is employee turnover in a trust department. Go-getters on the rise use trust departments as springboards to bigger and better things. This turnover can be disconcerting and disruptive to your loved ones. Furthermore, because of their liability, institutional trustees tend to be conservative at times. They analyze, consider, and have meetings. Their conservatism is also reflected in their investment results. The bad news is that they may not significantly outperform the market. The good news is that they seldom lose or squander their funds. They rightly believe that it is more important to preserve the principal of their trust accounts with modest rates of return than to invest in high-yield, high-risk investments. Many of our clients look at this conservative mandate as a definite and reassuring advantage.

Using Individuals as Trustees

Family members, friends, colleagues, and advisers are often named as Loving Trust trustees. Since they are not professional trustees, they are free from much of the cumbersome apparatus that goes with an institutional trustee. Like institutional trustees, they have their advantages and disadvantages. By their very nature, individual trustees are less likely to be objective than are institutional trustees. Any individual you would select will most likely know you and your family. He or she may even know a great deal about your business and investment affairs. The odds are good that your individual trustees will be subject to beneficiary pressures and that they will be more likely to make decisions based on a touched heart than on an objective and dispassionate intellect.

You have the opportunity, while you are alive and healthy, to share your Loving Trust with your individual trustees in order to communicate the essence of your beliefs and desires with respect to your loving instructions. Your trustees can be schooled in becoming knowledgeable about your Loving Trust. They should read this book and our *Handbook of Estate Planning*. They should have an opportunity to read your Loving Trust and to ask you and your other advisers any questions they may have.

You can certainly name your lawyer, your accountant, your financial planner, and your life insurance agent as trustees of your Loving Trust. Any one or more of them may have the knowledge and expertise to act as your trustee. Each of them may also have invaluable knowledge with respect to your business and financial affairs. They may also be close to and have a particular empathy for your family members. It is likely that they will also have a professional objectivity that will temper their emotions. In our opinion, many advisers make excellent co-trustees. They are often an overlooked trustee source.

Almost all individual trustees have some drawbacks. Their lack of objectivity can cause squabbles among your loved ones. They may do too much reading between the lines in your Loving Trust and fail to follow your instructions. They may try too hard and get so close to the trees that they can't see the forest.

Individual trustees—and this is a major drawback—may not be collectible for their mistakes. When a trustee makes a mistake such as failing to follow trust instructions or acting in a negligent manner, that trustee must pay any damages incurred by the beneficiaries. For individual trustees, this means that their personal property can be used to pay for these damages if they have no liability insurance. Does your sister or brother have the resources to make good on his or her mistakes if they lose or squander your trust funds? What about Joe, your best friend and colleague? Does your lawyer, CPA, investment adviser, and trusted life insurance agent have the requisite resources? If they don't, you should think twice about naming one of them as a sole trustee.

If you are thinking that you or your individual trustees can purchase trustee liability insurance, think again. Obtaining liability insurance is a growing problem, and it is next to impossible to purchase liability insurance to cover a trustee. Even if you could purchase it, say from Lloyd's of London, it would be prohibitively expensive. The cheapest coverage that we have found, therefore, is for you to name a large bank or trust company as one of your co-trustees.

By law, institutional trustees must post all their assets as their performance bonds. These professionals usually charge less than two percent annually on the value of your property to provide their services. We think of their fee as the cost of an insurance policy, and in today's market it is a bargain.

Individual trustees are mortal. They can go bankrupt or become disabled. They can die prematurely. They can become embezzlers, drug addicts, or alcoholics. They can move to distant lands. They can decline to be your trustee when their time comes to serve.

We recommend that you name more than one individual as your successor trustee. We also recommend that you give serious consideration to naming a professional trustee to serve with them because of the insurance factor professional trustees bring to the table. Name your trustees in teams that will work best for you and your loved ones in the event of your death or disability.

Selecting Your Trustees

While you are alive and well, you should be a co-trustee of your Loving Trust. If you are happily married, your spouse, barring exceptional circumstances to the contrary, should be your co-trustee.

If you are single, or you do not choose to name your spouse as your initial co-trustee, you may act as sole trustee, but you would be better advised to name a close family member, friend, colleague, or one of your closest advisers as a co-trustee.

Upon your disability, you should provide for successor trustees as your replacement. You can name any number of successor trustees to act in your stead. They can join your spouse or other individual co-trustee, or they can replace him or her as well as yourself.

It is important that your Loving Trust instructions list who you wish your disability trustees to be. It is equally important that you provide for their replacements in the event they cannot serve.

You must stipulate who your Loving Trust trustees will be following your death. They can be the same as your disability trustees, or they can be entirely different. Do not forget to provide for their replacements. It is critical that your Loving Trust always have a succession of trustees to assure continuity in its administration.

In the event a trust fails to provide for replacement trustees or if the replacement trustees named in a trust cannot serve, the trust is still valid. The same is true if replacement trustees refuse to serve, which is their prerogative. (There is no law that forces any trustee named in a trust to actually serve.) "No trust shall fail for want of a trustee" is one of the cornerstones of trust law. Beneficiaries of a trust that does not have a trustee, no matter the reason why, can always go to a court and have the court appoint a trustee. The trust is still valid. Happily, the court only names a trustee; it does not have the right, in most cases, to exercise any control over either the terms of the trust or its beneficiaries.

If you are fortunate, you will have the opportunity to select among several well-qualified individuals in whom you have much faith. But if you are like most of our clients, you will not have this luxury. You may have only one or two individuals you would feel comfortable naming. You may feel uncomfortable naming any individual trustees, in which case you may choose to name an institutional trustee to act when you die or become disabled.

In designing your trustee team, please remember that institutional trustees offer distinct advantages and that they often blend well with individual trustees as co-trustees. By combining an individual trustee with an institutional trustee, you can maximize the advantages and minimize the disadvantages of each. By working together, they can provide expertise, collectibility, and administration tempered with love, empathy, and caring. We highly recommend that you consider such an option.

Before we offer you those alternatives most commonly selected by our clientele over the years, there are still two issues that you need to address when selecting your trustees: control and cost.

Control

Your trustee is controlled by the terms of your Loving Trust and by the law governing trustees in your state. However, when you name a trustee in a Loving Trust, you are not going to be around to see that trustee in action. It may be that even with much thought and the best of intentions, you have made a bad choice.

Most of the "bare-bones trusts" that we have reviewed over the years fail to take into consideration that a trustee may do a bad job. These trusts do not have any method for the beneficiaries to terminate a trustee who just isn't doing a very good job.

While you are alive and well, you can terminate any trustee at any time, for any reason. If you are happily married, we suggest that you give this same termination right to your spouse upon your disability or death. If you have adult children, we suggest that you next give these termination powers to a majority of your children. If your children are minors, you should consider giving termination powers to your children's guardians. The same would hold true for a majority of your beneficiaries, regardless of who they are.

By always giving your loved ones the power to terminate a trustee, you continue to control through their control. A trustee doing a poor job ought to be replaced. In fact, if your trustees know they can be terminated they will probably do a better job and be more responsive to the needs and sensitivities of your beneficiaries. If you *do not* wish your beneficiaries to have this right—this is clearly your prerogative—don't give it to them.

You should give your loved ones the power to terminate your trustees only if you place substantial restrictions on its use. We strongly suggest you provide instructions that if a trustee is terminated, that trustee must be replaced with another trustee whom you have named in your Loving Trust.

We are often asked, "What happens if my beneficiaries fire all of the trustees I have named?" Our last line of defense provides that, in that event, an institutional trustee must be named. We know that your beneficiaries will not dupe or unduly take advantage of one of these professionals. We even give our beneficiaries the power to terminate professional trustees, but if they do that, they have to name another institutional trustee as a replacement.

Giving your beneficiaries termination powers, so long as they are coupled with the power to appoint your replacements, is good planning. It provides a system of checks and balances and adds significant flexibility to your Loving Trust planning.

Cost

Your Loving Trust should provide that your individual trustees get paid for acting as your trustees. Trustees work hard and have significant responsibilities and significant personal liabilities.

When it comes to a close friend or family member, many of us will take on responsibility, work hard, and even endure some personal liability, regardless of whether we are paid or not. Somehow, though, this kind of work all too often gets shuffled to the bottom of our stacks, left undone until all of our profitable work is finished. We believe that you will get better performance from your individual trustees if you provide Loving Trust instructions that your trustees are to be paid. If they are family members or friends, they may decline their compensation. The key to such instructions is that they can receive a trustee's compensation if they earn it and elect to receive it.

Every state has laws regulating trustee fees. Some states' laws specify that trustee fees will be a certain percentage of the trust property. Others provide that trustee fees will be governed by whatever fees are customarily charged in a given area or that they will be governed by whatever is reasonable in a particular community.

Institutional trustees always charge a fee for their services. All of them have written fee schedules that they will be happy to provide to you. We believe that their fees are very reasonable for the liability they assume and the work that they do. Most fee schedules provide for higher percentage charges for smaller trusts; many do not take trusts below a certain dollar value. You can readily find out what your bank or trust company charges by asking for their fee schedule.

We have listed those alternatives that are commonly selected by our clients, plus an alternative that you can use to create your own motive. Please take a moment to check the alternatives that most nearly coincide with your desires and motives. For your convenience, we have broken these alternatives into four categories:

1) Naming my trustees while I am alive and well.

2) Naming my successor trustees on my disability.

3) Naming my successor trustees on my death.

4) How my beneficiaries may terminate my trustees.

Naming my trustees while I am alive and well

( ) 15-1   I will act as my sole trustee.

( ) 15-2   My spouse and I will act as my co-trustees.

( ) 15-3   I will act as a co-trustee along with:

_____

_____

_____

_____

( ) 15-4   My own alternative:

_____

_____

_____

_____

Naming my successor trustees on my disability

( ) 15-5   The following individuals or institutions will act as my successor trustees in the order I have set out (if I do not name an institution, at least two individual trustees must always serve):

_____

_____

_____

_____

( ) 15-6   The following individuals or institutions will *replace all my initial trustees* and will act in the order I have set out (if I do not name an institution, at least two individual trustees must serve):

_____

_____

_____

_____

( ) 15-7   My initial co-trustee must choose a major institutional trustee to serve as successor co-trustee. When my initial co-trustee can no longer serve, this institutional trustee shall continue to serve alone.

Naming my successor trustees on my death

( ) 15-8   My disability trustees will continue to serve. They will be replaced by the following individuals or institutions in the order I have set out (if I do not name an institution, at least two individual trustees must serve):

_____

_____

_____

_____

( ) 15-9　　My disability trustees will be replaced by the following individuals or institutions in the order I have set out (if I do not name an institution, at least two individual trustees must serve):

_____

_____

_____

_____

( ) 15-10　　My initial co-trustee must select a major institutional trustee to serve as co-trustee. When my initial co-trustee can no longer serve, this institutional trustee can serve alone.

How my beneficiaries may terminate my trustees

( ) 15-11　　My spouse can terminate any of my successor trustees. After my spouse is no longer a trustee, a majority of my beneficiaries can terminate any of my successor trustees. When all my successor trustees have either been terminated or they are no longer available, my beneficiaries must choose a major institutional trustee.

( ) 15-12　　A majority of my beneficiaries can terminate any of my successor trustees. When all my successor trustees have either been terminated, or they are no longer available, my beneficiaries must choose a major institutional trustee.

( ) 15-13　　My own alternative:

_____

_____

_____

_____

16

How to Save
Federal Death Tax

Just as most of us have come to accept the old adage that "nothing is certain but death and taxes," many of us have come to believe that death *means* taxes. Fortunately, for most Americans, death taxes, or at least the federal death tax, are not inevitable.

In 1981, the Economic Recovery Tax Act significantly reduced the federal government's taxation of estates. Today the value of an estate, less all its liabilities, must exceed $600,000 to be subject to the federal death or estate tax. Recent statistics show that a mere 3½ percent of estates pay federal estate tax.

If You Have Not Changed Your Federal Estate Tax Planning Since 1981

The Economic Recovery Tax Act so changed the precepts of federal estate tax planning that any planning you accomplished prior to its enactment is probably totally obsolete. If you did federal estate tax planning before the Economic Recovery Tax Act was passed, you must change your planning now. Your current planning very likely creates unnecessary federal estate taxes upon your death. This is especially true if you live in Arizona, California, Idaho, Louisiana, Nevada, New Mexico, Texas, or Washington. The new law has had its greatest impact on these community property states.

We can't emphasize enough the urgency and importance of our request. We have observed that only a small percentage of people with pre-1981 plans have bothered to change their planning. We suspect most people believe that the Economic Recovery Tax Act's benefits automatically apply to them. Unfortunately, the truth is just the opposite. If you want to take advantage of its ample benefits, you need to redo your planning.

How Big Does Your Estate Have to Be?

For tax to be one of your planning motives, the value of all your property, including your life insurance proceeds—reduced by the value of all your debts—must approach or exceed $600,000. If you are married, the combined net value of your and your spouse's property must approximate $600,000 to warrant federal estate tax planning.

Federal Estate Tax Planning for Single People

If you are single and you wish to do federal estate tax planning, you are faced with a very difficult task. The federal government does not give any special federal estate tax breaks to single people. Most federal estate tax planning done for singles deals with sophisticated lifetime gifts, special life insurance trusts, and other complex measures beyond the scope of this book.

We strongly recommend that you concentrate on designing your Loving Trust, as explained in Chapter Eighteen, "How to Plan if You Are Single," and that you work closely with a good tax lawyer. We would also recommend that you read *The Handbook of Estate Planning*. We wrote this text primarily with larger estates in mind. It will provide you with estate tax planning strategies by acquainting you with many of the finer tax-planning points.

Given the difficulty of planning for a single person's federal death taxes, most of our single clients ultimately opted to purchase considerable amounts of additional life insurance to cover their tax liability. In effect, they viewed federal estate tax as a liability that could only be covered or offset by adding more money to their Loving Trust.

If you are single and wish to cover your federal estate tax liability with additional life insurance, you should be absolutely sure that you work closely with your lawyer and your insurance agent in dovetailing your insurance into your Loving Trust planning; absent good planning, your life insurance will be subject to federal estate tax.

The Unlimited Marital Deduction

If you are married when you die, the federal government gives your spouse a significant tax break called the unlimited marital deduction. If you leave your property to your spouse—it does not matter whether you do so outright or in trust—it will *not be subject to federal estate tax.*

In its simplest form, this is how the unlimited marital deduction works:

> Esther Feld is wealthy. She decides to leave all her property outright to her husband, Fred, at her death. When she dies, none of her property—regardless of its value—will be subject to the federal estate tax, as long as she and Fred are still married at the time of her death.

The marital deduction allows you to pass unlimited amounts of property to your husband or wife free of federal estate tax. This remains true even if you wish to leave your property to your spouse with severe restrictions placed on its use. The only requirement you must meet in order to qualify for this wonderful tax benefit is that you must give your spouse the right to all the income your property produces each year.

> Esther left all her property to her husband, Fred, in trust. Her trust instructions could have stated that Fred was to receive only the interest, dividends, and other income that Esther's trust property produced each year.
>
> Even with Fred's receiving this meager benefit from his wife's inheritance, it would qualify for the unlimited marital deduction. Esther's property would not be liable for federal estate tax.

The only right you must give your husband or wife with the property you leave him or her in order to qualify for the unlimited marital deduction is the right to the income from that property, paid at least annually, for the rest of his or her life.

You may certainly choose to be more liberal in providing for your spouse and still have your inheritance qualify for this tax bonanza. The law only requires that your spouse annually receive the income.

The property that you leave your spouse will, however, be subject to federal estate tax when your spouse dies. The reason that the federal government is so kind to married couples is that they know that if the value of a husband and wife's property is large enough, there will eventually be an estate tax. Like circling vultures, the federal tax collectors know it is only a matter of time before they can feed.

Your $600,000 Tax-Free Amount

Every person gets a $600,000 tax-free amount that they can pass to loved ones. If this amount is not wisely used, it can be "lost" and tax paid where it doesn't have to be paid. For example:

> Let's assume that Esther leaves her entire estate of $1,000,000 directly to Fred and that Fred has no property of his own. He would receive the money tax-free because of the unlimited marital deduction. But keep in mind that Esther did not use her $600,000 tax-free amount.
>
> However, on Fred's subsequent death, his federal estate tax on the $1,000,000—even after his $600,000 tax-free amount is used to offset it—would be $153,000!

Had Esther properly planned her tax strategy and used her $600,000 tax-free amount, there would absolutely be no federal estate tax on either her or Fred's deaths. Esther could have designed her Loving Trust something like this:

> My Loving Trust will take care of me first. When I die, it will create two subtrusts. One will be a Family

Trust for our children. I will leave my tax-free amount of $600,000 to this Family Trust.

I want the remainder of my property to go to Fred in a Pocketbook Trust. He can have all the income and all the trust property for whatever he wants. My trustees shall take care of him if he is ill or disabled. He can leave what is left in this Trust to whomever he wants on his death. If he doesn't, its remaining funds will go to my Common Trust for our children.

A diagram of this Loving Trust would look like this:

"Me" Trust
$1,000,000

"Pocketbook" Trust   Family Trust
$400,000 $600,000

Esther's Loving Trust totally avoids federal estate tax because it fully uses the unlimited marital deduction and her $600,000 tax-free amount. It accomplishes this because:

All the property in Fred's Pocketbook Trust qualifies for the unlimited marital deduction.

The $600,000 in the Family Trust is subject to federal estate tax, but is offset by Esther's $600,000 tax-free amount.

When Fred dies, the property in the Pocketbook Trust will be more than offset by Fred's $600,000 tax-free amount. The $600,000 in the Family Trust will not be subject to tax because it was subject to federal estate tax on Esther's death.

Esther's federal estate tax planning utilized both her and Fred's tax-free amounts in addition to Esther's unlimited marital deduction. Her situation clearly demonstrates that despite the lure of the unlimited marital deduction, it is better to use Pocketbook and Family Trusts than it is to leave everything directly to your spouse.

Your Pocketbook and Family Trusts

If you are married and one of your desires is to achieve federal estate tax planning, your Loving Trust will always have a Family Trust and one or two Pocketbook Trusts.

Whether your Loving Trust has one or two Pocketbook Trusts will be determined by your non-tax motives, and will, to a large degree, depend upon the value of your property. If the value of your property exceeds $1,200,000, you should consider using two Pocketbook Trusts. If the value of your property lies somewhere between $600,000 and $1,200,000, you will usually utilize a single Pocketbook Trust for your spouse's benefit.

Whether you have one or two Pocketbook Trusts in your Loving Trust is irrelevant for federal estate tax savings purposes. One Pocketbook Trust and one Family Trust will always maximize federal estate tax savings for married couples. The number of Pocketbook Trusts that you create will be based solely on your non-tax motivations.

Non-Tax Motives

Even though reducing federal estate tax is one of your primary motives, your non-tax motives will totally influence the Pocketbook and Family Trust alternatives you ultimately select.

> Let's assume that Esther has $2,000,000 and that Fred is still penniless. Let's further assume that the couple's state law mandates that a spouse has an absolute right to half of a deceased spouse's property. In our situation, Fred would have legal right to $1,000,000 of Esther's property at her death.
>
> Esther has confided to us that she loves Fred and her children, and she wishes to leave everything she owns to them. She also desires to avoid every last dollar of federal death tax possible. Esther also shares her concern that she doesn't want Fred to disinherit the children because he is taken in by another woman or because of some other equally aberrant behavior. Given Esther's desires, we would recommend two Pocketbook Trusts and a Family Trust within Esther's Loving Trust:

Esther's Family Trust would have her tax-free amount
of $600,000 in it. It would provide for Fred and their
children, but would remove Fred as a beneficiary if he
remarried. Its funds would automatically pass to the
children's Common Trust—free of federal estate tax—
on Fred's subsequent death.

Esther's First Pocketbook Trust would be funded
with the amount Fred would be entitled to under state
law, in this case, $1,000,000. Its instructions would pro-
vide that he could have whatever he wanted, whenever
he wanted it. It would be tax-free because of Esther's
unlimited marital deduction.

Esther's second Pocketbook Trust would be funded
with $400,000. It would give Fred all its income at least
annually. It would also instruct the trustees to provide
for Fred's needs out of the principal of the trust so
long as he didn't remarry. It would further provide
that its funds automatically pass to Esther's Common
Trust for the children on Fred's subsequent death.
It would also be tax-free because of the unlimited marital deduction (all it has to give Fred is its annual
income).

Esther used two Pocketbook Trusts because they served her
desires better than just one. She used the first to liberally
provide for Fred with what he was otherwise entitled to under
state law. She created the second to provide for him on a
more regulated basis in order to protect their children's inheritance.

Given Esther's desires, you can see how your non-tax motivations will greatly affect the design of your Loving Trust tax
strategies.

The instructions you choose to place in these various trusts
will be determined by the alternatives you selected in Chapter
Ten, "How to Provide for Your Spouse," and Chapter Eleven,
"How to Provide for Your Family."

Allocation of Your Property Between Your Subtrusts
Federal estate tax planning is primarily concerned with how
much of your property you place in your Family Trust and

how much you place in your respective Pocketbook Trusts. It is purely a numbers game. The amounts that you will allocate between these various subtrusts will be based on the size of your estate and your non-tax desires.

As we set out the various allocation alternatives for estates between $600,000 and $1,200,000, and for those over $1,200,000, you will see you have only a few choices.

Please keep the following concepts in mind as you review these allocation alternatives:

- If you are married, all the alternatives will totally eliminate federal estate tax on your death.
- State and local death taxes may not be eliminated. Your lawyer may have to make modifications to your Loving Trust to reduce or eliminate them.
- There will be a federal estate tax due on your spouse's subsequent death if the combined value of your estates exceeds $1,200,000.
- For easy calculation purposes, we are assuming that the value of your Loving Trust property does not increase after your death.

Federal estate tax planning, although at times complex, can usually be easily accomplished by most lawyers with the help of an accountant, a sharp insurance agent, or a financial planner who is familiar with federal estate tax planning. Our goal is to give you an overview of the process, to acquaint you with the concepts, and to provide you with the basic planning alternatives.

Our clients have often been concerned about the specifics of how their property will be allocated among their various subtrusts. "Will our home go in the Family Trust or in one or the other of the Pocketbook Trusts? What about my bank accounts, retirement benefits, and other property? In which trust will my life insurance proceeds be placed?"

The answer to all these questions is that your trustees will make all those decisions by taking into consideration your family members' respective needs and the federal estate tax laws at that time. In Chapter Six, "Our Loving Trust," we provided that our residences should be placed in Pocketbook Trust One. Other than that, we left the process of allocating specific property to our trustees, and so should you.

The Value of My Estate Is Between $600,000 and $1,200,000

If the value of all your property is between $600,000 and $1,200,000, you should most likely create a single Pocketbook Trust to accompany your Family Trust, although you can create two under certain circumstances. We have already discussed the instructions that you should place in these respective trusts in Chapter Ten, "How to Provide for Your Spouse," and Chapter Eleven, "How to Provide for Your Family."

If saving federal estate tax is one of your primary desires and the value of your estate is between $600,000 and $1,200,000, there are four alternatives for allocating your property between your Pocketbook and Family Trusts. Because of the complexity of federal estate tax planning, we do not suggest that you invent your own alternative in this area.

Following are the motives that our clients have commonly selected over the years. Each is designed to put different amounts in your different subtrusts in order to avoid federal estate tax. Which alternative you select will depend upon your own desires and motives.

16-1 I want my first $600,000 to pass to my spouse in my Pocketbook Trust and the remainder to go to my Family Trust.

16-2 I want up to my first $600,000 to pass to my Family Trust and the remainder to go to my spouse in my Pocketbook Trust.

16-3 I want my property equally divided between my Pocketbook and Family Trusts.

16-4 I want my spouse to receive whatever he or she is entitled to under our state law, with the next $600,000 of my property passing to my Family Trust, and whatever is left—if any—passing to my Pocketbook Trust Two.

16-1 *I Want My First $600,000 to Pass to My Spouse in My Pocketbook Trust and the Remainder to Go to My Family Trust*

This alternative uses your unlimited marital deduction and both your and your spouse's tax-free amounts to save federal estate tax. There is no federal estate tax on the $600,000 going to your Pocketbook Trust because of your unlimited marital deduction. On your spouse's subsequent death, this $600,000 would also be offset by his or her tax-free amount. There is no tax on the Family Trust because of your tax-free amount. On your spouse's subsequent death, whatever is left in the Family Trust will pass to your children free of federal estate tax.

A few allocation examples should help you to see how this alternative works:

> If you have $600,000 of property, it would all go to your Pocketbook Trust. If you have less than $600,000 it would do likewise.
> If your property is valued at $700,000, the first $600,000 would pass to your Pocketbook Trust and $100,000 would go to your Family Trust.
> If your property is valued at $900,000, $300,000 would go to your Family Trust; at $1,100,000, $500,000 would go to your Family Trust; at $1,200,000, $600,000 would pass to your Family Trust.

This alternative is commonly selected by people who love their spouses and want them to have and control as much of their property as possible, while still achieving federal estate tax planning. By selecting this alternative you would be emphasizing your desire to provide liberally for your spouse.

16-2 *I Want up to My First $600,000 to Pass to My Family Trust and the Remainder to Go to My Spouse in My Pocketbook Trust*

This alternative also uses your unlimited marital deduction and both your and your spouse's tax-free amounts to save federal estate tax. In fact, it is exactly the same as alternative 16-1 except that it funds your Family Trust before your Pocketbook Trust.

It is commonly selected by people who love their spouses but who are concerned that their spouses' subsequent behavior or mistakes may squander their children's inheritance. It assures you that your children will be cared and provided for with your $600,000 tax-free amount.

This alternative is often used in community property states. In a community property state, one-half of the property acquired in a marriage is owned by each spouse. By state law, each spouse has full control over his or her half and may dispose of this property in any manner.

If you live in a community property state, your share of the community property, plus all your sole and separate property, is yours to dispose of as you see fit. Since your spouse already owns one-half of your marital property, you would allocate the first $600,000 of your community share to your Family Trust. This will maximize your federal estate tax savings and assure that your children are provided for with your tax-free amount.

16-3 *I Want My Property Equally Divided Between My Pocketbook and Family Trusts*

This alternative also uses your unlimited marital deduction and both your and your spouse's tax-free amounts to save federal estate tax. It divides your property equally between your Pocketbook and Family Trusts. As a result, your Pocketbook funds will be free of tax because of your unlimited marital deduction. Your Family Trust funds will avoid federal estate tax up to your $600,000 tax-free amount. On your spouse's subsequent death, the first $600,000 in the Pocketbook Trust would be tax-free because of his or her tax-free amount; the Family Trust funds will automatically pass tax-free to your children's Common Trust.

In "Our Loving Trust" in Chapter Six, we wanted at least half of our property to pass to our children. This is not an uncommon motive. Many of our clients have expressed the desire that their children receive at least half of their property. People who express this desire usually view the marriage as a partnership, a fifty-fifty proposition. They express their love for their spouse and children equally, and wish to leave their property to them equally. If that is your desire, this alternative may be for you.

16-4 *I Want My Spouse to Receive Whatever He or She Is Entitled to Under Our State Law, with the Next $600,000 of My Property Passing to My Family Trust, and Whatever Is Left—if Any—Passing to My Pocketbook Trust Two*

If you use this alternative you may have to create two Pocketbook Trusts if the value of your property—after your spouse's state-mandated share is placed in Pocketbook Trust One—exceeds your $600,000 tax-free amount. Here is how this happens:

> You have $1,000,000 of property. Under your state law, your spouse is entitled to one-third of your property, or $333,333. You place that amount in your Pocketbook Trust One.
>
> You would like your remaining $666,667 to go into your Family Trust. Unfortunately, this is $66,667 more than your tax-free amount. If you put it all in your Family Trust, $66,667 will be subject to federal estate tax.
>
> To avoid this tax, you create a second Pocketbook Trust for the remaining $66,667. Your instructions in Pocketbook Trust Two are very restrictive. They give your spouse only the Trust's annual income for his or her lifetime (you'll recall that this is the minimum requirement for the unlimited marital deduction).
>
> Upon your spouse's death there will be no federal estate tax, just as there wasn't any at your death. The $333,333 in Pocketbook Trust One plus the $66,667 in Pocketbook Trust Two are offset by your spouse's tax-free amount. The property in your Family Trust automatically passes to your children tax-free.

This alternative will automatically adjust for your state's law. You should consider selecting it if you desire to give your spouse the absolute minimum amount of your property possible under your state's law.

The Value of My Estate Is Over $1,200,000

If you wish to reduce your federal estate tax, and the value of your property is over $1,200,000, you will always allocate $600,000 worth of your property to your Family Trust on your death. This will assure that your $600,000 tax-free amount will be used. It also keeps that sum, plus any increase in its value, out of your spouse's estate on his or her subsequent death.

If the value of your property is over $1,200,000, your family will pay some federal estate tax on your spouse's subsequent death. If your desire is to ultimately pass your property to your children or other loved ones, there is no way to avoid second-death federal estate tax. This certain tax reality can be illustrated as follows:

> John Miller has $1,500,000. He is bound and determined to totally avoid federal estate tax while still totally providing for his wife, Mary Kay, and his three children.
>
> He was exasperated when we told him that the best tax planning we could do, while still meeting his other desires, was to have his children pay $153,000 of tax after his and Mary Kay's deaths. He challenged us to prove it.
>
> We explained that there were only so many ways he could allocate his property within his Loving Trust:
>
>> He could leave all $1,500,000 to Mary Kay. There would be no tax on his death because of the unlimited marital deduction. On Mary Kay's death, tax would have to be paid on the $900,000 left after setting off Mary Kay's tax-free amount.
>>
>> He could leave half of his property, or $750,000, to his respective Pocketbook and Family Trusts. On his death that would generate an immediate tax on the $150,000 left to the Family Trust over his tax-free amount.
>>
>> He could leave his $600,000 tax-free amount to his Family Trust and $900,000 to his Pocketbook Trusts. That would only generate tax on Mary Kay's subse-

quent death on the $300,000 over her tax-free amount or $153,000, by far the best tax alternative.

We told John what we have told countless clients. "We can keep all your property free of federal estate tax on your death if your spouse survives you. We can keep your Family Trust and $600,000 of your spouse's tax-free amount free of federal estate tax on his or her subsequent death. Any funds in addition to that $600,000 tax-free amount will be liable for federal estate tax."

Popular federal estate tax planning strategies involve deferring your taxes to your spouse's subsequent death and making sure that your $600,000 tax-free amount immediately funds your Family Trust.

People with property valued at over $1,200,000 should consider using two Pocketbook Trusts. The larger your estate, the more likely it is that you would do so. You would elect to use two Pocketbook Trusts in order to better control what happens to your property subsequent to your death. The case of Earl and Debbie illustrates such a need:

Earl Johnson has worked hard in a real estate development career and has amassed property worth $2,000,000. He loves his wife, Debbie, and his three children. He wants Debbie to be fully cared for after his death. He also wants to make sure that his children will receive half of his property on her death.

In achieving his objectives, Earl would first allocate his $600,000 tax-free amount to his Family Trust. As you know by now, it will be tax-free on both his and Debbie's deaths. Because he loves Debbie and views that half of his property is attributable to her efforts, he leaves $1,000,000 to her in his Pocketbook Trust One, with liberal instructions for her care.

Earl leaves the balance of his property, $400,000, to his Pocketbook Trust Two. Debbie will receive all its income and whatever amounts of the property itself as will be needed to care for Debbie.

On Debbie's subsequent death, all the funds in both

Earl's Pocketbook Trust Two and his Family Trust will automatically pass to his children in his Common Trust. Please note that the sum of the two are $1,000,000; half of Earl's property will pass to his children just as he desired.

A second Pocketbook Trust is used both to qualify for the unlimited marital deduction and to control where and how that property is distributed. In most cases it is used to make sure that your children receive its funds on your spouse's subsequent death.

The following alternatives for allocating your property to your respective Pocketbook and Family Trusts are designed to avoid federal estate tax on your death and to minimize it on your spouse's subsequent death. Whether you use one or two Pocketbook Trusts will depend upon your "people motives" rather than technical tax motives.

16-5 I want to save federal estate tax and thereafter care for my spouse as much as possible with a single Pocketbook Trust.

16-6 I want to save federal estate tax; I also want to take care of my spouse and to be assured that my children will have one-half of what's left of my property on my spouse's subsequent death.

16-7 I want to save federal estate tax, while giving as much of my property to my children as possible.

16-5 *I Want to Save Federal Estate Tax and Thereafter Care for My Spouse as Much as Possible with a Single Pocketbook Trust*

Since your motives indicate that you will not be particularly concerned with what your spouse does with your property subsequent to your death, you will need only one Pocketbook Trust under this alternative.

This alternative first allocates $600,000 to your Family Trust and then places the balance of your property in your spouse's Pocketbook Trust.

If the value of your property is $2,000,000, this alternative would be diagrammed as follows:

Pocketbook Trust   Family Trust
$1,400,000 $600,000

This alternative is commonly used by people without children and by those who have extraordinarily good marriages and faith in their spouses.

16-6 *I Want to Save Federal Estate Tax; I Also Want to Take Care Of My Spouse and to Be Assured That My Children Will Have One-half of What's Left of My Property on My Spouse's Subsequent Death*
This is the alternative that we chose in our Loving Trust in Chapter Six. It first allocates your $600,000 tax-free amount to your Family Trust. It then allocates one-half of your total property to your Pocketbook Trust One. The balance of your property will go to your Pocketbook Trust Two. This is the alternative that Earl and Debbie Johnson chose in our earlier example.

If your property is valued at $2,000,000, this alternative can be diagrammed as follows:

Pocketbook   Pocketbook
Trust One   Trust Two   Family Trust
$1,000,000 $400,000 $600,000

Upon your spouse's subsequent death, the funds in Pocketbook Trust One will pass to whomever your spouse leaves them to. If he or she neglects to do so, they will automatically pass to your children's Common Trust. All your funds in Pocketbook Trust Two and all your Family Trust property will automatically pass to your children's Common Trust on your spouse's subsequent death. And there you have it, at least one-half of your remaining property—$1,000,000—will be locked-in for the benefit of your children.

16-7 *I Want to Save Federal Estate Tax, While Giving as Much of My Property to My Children as Possible*
Two Pocketbook Trusts and a Family Trust are created by this alternative. It first allocates the amount required by your

state's law to your Pocketbook Trust One. It then places your $600,000 tax-free amount to your Family Trust. The balance of your property is placed in your Pocketbook Trust Two.

This alternative is exactly the same as its counterpart for estates between $600,000 and $1,200,000. If your state's law mandates that your spouse receive one-half of your property, and you have $2,000,000, it would be diagrammed as follows:

Pocketbook Trust One $1,000,000	Pocketbook Trust Two $400,000	Family Trust $600,000

If your state's law mandates that your spouse receive one-third of your property, it would be diagrammed like this:

Pocketbook Trust One $666,667	Pocketbook Trust Two $733,333	Family Trust $600,000

Your spouse would receive only the amount required by your state's law in Pocketbook Trust One and only the income from Pocketbook Trust Two. He or she would not receive any benefits from your Family Trust. At your spouse's death, all the funds in Pocketbook Trust Two and your Family Trust will automatically pass to your children's Comon Trust. Should your spouse neglect to dispose of Pocketbook Trust One's funds, they, too, would automatically pass to your children's Common Trust.

Because the complexities of providing for loved ones increases as your estate grows larger, it is imperative that you seek the services of a lawyer who understands federal estate tax planning. Chapters Twenty, "How to Find a Loving Trust Lawyer," and Twenty-one, "How to Work with and Pay Your Lawyer," will be of great help to you in this endeavor. You should also utilize the services of your other advisers; Chapter Twenty-three, "How To Get Your Advisers Involved to Save Your Time and Money," will tell you how to do just that.

The Handbook of Estate Planning explains sophisticated federal estate tax planning techniques in nontechnical terms. We suggest that you read it if you wish to get a better grasp of how you can reduce your federal estate taxes.

The tax allocation alternatives that we have discussed for estates between $600,000 and $1,200,000 and those over $1,200,000 are listed below so that you may check that alternative that most closely meets your desires and motives.

The Value of My Estate Is Between $600,000 and $1,200,000
( ) 16-1   I want my first $600,000 to pass to my spouse in my Pocketbook Trust and the remainder to go to my Family Trust.

( ) 16-2   I want my first $600,000 to pass to my Family Trust and the remainder to go to my spouse in my Pocketbook Trust.

( ) 16-3   I want my property equally divided between my Pocketbook and Family Trusts.

( ) 16-4   I want my spouse to receive whatever he or she is entitled to under our state law, with the next $600,000 of my property passing to my Family Trust, and whatever is left— if any—passing to my Pocketbook Trust Two.

The Value of My Estate Is Over $1,200,000
( ) 16-5   I want to save federal estate tax and thereafter care for my spouse as much as possible with a single Pocketbook Trust.

( ) 16-6   I want to save federal estate tax; I also want to take care of my spouse and to be assured that my children will have one-half of what's left of my property on my spouse's subsequent death.

( ) 16-7   I want to save federal estate tax, while giving as much of my property to my children as possible.

17

How to Leave Your
Personal Property

You might have some very special personal possessions that you wish to provide for in your Loving Trust. Jewelry, collections, keepsakes that have been in the family for generations, or even personal papers or diaries are just some of the items our clients have been particularly concerned about when planning for their loved ones. Or you may want to leave your personal property in a special manner, even though it may not be of special value or significance. In either case, your Loving Trust can be designed to pass your personal property to whom and in what way you want.

Maintaining control of personal property is exceedingly difficult for people who choose to do will planning. The legal complexities and requirements of wills make them inconvenient and expensive methods for passing personal property. Here's why.

> Before we began practicing law, we knew a woman named Marian who had several pieces of jewelry and some antique furniture that had been in her family for generations. It was very important to Marian that certain members of her family inherit these heirlooms so they could be passed from generation to generation.
>
> Marian had a will that spelled out exactly which family member would get which item of jewelry or

furniture. Unfortunately, Marian constantly kept changing her mind as to who should get what. Each time Marian wanted to make a change, she would go to her lawyer's office and have him make a codicil to her will. On each occasion, she would have to go through all the formalities of changing her will, a process that is complex and time-consuming. It is also expensive. The lawyer had to charge Marian for the time it took to make the changes. Marian was not happy with the expense, and her lawyer wasn't happy with what he viewed to be unimportant nuisance work.

Making Changes to Your Loving Trust

A Loving Trust is a very simple document to change. It does not require complex legal formalities, nor does it require a trip to the lawyer's office each time a change is necessary.

A change to a Loving Trust is called an amendment. You only need to make your changes in writing. That is all there is to it. This simple process effectively amends your Loving Trust.

There are dangers in being able to make changes so easily. Changes in the technical provisions of your Loving Trust may invalidate other provisions or so confuse your trustees as to make your Loving Trust virtually impossible to interpret. Even baby-sitters get confused if you leave them conflicting or cryptic changes. That is why you should be very careful about what you change and why. You should send any changes you want to make to your lawyer to make sure that the change is not going to inadvertently affect some other portion of your Loving Trust.

Luckily, however, changes in how you want to leave your personal property will almost never affect the other provisions of your Loving Trust. They can frequently be made with little cost or no involvement by your lawyer. Your lawyer should simply be notified each time you make changes in who is to receive personal property. It will take only a few minutes for your lawyer to review and file such changes. This protection will cost you little or nothing and will help both you and your lawyer make sure your Loving Trust is still in good operating order.

What Is Personal Property?

Personal property is property such as furniture, jewelry, clothes, antiques, books, and collections of all kinds. It is not business property, cash, investments, land, or any other income-producing property. The kind of personal property we are talking about is technically called "tangible personal property." If you have a question as to specific property, ask your lawyer. You will quickly find out the answer. Most states have very specific definitions of what constitutes tangible personal property.

Because this type of property is so "personal" in nature, well-drafted Loving Trusts contain an entire section dealing specifically with it. In our Loving Trusts, this section is in three parts:

> Leaving your special personal property to special loved ones.

> Leaving the remainder of your personal property to loved ones.

> Instructions for resolving disputes over who is to get what personal property.

Leaving Your Special Personal Property to Special Loved Ones

Leaving special personal property to special loved ones is accomplished by a Memorandum of Personal Property that itemizes your special property and names whom you would like to leave it to. A copy of the Memorandum of Personal Property that we used in our practice can be found on page 186.

As you can see, all you have to do is write down a description of the property you wish to leave and the name of the person who is to receive it. Not only does it look simple, it is simple to use. You only need to make sure that you sign and *date* several copies, one of which is to be sent to your lawyer.

The date is critical, because if you change your mind, the Memorandum of Personal Property that is the most recent will prevail. Failure to date the Memorandum of Personal Property may well invalidate it.

We have a suggestion that many of our clients have used very successfully. Sometimes, even though you write down a short description of property, it is hard for some people to determine exactly what you mean. On larger pieces of personal property—furniture, paintings, and the like—take some white adhesive tape and write the name of the person who is to receive it on the tape. Attach the tape to the back or underside of the property so it can be identified.

Some of our clients have used photographs for the same purpose. The point is, be as clear as you can about what's what and who gets it. Confusion is not what trustees and loved ones need.

Leaving the Remainder of Your Personal Property

Property you do not specifically leave by Memorandum can be passed by more general instructions contained in your Loving Trust.

Most married people prefer to leave most of their personal property to their spouses. Our Loving Trust instructs the trustees to give all personal property not specifically left to loved ones by Memorandum of Personal Property to the surviving spouse.

What if you are single or your spouse dies before you do? Then personal property can be divided among your children equally, or in any manner you choose. You can even have it pass exactly like the other property that is in your Loving Trust. How you leave the remainder of your personal property, just like how you leave specific items of personal property, is entirely at your discretion. You only need to make your lawyer aware of your desires.

Resolving Disputes Over Who Gets What Personal Property

In our experience, some of the most intense and angry battles that heirs get into involve personal property. Because it is so personal in nature, and because it can be very valuable, disputes inevitably arise. Prevention is the best medicine when it comes to avoiding these kinds of disputes.

For example, let's say that you have three children and your spouse is no longer living. You instruct your trustees to divide your personal property equally among your children. Your two daughters both want your jewelry. Your son and one daughter both want your collection of feather hats. Then there is the furniture, the photographs . . . well, you get the idea. Everybody is mad and makes a mountain out of a molehill.

We solve this problem by instructing the trustees to do the following:

> If my children cannot agree as to how they would like to divide my personal property within a reasonable period of time, then you, trustees, divide it the way you think is fairest. If there is no fair way, and no agreement can be reached, sell it and divide the proceeds equally among my children.

When faced with the "O.k., we'll sell it!" choice, children usually find it prudent to reach an agreement. We highly recommend that you insist that this language, or language similar to it, is contained in your Loving Trust.

Minor Children

Minor children, as we stated in Chapter Thirteen, "How to Distribute Your Children's Property," cannot effectively own property, even personal property. Your Loving Trust should contain instructions so that if you have minor children, your trustees can select which personal property they will immediately receive and which will be held for them until a later date. For instance, you may instruct your trustees to divide your personal property among your three children as they work it out among themselves, but if one of them is only ten years old, he or she will be outnegotiated by his or her older brothers and sisters. To protect the ten-year-old, the trustees will act for him or her.

In our Loving Trust, we instruct the trustees to be mindful of the desires of the minor children. Even minors can be attached to certain items of their parents' personal property.

Property that is not directly passed to minor children will

be added to their trusts or given to their guardian for safe-keeping.

Bare-bones Boilerplate Trusts and Personal Property

Most bare-bones living trusts ignore personal property. More often than not, these trusts leave it to be taken care of by the provisions of a pour-over will (a pour-over will is a special will that leaves property to a living trust, but like any other will, it is controlled by the probate process). Not only is the personal property subject to probate, but the bare-bones boilerplate trust usually has terse or nonexistent terms as to how to give that property to loved ones. Whether this is an oversight or a product of preoccupation with short documents, we do not know. We do know that how you wish your personal property to pass to your loved ones is something that should be addressed in your Loving Trust.

Neither wills nor bare-bones boilerplate trusts can effectively and simply leave your personal property to your loved ones. In a will, leaving your special personal property generally creates problems when you want to make changes and assures that all your personal property will go through the probate process. Bare-bones boilerplate trusts dismiss personal property as part of the domain of wills, making the bare-bones boilerplate worthless to those who have special personal property for special people. Your Loving Trust can make leaving this property convenient for you, your loved ones, and your trustees.

MEMORANDUM OF DISPOSITION
OF TANGIBLE PERSONAL PROPERTY OF

Pursuant to the terms of my Loving Trust dated _____,
I hereby request my Trustee(s) to distribute the following
items of nonbusiness tangible personal property as follows:

Description of Tangible   *Recipient of Tangible*
Personal Property   *Personal Property*

If a recipient of a particular item of nonbusiness personal
property does not survive me by thirty days, such item shall
be disposed of as though it had not been listed in this memorandum.

Dated: _____

_____   _____
         Witness   [Your Full Name]

18

How to Plan if You Are Single

Most of the literature that deals with wills, trusts, and planning for loved ones ignores the needs of the single person. It's almost as if the single person were purposefully shunted to the side. Commentators seem to forget that single people also have loved ones who need to be provided for. With the divorce rate continually hovering at 50 percent levels, and with increased numbers of widows, widowers, and individuals who simply prefer to remain unmarried, it seems a shame that more is not written about how the single person can plan for loved ones.

If you are single, you should have a Loving Trust. Whether you are elderly with adult children and grandchildren, divorced with children of your own, or unmarried for any other reason, it is imperative that your concern and instructions for your loved ones survive your disability or death. Even if you are completely career-oriented, and have no thoughts of family or marriage, a Loving Trust is something you should seriously consider; it can provide for your disability and for your parents or other loved ones on your death.

Every Loving Trust need and benefit that we discussed in Part One applies as much to you as it does to married people. In fact, its benefits may well be more important to you, since you have only yourself to depend upon.

Without a surviving spouse to temper the greed and bitterness that often occur in death's aftermath, disgruntled heirs can be more aggressive, belligerent, and avaricious than they might otherwise be. It is very possible that your heirs may be more hostile than those of a married person.

Because your Loving Trust is governed by significantly less complicated legal rules than a will, and because it avoids both living and death probates, it is not likely that there will be expensive and bitter court battles over you or your property "à la Groucho." Your Loving Trust allows you to continue to provide for yourself and your loved ones following your disability or death.

Unfortunately, single people are often mistakenly characterized as loners whose thoughts and feelings center only on themselves. In our experience, nothing could be further from the truth. Your Loving Trust can quickly dispel any such stereotype by conveying your hopes, fears, dreams, and ambitions for your loved ones with a dimension that simple wills or bare-bones living trusts rarely accomplish.

It is critical that you plan for your potential disability. Without a spouse to watch over you and provide for your welfare, you should rely upon your Loving Trust instructions for your care.

Your Loving Trust begins with a "Me" Trust, as do all Loving Trusts. At your death, it will either immediately create a Common Trust or Separate Trusts for your children or grandchildren, or Separate Trusts for your other loved ones.

Your "Me" Trust

Your "Me" Trust may well be more necessary for you than its counterpart for a married person. You will not have a mate to rely on during the period of your disability. You will not be able to depend upon a spouse's judgment with respect to decisions about nursing-home care, institutionalization, and other equally grave matters. Because spouses often share their feelings about what they want to occur if they become disabled, many decisions can be made in the absence of written instructions.

If you become disabled, it is likely that you will not have a "partner" to look after you and handle the myriad problems that will arise as a result of your disability. You may or may not have close relationships with mature and responsible loved ones. Either way, you will be at the mercy of the probate court and may be at the mercy of self-serving supposed friends and acquaintances.

Your "Me" Trust can empower true friends and close loved ones to act as your trustees or "surrogate mates," following your desires and protecting you and your interests.

A business or marital partner is supposed to look after the partnership's pocketbook in order to make sure that expenses are kept to a minimum. We have seen too many cases where no one was around to monitor the expenses of a disabled single person. As a disabled single person, you would be more liable to be fleeced of your property than a disabled married person. Bluntly, our society seems to be less concerned about the well-being of a single person and his or her money.

A Loving Trust is tailored primarily to take care of you and your money. It preserves your property for your use and care by reducing your expenses. By avoiding lawyers and the other costs of a living probate, your Loving Trust goes a long way in reducing those costs. Having trustees to implement your instructions also saves expenses; they are legally charged with protecting you and your trust property, and they are liable for any excesses or irregularities as a matter of law.

In Chapter Nine, "How to Provide for Yourself," we provided two alternatives that you could use as a single person. However, it is likely that you will have to create your own alternative for your disability. Enhance your Loving Trust with your hopes, fears, dreams, and ambitions for your loved ones.

We all become incredibly vulnerable when we are disabled. There is no reason to augment your vulnerability by failing to protect yourself and your loved ones with Loving Trust instructions.

Probate Avoidance

Your Loving Trust will avoid probate at your death. Single people can generate significant probate fees. That is why it is most important that you use your Loving Trust to avoid all probate fees on your death. The main probate-avoidance gimmick suggested for married people—joint tenancy with right of survivorship—does not work at all for single people. Your Loving Trust provides the only effective method by which you can safely avoid probate.

Your Children

In Chapter Twelve, "How to Provide for Your Minor Children," and Chapter Thirteen, "How to Distribute Your Children's Property," we provided you with planning alternatives for your children. Each of these chapters discussed several alternatives for caring for and distributing your property to your children and grandchildren. You will want to review each of them before designing your Loving Trust.

If you want to leave your property to children who are not your own, you would still utilize the alternatives in Chapter Thirteen. In your plans for providing for your children, nieces and nephews, or others, you must always give consideration to their ages and experience.

Other Loved Ones

It is our contention that leaving property of any value outright to a loved one is a mistake. It cannot protect them from:

- The claims of their creditors.
- Their disability and resulting need for a living probate.
- The avarice of the many hucksters of the world.
- Their own inexperience or inability to wisely handle their inheritance.

A Loving Trust can guide, protect, and teach them. It can pass your wisdom along with your property.

Leaving Property to Charity

There are innumerable methods for leaving your property to charity upon your death. We discuss charitable giving in *The Handbook of Estate Planning*. If you plan to leave property to charity you should employ your Loving Trust. If you do, more of your property will go to the charity, and less will end up in the hands of noncharitable advisers. There is absolutely no reason for any of the property you have earmarked for charity to go through the probate process.

Your Loving Trust should be filled with your charitable instructions. Do you want to create a scholarship in your name? How about a charitable foundation? Do you want publicity, or do you want your gift to be anonymous? Do you want to restrict how your gift is used or who may benefit from it? Allow yourself the luxury of completely setting forth your charitable desires in your Loving Trust.

Federal Estate Tax

If the value of your property is $600,000 or more, it will be subject to federal estate tax. As we discussed in Chapter Sixteen, "How to Save Federal Death Tax," it will be very difficult for you to save this federal death tax. The federal government does not give any special estate tax breaks to single people. Most federal estate tax planning done by singles deals with sophisticated lifetime gifts, special life insurance trusts, and other complex measures beyond the scope of this book.

We strongly recommend that you read *The Handbook of Estate Planning*. We wrote this text primarily with larger estates in mind. It will provide you with estate tax planning strategies by acquainting you with many of the finer tax-planning points.

Given the difficulty of planning for a single person's federal death taxes, most of our single clients ultimately opted to purchase considerable amounts of additional life insurance to cover their tax liability. In effect, they viewed federal estate tax as a liability that could only be covered or offset by adding more money to their Loving Trust.

If you wish to reduce your federal estate tax, you should work closely with a tax attorney and your other advisers in reviewing the available alternatives.

Single people have traditionally been ignored in the planning arena. This neglect may be because of an inability to save meaningful amounts of federal estate tax. We hope that you realize that saving federal estate tax is only one of your many Loving Trust desires. In reviewing your Loving Trust needs, you will want to give particular attention to the following chapters: Chapter Nine, "How to Provide for Yourself"; Chapter Twelve, "How to Provide for Your Minor Children"; Chapter Thirteen, "How to Distribute Your Children's Property"; Chapter Fourteen, "How to Ultimately Distribute Your Property"; Chapter Fifteen, "How to Select Your Trustees."

19

How to Provide for Your Loved Ones Upon Remarriage

With the national divorce rate so high, it should come as no surprise that second marriages are extraordinarily common. It also should come as no surprise that it is difficult to decide how to provide for loved ones in second marriages because, more often than not, there are children from prior marriages, as well as children from the current marriage. "Yours, mine, and ours" situations mean that tough decisions have to be made, but they are usually postponed due to conflicting emotions and a lack of guidance.

Rather than make a potentially wrong or unfair decision when planning for our loved ones, most of us make no decisions at all. As you can imagine, when there is a death or disability in a second marriage, the problems are often horrendous, and the resulting dissension can tear families apart.

Spouses in a second marriage are often paralyzed in terms of planning because their desires are thwarted by significant planning conflicts. Letting your Loving Trust planning languish because you cannot—or will not—make planning decisions is absolutely the worst thing you can do. Without the protection of a Loving Trust, the tragedy of your disability or death can be many times greater than it needs to be. If you have children by a first marriage and you die or become disabled without providing Loving Trust instructions, you may have condemned yourself and your loved ones to potential economic and emotional disaster.

When in doubt, make a planning decision and use a Loving Trust. Your Loving Trust can always be changed if you change your mind at a later date. Your planning options may not be perfect, but even in their imperfection, they will be far better than the options the probate judge will utilize in rendering his decisions for your loved ones.

There are many proven methods to plan for loved ones in second marriages that are not unlike those we have already covered in Part Two. Those thoughts and techniques that we have found particularly relevant to the remarriage problem will be covered in this chapter.

Your "Me" Trust

As we discussed in Chapter Nine, "How to Provide for Yourself," your Loving Trust should present a hierarchy of beneficiaries. This hierarchy can cause emotional complications when you have children by a prior marriage. Will their natural father or mother take care of them following your disability or death? Will your current spouse provide for them? Should you provide for them to the exclusion of your spouse? Should they be treated any differently than their stepbrothers or stepsisters?

These are serious questions that are difficult to answer. You must thoroughly analyze the specific economic and emotional factors in your situation and make those decisions that honestly reflect your thinking.

The needs of most spouses that we have helped in this circumstance fall into two general categories—the breadwinner spouse and the homemaker spouse. Most of our breadwinner spouse clients opted to provide for themselves, their spouses, and their children—regardless of what marriage they were from—in that order. If their current spouses had independent financial means, they frequently placed their children ahead of their spouses on the disability hierarchy. If their children by a prior marriage were adults, they often excluded them in favor of their spouses or their minor children.

The needs of the homemaker spouse clients were significantly different from those of breadwinner spouses. They were always concerned about their children—particularly their minor children—by prior marriages, and generally put their spouses' needs well below their children's.

If you have children from more than one marriage, do you want all your children taken care of equally? Is there a significant difference in their ages? Do you want your younger children provided for first? Will your ex-spouse provide for your first family? Will your spouse provide for your current family? Will your spouse provide for your previous marriage's children? These are practical questions that you must answer when deciding the hierarchy of how you want your loved ones provided for on your disability.

In planning the disability portion of your Loving Trust, you must also consider any child support or alimony obligations that you may have. You should provide your trustees with notice of such agreements so those obligations can be continued from your trust funds. In some agreements, payments end upon disability, but in others they do not. In either case, it is important that you alert your trustees so they will be prepared to honor your obligations if it becomes necessary.

You must prepare your trustees to step into your shoes should you become disabled. While disability, in and of itself, engenders significant confusion, its aftermath can be made much worse if there are lawsuits over your property and your obligations.

Explicit instructions are much more important when you have children by a prior marriage.

Settlement Agreements for Divorces

Divorces sometimes create very confusing and unique settlement agreements. There are agreements as to who receives property at what time, and agreements to keep life insurance policies in force. There are even agreements that provide for financial arrangements for the education of the children. The terms of these agreements will greatly affect how you design your Loving Trust.

Because of the wide variety and content of settlement agreements, it is impossible for us to deal with their ramifications on even an overview basis. You need to discuss any divorce agreements you may have with your lawyer as part of your Loving

Trust design criteria. Failure to coordinate your divorce settlement agreements with your Loving Trust instructions may end up haunting your loved ones. Lack of planning in this area has created many a lawsuit, something that can easily be avoided with a little foresight.

Premarital and Postmarital Agreements

When you marry, your property may become marital property. That means that your spouse may have certain claims to your property on your death. Many states give a surviving spouse substantial rights to a deceased spouse's property.

If both spouses sign a valid contract that sets out the rights each has to the other's property, it can usually override the state's requirements. These contracts can be entered into before marriage and, in some cases, after marriage. Each state has its own requirements as to the content and validity of these premarital and postmarital agreements. These agreements are frequently used in second marriages.

If you have signed one of these agreements, it can substantially affect how you plan for loved ones. Your marital agreement will probably restrict what you receive from your spouse on death and vice versa. It may also affect your federal estate tax planning in that it may reduce or eliminate your, or your spouse's, unlimited marital deduction and tax-free amounts.

If you have signed such an agreement, be sure to have your lawyer review it as part of your Loving Trust guidelines. If there are conflicts between your Loving Trust instructions and your marital agreement, they will very likely have to be resolved in the courts.

Even if you have signed a marital agreement, it is still possible for you to save federal estate taxes in your Loving Trust. Working with seasoned professionals will make the task easier, less expensive, and more effective. To facilitate your lawyer's work, you should provide him or her with a copy of it.

Since a marital agreement will restrict what you and your spouse receive from each other on your respective deaths, you very well may want to make a diagram of what your marital agreement says. You can then compare its terms to the alternatives you have selected in your Loving Trust. This review will give you a good idea of the conflicts, if any, between the two. Diagramming your marital agreement and filling in "My Checklist for Designing My Loving Trust" (at the end of Part Two) should enable you to communicate to your lawyer precisely what your Loving Trust instructions are.

Separate Loving Trusts for Separate Planning

When we say that everyone needs a Loving Trust, we mean exactly that. You and your spouse should each have your own separate Loving Trust. Your Loving Trusts may be identical, but they do not have to be. You and your mate may have different ideas as to how your property is to be used upon your disability. You may each have different feelings as to who should receive your property or how it should be provided for on your death. You may have different beneficiaries, beneficiaries of different ages, or beneficiaries who have widely varying needs. You may also be subject to different divorce settlement agreements.

Separate Loving Trusts control separate property. Your Loving Trust controls only that property that you own in your name. It also controls property that is paid to your Loving Trust on death, like life insurance proceeds or death benefits from a retirement plan. Joint tenancy with right of survivorship, life insurance, and death benefits *not payable to your Loving Trust* are not controlled by your Loving Trust.

In second marriages, we emphasize that separate Loving Trusts can and should be done. It is likely that you and your spouse have brought separate property into your marriage. The property you have brought into the marriage is yours, and you should plan to do with it as you desire.

You and your spouse may each have different loved ones you wish to care for. This reflects the "yours, mine, and ours" planning requirements that often need to be accomplished when a second marriage involves children from prior marriages as well as from the current marriage. Having different loved ones to plan for dictates that you and your spouse establish your own Loving Trusts.

You and your spouse should each come to grips with your own situation and design a plan to meet—as closely as possible—

all of your separate needs and desires. You may find it easier to make decisions and to determine what you would like to do, knowing that you only have to worry about your Loving Trust.

To help you address your own unique circumstances, we will give you a planning idea that has worked well for us over the years. It is an ideal solution to a major second marriage dilemma.

A Gift of Love

Many second marriages involve spouses with children from their previous marriages. Oftentimes the husband's children are with his former wife. He sees them occasionally on visitation days, but their relationship is not especially close. His new wife is often younger than he, and she either desires a family or already has one from her first marriage. In the latter case, her children are usually living with the two of them. She generally views her first husband as an ogre, someone who is irresponsible and not very loving.

There are many instances where an ex-wife and mother has very little property from her first marriage; what she does have may consist of furniture, a car, and personal effects. Rarely does she have much cash or many real assets. In many cases, her first husband is delinquent on his child support payments. Until her second marriage, she has lived on what she could earn while taking care of her children. Her new husband may have property and a better income than she has been accustomed to having.

A divorced mother's children can be a problem. Those children lost a father and gained a competitor for their mother's affections. They have been the focus of their mother's life ever since the divorce and are not happy with her attempt at refocusing on another man. They generally do not behave kindly to the stranger they must now call "Dad."

The mother's new husband is in a bind; his relationship with his wife's children may not be good. They seem to go out of their way to create tension between him and their mother. He tries to get the children to like and respect him, but the harder he tries, the worse their behavior seems to get. He is afraid that his discipline may trigger significant turmoil between himself and their mother, so he endures their distemper with some distemper of his own.

Meanwhile, the new wife is facing a dilemma. She may know that her husband does not care for her children as much as she does and that there is real competition between him and her children. She is faced with lose-lose situations daily, and can only hope to keep everyone happy.

When such a newly married couple decides to look into Loving Trusts, it is usually at the wife's insistence. She is probably more insecure with the situation than he is and needs the security that she perceives planning will give her. He goes along with the idea, hoping to establish a little more harmony between them.

When we encountered a couple like this, we knew from experience that the wife's real concern was for her children. She knew that if something happened to her, their real father might not be capable of providing for them—especially if he couldn't even stay current on his child support payments. She also knew, regardless of his protestations to the contrary, that her current husband wasn't likely to care for them either. She may have observed how poorly the children treated him and how he controlled his anger with only the greatest difficulty. She had no confidence that his feelings would change after her disability or death. She usually became even more agitated when she realized that she didn't have enough property to begin to provide for her children's well-being.

She was in a terrible planning bind and considerable emotional distress when we told her that her ex-husband would more than likely be named as the children's guardian, even if she provided instructions to the contrary.

Given this situation, we explained that a Loving Trust, coupled with a loving act, could solve her dilemma. We helped her design her Loving Trust to totally take care of her children on her disability or death. We encouraged her to name her current husband as one of its trustees. This, we assured her, would keep her ex-husband from seizing her children's funds. We then encouraged her husband to make a loving act by purchasing a life insurance policy on her life. The policy would be hers to own, and its proceeds would immediately pass on her death to her Loving Trust for her children.

Her husband would pay the annual premium on her policy on their anniversary, as his way of saying, "I love you and want to provide a means by which your children will be provided for." So long as they stay married, this loving act could continue. If, however, they should separate or divorce, there would be no requirement that the husband continue the premiums.

Let's now look at the dynamics of the situation. Even if her first husband is named as the guardian of the children, her new husband controls the money as one of his wife's trustees. Her ex-husband would have no way to get any of his children's money for his benefit. This fact alone might deter the children's natural father from seeking their custody. If he does get custody, he will have to interact with the new husband, who will generally go out of his way to make sure that the first husband acts responsibly for the well-being of the children.

The new husband is usually more than content with this arrangement. He is delighted that, for the cost of an insurance policy that provides her with a means to provide for her children, he can make his wife so happy, loving, and secure. He is also happy with being a trustee of the children's trust. He usually believes that he can financially raise the children better than their natural father.

Everyone—the new wife, the new husband, the new wife's children—is protected remarkably well under this Loving Trust arrangement.

When we presented this idea to clients, we ended by explaining why this is a gift of love. Each year on the anniversary of their marriage, the husband—through his love—will make another year's premium payment. It is a token of his love, a reminder that he loves her enough to give her the cash to fuel her Loving Trust. Yes, it sounds corny, doesn't it? Yet, not once in the countless times we have presented it was this Loving Trust idea rejected.

A gift of love is not the only method of using a Loving Trust in a second marriage. As you have likely realized, there are many different ways to combine the various subtrusts of a Loving Trust to meet your every planning objective. By selecting and designing your various subtrusts, you can build a Loving Trust that will not only care for you, but will also carry your love to others long after you are gone.

The first step in second-marriage Loving Trust planning is to solidify your thinking. Examine your motives in detail and determine what you really want to accomplish. You are going to run into some issues that will be very difficult to resolve. You will worry about fairness and jealousy and all the other very human aspects of planning for loved ones. Reduce your possible solutions to a few key alternatives, then choose the best of the lot. None of them may be perfect, but picking the "best of the worst" is certainly better than not acting at all. Do not insist on perfection, just do the best you can. No one can ask for more than that.

Please keep in mind that each marriage partner can design his or her own Loving Trust, and that they need not be alike. Each of you can have a Loving Trust that best meets your desires and financial situation.

My Checklist for Designing My Loving Trust

There are checklists at the ends of Chapters Nine through Sixteen that will quickly enable you to record your planning thoughts. We strongly suggest that you review each of those chapters and fill in each of their checklists before consolidating your desires on this master checklist.

This master checklist for designing your own Loving Trust is your Loving Trust blueprint. It will contain almost everything your lawyer needs to prepare your Loving Trust quickly and inexpensively.

Chapter Nine: How to Provide for Yourself
This checklist is appropriate for all Loving Trusts.

( ) 9-1   Take care of me and nobody else.

( ) 9-2   Take care of my needs first and then my spouse's needs.

( ) 9-3   Take care of my needs first, then my spouse's, and then my children's or dependents', in that order.

( ) 9-4   Take care of me, my spouse, and my children based solely on our needs, without any priorities among us.

( ) 9-5   Take care of me and my children based solely on our needs, without any priorities among us.

( ) 9-6   My own motive:

_____

_____

_____

_____

Chapter Ten: How to Provide for Your Spouse

You should disregard these alternatives if you do not want to directly provide for your spouse.

( ) 10-1 I want my spouse to have total control over my property.

( ) 10-2 I want my spouse totally taken care of, but I want to limit my spouse's right to leave my property on his or her death.

( ) 10-3 I want my spouse totally taken care of, but I will decide where my property goes on my spouse's death.

( ) 10-4 My spouse can have only the income my Pocketbook Trust earns and nothing more; I will say where my property goes on his or her death.

( ) 10-5 My spouse will get only whatever my state's laws require that I must leave him or her.

( ) 10-6 My own motive:

_____

_____

_____

_____

Chapter Eleven: How to Provide for Your Family

HOW TO ALLOCATE BETWEEN MY POCKETBOOK AND FAMILY TRUSTS

( ) 11-1 I want all my property to pass to my spouse in my Pocketbook Trust.

( ) 11-2 I want my spouse to receive whatever he or she is entitled to under state law with the balance passing to my Family Trust.

( ) 11-3 I want my property equally divided between my Pocketbook and Family Trusts.

( ) 11-4 I want ＿＿ percent to pass to my Pocketbook Trust and ＿＿ percent to my Family Trust.

( ) 11-5 I want all my property to pass to my spouse in my Family Trust.

( ) 11-6 My own alternative:

_____

_____

_____

_____

HOW I WANT MY BENEFICIARIES PROVIDED FOR
FROM MY FAMILY TRUST

( ) 11-7 I want primarily to care for my spouse by providing him or her with as many benefits and as much control as possible.

( ) 11-8 I want to provide for my spouse and my children based upon their respective needs, while giving priority to the needs of my spouse. I want my children and grandchildren to get what is left after my spouse's death.

( ) 11-9 I want to provide for the respective needs of my spouse and my children, but if my spouse remarries, I want to provide only for my children.

( ) 11-10 The same as alternative 11-9, except that I want my spouse taken care of during any period of time that he or she is single.

( ) 11-11 I want to provide for the respective needs of my spouse, my children, and other loved ones, and will set forth my priorities.

( ) 11-12 I want to provide for loved ones other than my spouse.

( ) 11-13 My own motive:

_____

_____

_____

_____

Chapter Twelve: How to Provide for Your Minor Children

( ) 12-1   All my children are adults. I do not want a Common Trust.

( ) 12-2   I want my Common Trust to end when my youngest child is twenty-one years of age.

( ) 12-3   I want my Common Trust to end when my youngest child is twenty-three or completes college, whichever happens first.

( ) 12-4   I want my Common Trust to end when my youngest child is _____ years of age.

( ) 12-5   My own motive:

_____

_____

_____

_____

Chapter Thirteen: How to Distribute Your Children's Property

ADVANCEMENT DISTRIBUTIONS

( ) 13-1   I want my trustees to liberally provide for each of my children.

( ) 13-2   I want my trustees to provide only for the health, education, support, and maintenance of each of my children.

( ) 13-3   My own motive:

_____

_____

_____

_____

PREMATURE DEATH OF A CHILD

( ) 13-4   I want my child's trust property to pass pursuant to my child's directions.

( ) 13-5   I want my child's trust property to pass to my child's children or, if none, to my other children.

( ) 13-6   My own motive:

_____

_____

_____

_____

DISTRIBUTION ALTERNATIVES

( ) 13-7   I want my property distributed to my children immediately.

( ) 13-8   I want my children to have immediately whatever they want from their Separate Trusts.

( ) 13-9   Make two distributions to my child, one-half at a minimum age, the remainder at another stated age.

( ) 13-10   Make two distributions to my child, the first at a minimum age, or immediately if that age has been met, the second to occur five years from the date of the first distribution.

( ) 13-11   Make four distributions to my child, the first to occur at a minimum age, or immediately if that age has been met, the second through the fourth to occur every five years.

( ) 13-12   Make multiple unequal distributions, the first to occur at a minimum age, or immediately if that age has been met, the others at stated ages.

( ) 13-13   Make no mandatory lifetime distributions to my child, but take care of my child in whatever way he or she needs, whenever he or she needs it from the trust funds.

( ) 13-14   Make entirely different distribution patterns for each of my children.

( ) 13-15   My own motive:

_____

_____

_____

_____

Chapter Fourteen: How to Ultimately Distribute Your Property

( ) 14-1   I want one-half of my property to pass to my heirs and one-half of my property to pass to my spouse's heirs under my state's laws.

( ) 14-2   I want all my property to pass to my heirs under my state's laws.

( ) 14-3   I want my property to pass to certain individuals.

( ) 14-4   I want all my property to go to charity.

( ) 14-5   My own motive:

_____

_____

_____

Chapter Fifteen: How to Select Your Trustees

NAMING MY TRUSTEES WHILE I AM ALIVE AND WELL

( ) 15-1   I will act as my sole trustee.

( ) 15-2   My spouse and I will act as my co-trustees.

( ) 15-3   I will act as a co-trustee along with:

_____

_____

_____

( ) 15-4   My own alternative:

_____

_____

_____

NAMING MY SUCCESSOR TRUSTEES ON MY DISABILITY

( ) 15-5   The following individuals or institutions will act as my successor trustees in the order I have set out (if I do not name an institution, at least two individual trustees must always serve):

_____

_____

_____

_____

( ) 15-6   The following individuals or institutions will *replace all my initial trustees* and will act in the order I have set out (if I do not name an institution, at least two individual trustees must serve):

_____

_____

_____

_____

( ) 15-7   My initial co-trustee must choose a major institutional trustee to serve as successor co-trustee. When my initial co-trustee can no longer serve, this institutional trustee shall continue to serve alone.

NAMING MY SUCCESSOR TRUSTEES ON MY DEATH

( ) 15-8   My disability trustees will continue to serve. They will be replaced by the following individuals or institutions in the order I have set out (if I do not name an institution, at least two individual trustees must serve):

_____

_____

_____

_____

( ) 15-9   My disability trustees will be replaced by the following individuals or institutions in the order I have set out (if I do not name an institution, at least two individual trustees must serve):

_____
_____
_____
_____

( ) 15-10   My initial co-trustee must select a major institutional trustee to serve as co-trustee. When my initial co-trustee can no longer serve, this institutional trustee can serve alone.

HOW MY BENEFICIARIES MAY TERMINATE MY TRUSTEES

( ) 15-11   My spouse can terminate any of my successor trustees. After my spouse is no longer a trustee, a majority of my beneficiaries can terminate any of my successor trustees. When all my successor trustees have either been terminated or they are no longer available, my beneficiaries must choose a major institutional trustee.

( ) 15-12   A majority of my beneficiaries can terminate any of my successor trustees. When all my successor trustees have either been terminated or they are no longer available, my beneficiaries must choose a major institutional trustee.

( ) 15-13   My own alternative:

_____
_____

Chapter Sixteen: How to Save Federal Death Tax

THE VALUE OF MY ESTATE IS BETWEEN $600,000 AND $1,200,000

( ) 16-1   I want my first $600,000 to pass to my spouse in my Pocketbook Trust and the remainder to go to my Family Trust.

( ) 16-2   I want my first $600,000 to pass to my Family Trust and the remainder to go to my spouse in my Pocketbook Trust.

( ) 16-3   I want my property equally divided between my Pocketbook and Family Trusts.

( ) 16-4   I want my spouse to receive whatever he or she is entitled to under our state law, with the next $600,000 of my property passing to my Family Trust, and whatever is left—if any—passing to my Pocketbook Trust Two.

THE VALUE OF MY ESTATE IS OVER $1,200,000

( ) 16-5   I want to save federal estate tax and thereafter care for my spouse as much as possible with a single Pocketbook Trust.

( ) 16-6   I want to save federal estate tax; I also want to take care of my spouse and to be assured that my children will have one-half of what's left of my property on my spouse's subsequent death.

( ) 16-7   I want to save federal estate tax, while giving as much of my property to my children as possible.

Our Loving Trust

Initial Trustees: My Wife And I

My Trust

Disability Trustees: My Wife, Jack & Jean

Take Care Of
Me Then
My Family

How I Allocate My Property To My Trusts:
At Least ½ To My Spouse, ½ To My Children With Maximum Tax Savings

Pocketbook Trust One

This Is My Wife's
Property To Do With
As She Pleases

Pocketbook Trust Two

Successor Death Trustees: Same As Disability Trustees

Income For My Wife's
Life And Principal For
Whatever She
Needs

Family Trust

Take Care Of
My Family's Needs But
Give 1st Priority To My
Wife's Needs

Our Common Trust

Divide My Property
When My Youngest
Son Is 23 Or
Completes College

How To Distribute Our Sons' Property For Advancements:
Advances For Extraordinary Needs

Bill's Trust

½ At Age 25 And ½ At
Age 30, Or 5 Years After
The Initial ½

How To Distribute My Son's Property On Premature Death:
My Son's Choice, Or If He Fails To Act, Then My Choice

Dan's Trust

½ At Age 25 And ½ At
Age 30, Or 5 Years After
The Initial ½

Where My Property Goes If I Have No Survivors:
½ To My Relatives, ½ To My Wife's Relatives

My Loving Trust Diagram
If I Am Single

My Trustees While I Am Well	ALTERNATIVE 15—

My Trust

My Successor Disability Trustees	ALTERNATIVE 15—

How To Provide
For Myself

ALTERNATIVE 9—

My Successor Death Trustees	ALTERNATIVE 15—

My Common Trust

How To Provide
For My Minor Children

ALTERNATIVE 12—

How To Distribute My Children's Property & Advance Funds To Them	ALTERNATIVE 13—

My Separate
Trust For

CHILD _____

ALTERNATIVE 13—

My Separate Trust For

Premature Death Of A Child	ALTERNATIVE 13—

CHILD _____

ALTERNATIVE 13—

My Separate
Trust For

CHILD _____

ALTERNATIVE 13—

How To Ultimately Distribute My Property	ALTERNATIVE 14—

My Loving Trust Diagram
If I Am Married

My Trustees While I Am Well   ALTERNATIVE 15—

My Trust

My Successor Disability Trustees   ALTERNATIVE 15—

How To Provide
For Myself
ALTERNATIVE 9—

How To Allocate My Property Among
My Sub-Trusts   ALTERNATIVE 11—

Pocketbook Trust One
How To Provide
For My Spouse

ALTERNATIVE 10—

My Successor Death Trustees   ALTERNATIVE 15—

Family Trust
How To Provide
For My Family

ALTERNATIVE 11—

My Common Trust
How To Provide
For My Minor Children

ALTERNATIVE 12—

How To Distribute My Children's Property
& Advance Funds To Them   ALTERNATIVE 13—

My Separate
Trust For

CHILD _____
ALTERNATIVE 13—

My Separate Trust For
Premature Death Of A Child   ALTERNATIVE 13—

CHILD _____
ALTERNATIVE 13—

My Separate
Trust For

CHILD _____
ALTERNATIVE 13—

How To Ultimately Distribute My Property   ALTERNATIVE 14—

My Loving Trust Diagram
If I Am Married And Wish To
Save Federal Estate Tax

My Trustees While I Am Well — ALTERNATIVE 15—

My Trust

My Successor Disability Trustees — ALTERNATIVE 15—

How To Provide
For Myself
ALTERNATIVE 9 —

How To Allocate My Property
To Save Federal Estate Tax — ALTERNATIVE 11—

**Pocketbook
Trust One**
How To Provide
For My Spouse
ALTERNATIVE 10 —

**Pocketbook
Trust Two**

My Successor Death Trustees — ALTERNATIVE 15—

How To Provide
For My Spouse
ALTERNATIVE
10-4

Family Trust
How To Provide
For My Family
ALTERNATIVE 11 —

My Common Trust

How To Provide
For My Minor Children

ALTERNATIVE 12 —

How To Distribute My Children's Property
& Advance Funds To Them — ALTERNATIVE 13—

My Separate
Trust For

CHILD _____
ALTERNATIVE 13 —

My Separate Trust For

Premature Death Of A Child — ALTERNATIVE 13—

CHILD _____
ALTERNATIVE 13 —

My Separate
Trust For

CHILD _____
ALTERNATIVE 13 —

How To Ultimately Distribute My Property — ALTERNATIVE 14—

PART THREE

How to Get Your Loving Trust Done

20

How to Find a Loving Trust Lawyer

The only obstacle that stands between your Loving Trust design and getting your Loving Trust implemented is finding a lawyer who will write it for you. Time and time again, we have been told by our lecture students and talk-show callers that it is almost impossible to find a lawyer who will do a Loving Trust. Our experience verifies their exasperation. There are no hordes of lawyers lined up to jump on the Loving Trust bandwagon, at least not yet.

However, the number of lawyers who want to prepare Loving Trusts is rapidly growing. Trusts of all types have become a topic of great interest to the public, and lawyers are taking notice. Competition among lawyers has been increasing as their number has been swelling. So has their inclination to extend their legal horizons.

Most lawyers are embroiled in daily conflict. They are under constant pressure to either create or mediate disputes. This constant sparring takes its toll. Many of our colleagues tell us that when their phone rings they often think, What's gone wrong now? A Loving Trust practice offers these lawyers a respite from the stress of their litigation practices.

Our Loving Trust lectures invariably generate great excitement among lawyers. The concept offers them an alternative to the traditional way of doing things.

With the help of our suggestions, you can easily find a lawyer to help you with your Loving Trust. Most any lawyer who is competent enough to draft a will or a revocable living trust is competent enough to draft your Loving Trust. Many lawyers already have the know-how to draft a basic Loving Trust. If your lawyer does not, you can provide it by using the techniques we describe in this chapter. There is no reason why your lawyer cannot easily and inexpensively produce your Loving Trust in a very short period of time.

The lawyers you talk with will generally fall into one of three categories:

1. Those who are familiar with the Loving Trust and who prepare them for their clients.

2. Those who are unfamiliar with them but are willing to learn.

3. Those who are convinced that wills and probate are the only way to plan and who dismiss the Loving Trust out of hand.

The first two will meet your Loving Trust needs. The last will not. He or she is the attorney that Dacey and Stock were talking about. Do not waste your time or money on these legal dinosaurs.

Contacting a Lawyer You Know But Have Not Used

Knowing a lawyer you like will give you a head start in getting your Loving Trust prepared. As you know by now, Loving Trust planning is very personal. Your lawyer will need to know what you own, how much you owe, and how all your property is titled. He or she will also be privy to your hopes, fears, dreams, and aspirations for yourself and your loved ones. It is important that you like the lawyer you ultimately select.

Do not approach your lawyer acquaintance or friend at a social function, other than to tell him or her that you will be calling to schedule an appointment. Most lawyers are sensitive about discussing legal business in a social setting, because many people abuse the conversation to obtain free legal advice. Resist the temptation to discuss your Loving Trust with your lawyer until you meet in his or her office.

If you know a lawyer you like, call and let him or her know that you are interested in using his or her services. Tell your friend that you want help preparing your Loving Trust and ask the following questions:

- Would you be interested in helping me put my Loving Trust instructions into a revocable living trust format?
- Have you read *Loving Trust?*
- Do you have experience in drafting revocable living trusts with Loving Trust instructions?
- Do you have expertise in federal estate tax planning? (You would ask this only if your estate approximates $600,000 or more.)
- Will you charge for our first meeting? If so, what will your charge be?

Give your friend the opportunity to expand and explain his or her answers. Resist the temptation to ask your questions in machine-gun fashion; take your time. Most lawyers are happy to talk with a potential new client—they need the business. You and your business are a precious commodity to your friend. Let him or her sell you on just how knowledgeable and good he or she is.

We believe that since you are just exploring whether or not you will be using your lawyer friend's services, good taste—and good business—should prevent him or her from charging for the first hour or so of your meeting.

If your friend does charge for an initial consultation, you must make the decision whether or not you are willing to pay for it. Your friend may convince you that he or she is the perfect lawyer for you and that your initial meeting will be so productive it will be worth whatever charge there is.

Whether you decide to proceed or not is up to you. However, you will not have that opportunity unless you first ask the question, "Do you charge for the initial consultation?" More problems are created between lawyers and their clients over miscommunication about fees than in any other area. Make sure you agree on the billing for your first meeting.

Your telephone conversation may not go well. The lawyer could very well become defensive about your Loving Trust requests. He or she may say that it can't be done or that you don't need it; that all you need is a will; that probate is not as bad as it is made out to be, and it isn't that expensive or time-consuming. He or she may even say that probate is different in your state and can be accomplished with streamlined efficiency.

There are responses that we hear about all too often. You now know as well as we do that they are absolutely wrong. A little bit of probate is not all right. That is exactly like a surgeon telling you that a little cancer won't hurt you. If you hear any of these timeworn arguments, politely but firmly end the conversation. You can do better elsewhere.

Another response you may hear is that a Loving Trust is "just an ordinary living trust." Don't fall for this line. There is a world of difference between a bare-bones living trust and a Loving Trust. The former has your lawyer's legalese in it; the latter has your complete instructions for your loved ones.

A bare-bones living trust is like a half-finished house. A skeleton of a home that is left half-built with the wind blowing through its unfinished walls. A Loving Trust is like the warm homes you see in the magazines during the holiday season. It is full of cheerfulness, good things to eat, and loved ones sharing the goodwill of the holidays. A Loving Trust is for loved ones, not hollow hopes and unfinished dreams.

Your friend may want to help you, but admit that he or she is not familiar with a Loving Trust. The really good lawyers will not attack what they do not know. If the lawyer seems genuinely interested in preparing your Loving Trust, tell him or her about the information in this book. You might also suggest that he or she review: *The Handbook of Estate Planning, Creating a Loving Trust Practice,* and *A Loving Trust Compendium.*

The Handbook of Estate Planning contains an overview of the process of planning for loved ones. It discusses the legal and tax ramifications of major estate planning techniques. It is a book written in relatively simple terms that can quickly initiate the nonspecialized professional or interested nonlawyer into major planning concepts.

Creating a Loving Trust Practice is a book for lawyers who are interested in serving clients just like you. It explains how a lawyer who is not in the business of preparing Loving Trusts can set up a successful Loving Trust practice. There are suggestions on how to find and service clients, how to keep fees down without sacrificing quality, and how to draft all the documents necessary to create a Loving Trust.

A Loving Trust Compendium allows your lawyer to draft your Loving Trust in the manner, and with all the clauses, that we have suggested in this book. It is a technical law text that provides the professional with a complete set of annotated forms that will facilitate his or her implementation of your Loving Trust. It contains specialist drafting suggestions and hints to aid your lawyer in honing his or her Loving Trust skills.

It will not take a lot of time or energy for your lawyer to master the information in these books. Most lawyers are intelligent, highly educated, and motivated individuals who are accustomed to studying. Learning the ins and outs of a Loving Trust practice will not be difficult for a lawyer who wants to learn.

Do not waste time; find out as quickly as possible if your friend is interested in a Loving Trust practice. If he or she is unwilling to work with you, thank him or her, ask for a recommendation, and move on. You can either initiate the process with another lawyer friend or utilize the other techniques we describe.

If your lawyer friend accepts the responsibility of preparing your Loving Trust, you should carefully read Chapter Twenty-one, "How to Work with and Pay Your Lawyer."

Contacting a Lawyer You Have Used

If you already have a lawyer, you should not assume that he or she is a Loving Trust lawyer. You can find out if your lawyer is a Loving Trust lawyer by following all the steps we have discussed when contacting a lawyer you know but have not used. You should use the same direct approach, and you should ask exactly the same questions as we described in "Contacting a Lawyer You Know But Have Not Used."

Your lawyer may refer you to another partner or associate in his or her firm. If that is your case, you should treat this colleague as if he or she were a complete stranger. You would approach this lawyer in the same manner you would approach a lawyer you don't know.

You Don't Know a Lawyer

We can help you find a Loving Trust lawyer. There are at least four good sources for finding one:

1. Ask friends, relatives, and business associates.

2. Ask your other professional advisers.

3. Contact your bank's trust department.

4. Contact your local Estate Planning Council.

We are confident that you will find a Loving Trust lawyer with one of these methods.

Ask Your Friends

Despite the fact that lawyers are far from popular with the public, Loving Trust lawyers usually rank high with their clients. A Loving Trust client generally perceives his or her lawyer as part of a planning team and associates him or her with good thoughts and feelings. Ask your friends if they have either a revocable living trust or a Loving Trust. If they do, ask them for the name and telephone number of the lawyer who prepared it.

Most lawyers rely on word-of-mouth advertising. They know that if they do a good job for a client, that client will recommend them to others. A happy client is a good indication that a lawyer has done a good job.

You may have friends, relatives, business associates, and colleagues who have revocable living or Loving Trusts. Question them as to how they found their lawyer and what they did to check out his or her credentials. Ask them how the lawyer conducted all meetings and on what basis he or she charges. Ask them *how long it took for their trust to be completed.* We emphasize this because too many lawyers take too much time to get their work completed.

Ask Your Advisers

Accountants, financial planners, bankers, and life insurance agents frequently deal with lawyers. They are immersed in the professional community and are usually knowledgeable on who is doing what and how well they are doing it. Most advisers are more than happy to direct you to other professionals with whom they have worked and whom they respect.

We realize that you might not know or work with any of these advisers. If you are in this situation, we suggest that you contact your insurance carriers and ask them for the names of a few of their better insurance agents. You could also ask your friends if they have a top-notch agent that they are happy with. In any case, insurance agents are generous with their time and in most cases should be helpful in assisting you to find the right lawyer.

Don't be surprised if they try to sell you some insurance. That is their job, and the good ones are always on the lookout for new clients. However, do not be put off by this aggressiveness. Take the time to listen to them because they usually have much to say.

If you plan to involve any of your other professional advisers in designing and implementing your Loving Trust (we explain how to do this in Chapter Twenty-three, "How to Get Your Advisers Involved to Save Your Time and Money") their recommendations can become even more meaningful.

Don't be afraid to ask your advisers whom they would recommend as a good Loving Trust lawyer. Your advisers are there to help you; they will be flattered and will usually go to great lengths to help you find just the right lawyer.

Contact a Trust Officer

Almost every city or town in the United States has a bank with a trust department. Larger cities also have trust companies. By law, trust departments, trust companies, and their employees cannot prepare trust documents. These institutional trustees administer trust documents that are prepared by lawyers engaged in the private practice of the law.

Before a trust department will accept the trusteeship of any trust, its officers will review the actual trust document to see if it meets minimum standards of clarity and legality. Some trusts are rejected because they are legally defective, others because their instructions are too vague or unclear.

Because trust officers review trust documents, they are in

constant contact with lawyers who prepare them. Some trust officers have the sole task of calling on lawyers and selling them on the idea of using the trust department as the trustee for the trusts they draft. Trust departments often provide assistance to lawyers who wish to prepare trusts but are insecure with their talents.

Contact the trust departments of your local banks or your local trust companies and make an appointment with one of their trust officers. Share this book with them and ask for a list of lawyers who have such a practice; it is likely that you will be given several names. If you ask, it is also likely that your trust officer will help you set up an appointment with your first choice.

If your bank has a trust department, ask your personal banker for an introduction. He or she will be glad to accommodate you. If your bank does not have a trust department, set aside a few hours and go trust-department shopping. If you arrive at their reception desk, the receptionist will usually arrange for you to meet with a trust officer without a prior appointment.

Remember, you are a potential client for that trust department and the officer you meet with. He or she will want to explain to you why you might wish to choose that trust department as a trustee in your Loving Trust.

You will not be charged for this referral service. Trust departments provide much information as a public service. They are a wonderful source of Loving Trust lawyer recommendations. In our opinion, they are the best and most professional source of Loving Trust expertise.

Contact an Estate Planning Council

Most major cities have an Estate Planning Council. Members of the Estate Planning Council include lawyers, accountants, life insurance agents, and financial planners. These professionals meet on a regular basis to discuss trends in estate planning, new laws, and new ideas. They are the professionals who spend much of their time planning estates.

Look in your telephone book to find the phone number of the Estate Planning Council in your area. If you cannot find the number in the telephone book, call your local bank's trust department for the number or for information on how you can contact officers or members of your local Estate Planning Council. Once you have located a member or an officer, you should be able to get a list of lawyers who are members. You can then begin the process of contacting its lawyer members.

Meeting a Lawyer You Do Not Know

Once you have the names of lawyers who prepare revocable living trusts or Loving Trusts, you need to make contact with them. We are advocates of the direct approach. Call the lawyer. This may not be as easy as it sounds. Lawyers are often unable to take calls and may not be able to return your call right away. You may not receive a return call at all unless you leave the proper message.

When a lawyer sees a telephone message from someone whose name does not look familiar, he or she may very well put your call slip on the bottom of the stack assuming thay you may be selling something. If you are unable to make contact, leave a message that you are interested in using his or her services and would appreciate a prompt call back. Most lawyers want new clients. When they see your "I'm a potential new client" message, they will likely put your slip on top of their stack.

When you talk with the lawyer, mention who gave you his or her name and state your business. Ask the questions and use the techniques that we described in "Contacting a Lawyer You Know But Have Not Used." If you feel good about your conversation, set an appointment; if not, cut the conversation short with a polite but firm "Thank you" and go to the next name on your list.

Many lawyers leave instructions with their secretaries as to how new clients are to be handled. If this is the case, listen to the secretary and follow his or her procedure. You can take the opportunity to ask about how the lawyer works, the charge for the initial meeting, and any other information you are offered. Secretaries often are better at explaining office procedures than their lawyer bosses. If you still want to talk to the lawyer, insist on it.

Not all lawyers will promptly return your telephone call. If a lawyer, or his or her secretary, does not call you back within a day and a half, go to the next name on your list. This is not the person you want to prepare your Loving Trust. Lawyers who are not prompt in returning their phones calls are usually not prompt in getting their work out.

Confirm in Writing

Neither you nor the lawyer wants to start off on the wrong foot. A great way to do so is for either of you to miss the time or day of the first meeting. Communications can go awry; confirm your appointment in writing. It is doubtful that the lawyer's office will do so.

Here is a sample letter for you to use:

> [Date]
> [Address]
>
> Dear [Lawyer's Name]:
> I look forward to meeting with you at your office on [date of first meeting] at [time of first meeting]. It is my understanding that there will be no charge for this meeting and that it will take between one and two hours.
> The purpose of our first meeting is to discuss the design and peparation of my Loving Trust. I am enclosing a copy of *Loving Trust,* as well as my completed *My Checklist for Designing My Loving Trust* and *My Personal Information Checklist.* My spouse will be attending our meeting.
> If there are any changes, or if any of my statements are not consistent with your understanding, please contact me at your earliest convenience.
>
> Sincerely yours,

Your objective is to find a lawyer you like and who is familiar with Loving Trust planning. Start the relationship with the attitude that you are employing the lawyer as your adviser. Advisers offer advice and make recommendations. They do not give orders. This letter should help you do just that.

We once hired a lawyer to represent us on some legal matters.

He was expensive and very well known. He was also egotistical. We had many disagreements with him over his recommendations, and he always put his recommendations in terms of what we *had* to do. On one occasion, when he stood up and said, "You *must* do the following things," we finally decided we had had enough. "You're fired! Now, what do we *have* to do?" Our legal "adviser" got the point. His job was to advise us; we would make the decisions. Advisers are supposed to advise; clients are supposed to make decisions.

You must now prepare for your meeting so that it will be as productive as possible.

21

How to Work with and Pay Your Lawyer

If you wish to reduce your lawyer's fees, you should take the initiative to do as much of your Loving Trust design as you possibly can. You will not want your lawyer to waste his or her time—and your money—on nonlegal matters.

You need to be organized so that you can quickly communicate your Loving Trust instructions to your lawyer. If you do a good job of this, your next meeting should result in a signed Loving Trust. You can, in a matter of weeks, have your Loving Trust in hand. You are the catalyst that will make your Loving Trust possible. How you work with your lawyer will also have a significant impact on the amount of his or her fee.

The First Meeting

Your first meeting with your lawyer is critical. You will need to cover much ground in ascertaining:

- Whether to hire him or her.
- How much he or she will charge.
- Whether you wish to modify or embellish your Loving Trust instructions.
- When the lawyer's work will be completed.

Your first meeting should take between one and two hours. Many people are surprised at this. You might expect it to be longer, but if you follow some of the simple procedures that we will explain, you can get your Loving Trust business efficiently communicated in this time. Please remember that the less time you spend with the lawyer, the lower your fee will be.

You should do most of the spadework so that your lawyer can concentrate on drafting your Loving Trust without having to waste time on information gathering and other ministerial functions. Your advance work will make it easier for you to accomplish the objectives of the first meeting and will facilitate your lawyer's grasp of what you want done.

What to Bring to the First Meeting
Bring this book with you. It will help your to make your points and give you confidence when making them. It will also give your lawyer the opportunity to see where you got your ideas so that he or she can better understand what you want accomplished. The book will give you and the lawyer a frame of reference to begin the meeting and will help set the tone of your meeting.

Make sure you bring copies of *My Checklist for Designing My Loving Trust* and *My Personal Information Checklist* (you will find this at the end of the book). It includes key family and financial information that your lawyer will need to know to quickly understand your planning situation. It will also allow him or her to affirm or correct your Loving Trust design. You should have sent copies of both of these checklists with your confirmation letter to give the lawyer a head start in preparing for your meeting.

You should also, if at all possible, bring your spouse. If you don't, you will waste a great deal of time and create unneeded conflict.

We have met too many times with people to discuss a Loving Trust design in the absence of the spouse. The result of such a meeting was that the husband or wife confidently made all the design decisions and assured us that "My wife or husband will love it!" Based on these assurances, we prepared the Loving Trust exactly as the person designed it. At the next meeting, when we met to review and sign the trust, everything went wrong. The excluded spouse was usually belligerent and made us go through the "how's" and "why's" of the first meeting all over again. The excluded spouse had no idea what was going on and was suspicious of us and his or her spouse. We spent twice as long as was necessary because we had to repeat ground that had already been covered. Because the excluded spouse was generally hostile, the ambience was ruined, and a fun exercise was turned into a chore.

Bring your spouse to the initial meeting with the lawyer. The only exception to this strict rule is when you do not want your spouse to know about your planning. If that is your situation, make no pretense of telling your lawyer that you are speaking for your spouse.

Interviewing the Lawyer

We use the phrase "interviewing the lawyer" because that is what you ought to be doing in the initial stages of your first meeting. The interviewing process begins as soon as you walk into the lawyer's office. How the reception room is kept up, the attitude of the receptionist, and the manner in which you are greeted are indications of what the lawyer is going to be like.

A dirty or shoddy reception room can be a sign that your lawyer is not very considerate of other people's feelings. If the receptionist or secretary who greets you is discourteous or uncaring, it is almost a sure thing that you will find the same attitude in the lawyer.

You should have to wait no longer than ten or fifteen minutes before you are ushered into the lawyer's office. If the wait approaches the fifteen-minute mark, you should inquire into the reason for the delay. If you cannot get a reasonable response or commitment as to when the lawyer will be ready to meet with you, it is time to leave.

Lawyers are busy and are not always in control of their calendars. However, you should not endure unreasonable delays or unfriendly treatment. Do not forget that you are hiring the lawyer; he or she is not hiring you.

The lawyer's demeanor should reflect courtesy and care. A convivial greeting may mean that you have found a person who is not under the gun and who has the time and the state of mind to concentrate on you and your Loving Trust. Regardless of whether he or she is busy or not, you have every right to expect that you will have his or her undivided attention during the course of your meeting.

There should be a minimum amount of time devoted to pleasantries about weather or hobbies, or "How about those Mets?" You are there for a purpose, and so is the lawyer. You have outlined that purpose on the telephone and in your letter confirming the appointment. Use the time wisely, and politely stick to the business at hand.

How the Lawyer Charges

Your first order of business should be to confirm how the lawyer is charging for your meeting. We do not believe that you should be charged for the first meeting or, at the very least, for the first hour or so of that meeting. You need to size one another up so that you can each decide whether you wish to work together.

You should also generally discuss the lawyer's billing procedure. Does the lawyer bill hourly, or does he or she have a set fee? There are very few situations where unexpected circumstances increase the number of hours needed to fully complete a Loving Trust. A fair fee should be quoted before the work begins, and you should have the opportunity to say "No, thank you" if it is more than you feel is reasonable or than you can afford.

If the lawyer normally bills hourly, we would suggest that you ask the lawyer to alter the normal billing procedure and quote a fee for your Loving Trust. If the lawyer insists on hourly billing, you should ask for a close approximation of the time he or she expects to devote to it and, of course, the hourly rate. Drafting a Loving Trust is not like a lawsuit where a lawyer has no control over the time it will involve. A lawyer should know the time it will take to prepare, explain, and get a Loving Trust signed. If that is not the case, you should extend your "Thank you, but no thank you," and find another lawyer.

One of the complaints that lawyers frequently hear these days is that they charge too much for pushing buttons on their computers; that they do not prepare documents, their machines do. Many people believe that computers do most of a lawyer's work; that the lawyer relies on boilerplate legal documents that are programmed into word processors; and that the lawyer does very little legal thinking. This is not an accurate picture.

We used to give our clients a tour of our word processing center. This was where our clients' Loving Trusts were produced. It contained all the boiler-plate that we had drafted and accumulated over the years. Our clients were somewhat taken aback when we actually admitted we used computers. They acted impressed, but we knew they were thinking, I suspected you guys had it made, now I know it. You just have a nonlawyer operator push a button and out comes a document. You sell paper by the pound and charge us full price, but your computers do all the work!

Knowing what they were thinking, we would say, "Every word in those computers is reviewed constantly by our lawyers. We are always updating and improving what we do. Can you imagine the time it has taken us to create all that legal boilerplate so that the computers can spit it back out? If we had to draft your Loving Trust from scratch and by hand—if we had to re-create all the words, phrases, and research just for your Loving Trust—your fee would be enormous. By using computers and word processors, we can spread the high costs of research and drafting over all our clients. They allow us to charge you far less than your Loving Trust is worth. Our technology allows us to spend more time with you, rather than on ministerial production functions. By using modern technology, we can give you your Loving Trust quickly and at a very fair price."

Don't complain when you see computers in your lawyer's office—rejoice. By having this type of technology, you can get a better Loving Trust at a lower cost. Drafting a Loving Trust with word processors is much more efficient and accurate than doing it by hand. Your lawyer can tailor his or her boilerplate to your Loving Trust needs, and eliminate wasted time on those aspects of a Loving Trust that do not have to be tailored for every client. Technology allows your lawyer to do a good job for you at a fair price and allows the lawyer to make a profit. There is nothing wrong with that. If your lawyer insists on reinventing the wheel, you're going to end up paying for its research and development.

Once you have discussed your lawyer's billing philosophy and method, do not expect that he or she will be able to quote you an exact fee at this juncture. In order to proceed, you still have to discuss your design parameters and make the commitment.

Getting Your Loving Trust Completed

Now is the time that your preparation will pay off. You should give your lawyer *My Checklist for Designing My Loving Trust* and *My Personal Information Checklist.* Explain to your lawyer that you want the Loving Trust described in *My Checklist for Designing My Loving Trust.* Remind your lawyer that you have done most of the design work and that you are there to have him or her review your checklists, point out any potential problems or opportunities you might have missed, and draft your Loving Trust.

Go over each of your checklists with your lawyer, emphasizing any information you think is particularly helpful to your lawyer's understanding of your Loving Trust. Ask any questions that you have with regard to your Loving Trust or trusts in general. This is the time for you to ask the lawyer *all* your questions.

Once your lawyer has reviewed the information in *My Checklist for Designing My Loving Trust* and *My Personal Information Checklist,* he or she should bring to your attention any opportunities or problems that he or she has spotted. Because you have given your lawyer complete information about your family, the design of your Loving Trust, and the property you own, he or she should be able to concentrate on the legal and tax implications of what you want to do and on the property you have to do it with. These are your lawyer's primary functions.

At this juncture of the first meeting, you and your lawyer should have an excellent idea of how your Loving Trust is designed, the elements it consists of, and what needs to be done to prepare your Loving Trust. Now it is time for the moment of truth—actually hiring the lawyer to prepare your Loving Trust.

The Fees and the Commitment

When you and your lawyer have agreed upon the terms of your Loving Trust, you should ask your lawyer how much it will cost. Your lawyer should know, based on the information you have provided, the amount of work required to draft your Loving Trust, and thus should be able to quote a fee. As we stated earlier, get a fee quote if possible. If he or she insists on hourly billing, get a range, with a promise that the Loving Trust will not exceed the top end.

If the fee staggers you, ask the lawyer why it is so high. See if you can find out from the lawyer why the fee is higher than you expected. It may be that you and your lawyer can work out a fee that is acceptable to both of you. Don't be afraid to question the fee and discuss it. Your lawyer is as interested in having you happy with the fee as you are.

We are frequently asked how much a Loving Trust should cost. Given the fact that fees vary dramatically from one locale to another, that is a tough question. However, through our seminars, we have been able to get some idea of what lawyers are currently charging for Loving Trusts.

Based on the information we have, it appears that about 90 percent of all Loving Trusts cost less than $1500. These Loving Trusts contain little, if any, federal estate tax planning. About half of these Loving Trusts cost $900 or less, because they are not particularly complex. The remaining 10 percent—usually prepared by attorneys who are tax and planning specialists— can cost anywhere from $1500 to an extreme of $50,000 or more for the humongous plan that involves tens of millions of dollars. If J. Paul Getty would have spent $50,000, he would have saved $27,000,000!

These fee estimates are based solely upon the drafting of the Loving Trust documents. They do not include the lawyer's time in transferring property into your Loving Trust, a topic we will discuss in Chapter Twenty-two, "How to Get Property into Your Loving Trust." These Loving Trust fees are more than reasonable. Keep in mind that probate fees can easily exceed 16 percent of smaller estates. Loving Trust fees are generally one of the great bargains to be found in a law office.

Should you and the lawyer not be able to agree on a reasonable fee, thank the lawyer for meeting with you and find another lawyer who will do the same work at a lower cost. It is no sin to decline a service that you feel costs more than you can afford or are willing to pay.

Once you have agreed upon the fee, you need to ask an additional question: "When will my Loving Trust be done and ready to sign?" No Loving Trust ought to take more than three weeks—or a month at the outside—to be completed. They are not that difficult to do if a lawyer is organized and has not overcommitted his or her time. If your lawyer cannot get your Loving Trust done in three weeks and set up a meeting for you shortly thereafter, you have the wrong lawyer. Except for vacation, illness, or other unavoidable delay, there is no excuse for taking longer than this to complete your work.

The actual preparation of your document is not that time-consuming. There is rarely any research required or any other process that should delay the work. If your lawyer is not willing to make a commitment to do your Loving Trust in this period of time, terminate your relationship before it starts and find a lawyer who wants your business and will get the work done in good time.

If you and your lawyer can agree on a deadline for completing your Loving Trust, you should also agree on the lawyer's retainer. Your lawyer has to commit people and other resources to the preparation of your Loving Trust. By requiring a retainer, your lawyer is assured that you have made a commitment too.

Your lawyer may not ask for a retainer; many do not. Whether your lawyer asks for a retainer or not, we believe that you ought to pay for your Loving Trust—in full—when it is completed to your satisfaction.

It is imperative that you and your lawyer schedule your next meeting before you leave his or her office. If you do not make a subsequent appointment at that time, you are asking for Murphy and procrastination to stall your Loving Trust. Keep the momentum going; set deadlines.

Make it clear to your lawyer that you do not want to see a "draft agreement" prior to your next meeting. When your lawyer sends you a "draft" of your Loving Trust, he or she is giving you a homework assignment—in effect, asking you to review it. Our clients were not interested in homework, and we assume you aren't either. You are not a lawyer, and you ought not have the responsibility for reviewing your lawyer's legal work. Your lawyer has all the information needed to successfully draft your Loving Trust. If your lawyer needs more information, he or she can call you. You will want your lawyer to review your entire Loving Trust document with you at the next meeting. You will then have the opportunity to ask your questions and to point out errors.

Confirm Your Agreement in Writing

You should confirm your agreement in writing within a few days after your meeting. It will put the burden on your lawyer to keep the commitments he or she made.

We have included a sample letter for you to pattern your letter after. It is well worth your time to write and send it. The letter is designed to protect both you and your lawyer from any misunderstanding that may have taken place as a result of your first meeting:

> [Date]
> [Heading]
>
> Dear [Lawyer's Name]:
> I enjoyed meeting with you and look forward to working with you on my Loving Trust.
> This letter is to confirm those agreements that we made in our meeting. For a total fee of ——, you are going to prepare my Loving Trust, based on *My Checklist for Designing My Loving Trust* that I discussed and left with you. On [date and time of day agreed at last meeting] I will meet with you in your office to review and sign my Loving Trust.
> If this is not your understanding, please get back to me as soon as possible.
>
> Sincerely yours,

The Last Meeting

We have deliberately chosen to call this second or follow-up meeting the last meeting. Except in extraordinary circumstances, no more than two meetings are necessary to discuss, agree to, and sign a Loving Trust. If you have completely filled in and presented *My Checklist for Designing My Loving Trust* and *My Personal Information Checklist,* two meetings are all that are needed to get the job done. Two meetings also conserve your lawyer's time and keep fees to a minimum.

Your last meeting should take no longer than two or three hours. It is likely to be somewhat longer than your first meeting because it will be devoted to reviewing your finished Loving Trust document. Your lawyer should take you through the entire document, answer your questions, and make needed corrections at that time. You shouldn't leave without signing your Loving Trust.

Don't forget to bring your spouse to your last meeting. You may also wish to invite your individual trustees to attend. The learning experience will be invaluable and will make them much better trustees. They can ask questions and become real participants.

You should also consider inviting your other advisers to this meeting. In Chapter Twenty-three, "How to Get Your Advisers Involved to Save Your Time and Money," we discuss just that.

Many times we have had last meetings where an insurance agent, accountant, or other adviser attended. These meetings were invariably more successful because of the adviser's participation. Whether other advisers attend or not is up to you, but you should allow them the opportunity to attend if you, and they, think it would be helpful.

Reviewing and Signing Your Loving Trust

Your lawyer should go through your Loving Trust with you. The review ought not to be a reading of the document word for word. Your lawyer should explain each paragraph in simple and easy-to-understand terms. As your lawyer reaches each part of your Loving Trust that presents one of your design alternatives, your lawyer should refer to *My Checklist for Designing My Loving Trust.*

You should also look at *My Diagram of My Loving Trust.* As your lawyer explains each subtrust, you can refer to the diagram and begin to become comfortable with how your Loving Trust is put together.

As you are taken through your Loving Trust, do not hesitate

to ask questions. Some of its legal phrases and terms may confuse you or be foreign to you. It is perfectly all right to ask questions about these confusing aspects of your Loving Trust.

As you and your lawyer review your Loving Trust, mistakes may be found. These can be typographical errors or substantive errors that change the meaning of your Loving Trust. Such errors, in this day of fast and efficient technology, can be corrected while you are in the lawyer's office.

After you and your lawyer have reviewed your Loving Trust, and you are comfortable with what it says, you should sign it.

You should sign a minimum of three Loving Trusts. Unlike a will, which should have only one original, a Loving Trust can have many duplicate originals. For your protection, you should have an original Loving Trust; so should your lawyer and your trustees. Who gets originals is up to you, but remember, you can have as many duplicate originals as you want.

You will also sign a "Pour-Over Will" and "Durable Special Powers of Attorney." Do not worry about these, they are just "fail-safe" mechanisms to make absolutely sure your property is put into your trust if you neglect to do so while you are alive and healthy. We will discuss these documents at length in Chapter Twenty-two, "How to Get Property into Your Loving Trust."

Finishing the Last Meeting

Once you have reviewed and signed your Loving Trust and the other documents related to it, there are still a few more matters to take care of. The first is a discussion you will have with your lawyer with regard to putting property into your Loving Trust. Chapter Twenty-two, "How to Get Property into Your Loving Trust," is devoted to explaining just how that is done.

Your lawyer can help you put your property into your Loving Trust. Your lawyer should review *My Personal Information Checklist* and point out any problem areas that may arise in doing this. He or she can answer any questions you may have about the procedure you must follow. You can either totally rely upon your lawyer to put your property into your Loving Trust, or you can involve him or her only on a limited basis.

The last order of your last-meeting business is to pay your

lawyer. As we previously mentioned, your commitment is to write a check for the services you received. You should also give him or her a sincere, "Thank you." This is just as important as being prompt in your payment. Your lawyer will very much appreciate your "Thanks." Many lawyers work for more than money, and this is especially true of Loving Trust lawyers.

If the Law Changes

You should ask your lawyer what happens if there is a subsequent change in the law that affects your Loving Trust. We are strong advocates of the position that by taking you on as a client, your lawyer should also take the responsibility for contacting you if there is a change in the law that affects your Loving Trust.

There have been very few changes in trust law as compared to other legal areas. Changes in trust law are extremely rare, and changes in the federal estate tax laws have not been so quick in coming as to be a burden to lawyers or their clients.

Your lawyer should contact you if there is a change in the law that affects your Loving Trust. He or she should also explain how it affects your trust, what needs to be done to make it current, and what the charge will be to get the amendment done. We have included a sample letter for you to use for this purpose.

[Date]
[Heading]

Dear [Lawyer's Name]:

I would like to thank you once again for preparing my Loving Trust. As you can imagine, I am vitally concerned that my Loving Trust is kept up-to-date with changes in the laws. While I recognize that I have a responsibility to apprise you of changes in my life that may affect my Loving Trust, I want to make sure that you will notify me whenever you believe a change in the law will affect my Loving Trust.

I will rely on you to keep me informed as to changes in the laws and with respect to your recommendations as well.

I understand that any changes I make in my Loving Trust will not be covered by my original fee and will be subject to a fee arrangement that we will agree on.

Sincerely yours,

Original Documents

When you leave your lawyer's office, take your original Pour-Over Will, your Loving Trust, and all your other original documents with you. Your lawyer can keep duplicate originals or copies of all the documents that he or she needs. There is no reason whatsoever to leave your original documents with the lawyer. You should keep them in your possession.

Since there will be several originals of most documents, and since they will be spread among several people, there is no reason to take special precautions to protect them. Keep them where you keep all your important papers. Do not put all of them in a safe-deposit box. If you die or become disabled, safe-deposit boxes can be difficult for other members of your family to get into.

You will have one original of your Pour-Over Will. Since there is only one original will, you should keep it in a safe place. If you have named an institutional trustee, it is likely that the institution will store a complete set of your documents, including your Pour-Over Will, in its trust vault, free of charge.

Make sure to tell your trustees and your beneficiaries where your original documents can be found. If anything happens to you, there should always be someone who knows where to look for your important papers. These precautions may seem a little silly, but the old saying that "an ounce of prevention is worth a pound of cure" certainly applies here.

Tune-ups

Our world is built around change. Circumstances change, people change, laws change. We cannot prevent change from occurring in our lives.

When changes occur that may affect your Loving Trust, it is quite simple to change or amend your Loving Trust to adapt to those changes. Unlike a will, a Loving Trust is made to readily accept change. Your lawyer can make such a change easily and quickly by preparing an amendment to your Loving Trust.

In most cases, a short letter to your lawyer explaining the change will enable the lawyer to draft it and send it back to you in a short period of time. There is generally no reason for a formal visit unless you want to redesign your Loving Trust on a massive scale. And, unless you have had major changes in your life, there is no reason for follow-up or regular visits.

If you take the time and make the effort to locate a good Loving Trust lawyer, and if you adequately prepare for your meetings with him or her, two meetings should suffice to create a Loving Trust that will serve your and your loved ones' needs for a long time to come.

22

How to Get Property into Your Loving Trust

Property that you own in your name, joint tenancy property, property owned in tenancy in common, and life insurance and retirement plan proceeds that name someone other than your Loving Trust as primary beneficiary will not be controlled by your Loving Trust. To make your Loving Trust work, you must get your property into it.

You have several choices as to how you can get your property into your Loving Trust. One choice is to do nothing and let the probate court do it. That choice is not acceptable to most of us. A Loving Trust is supposed to *avoid* probate, so letting the probate court put your property into your Loving Trust is self-defeating.

Another choice is for you to put property into your Loving Trust solely through your own efforts. That is what the traditional how-to books tell you to do. They give you a great number of forms to help you be your own lawyer. Norman F. Dacey, in *How to Avoid Probate!*, includes more than 550 pages of forms, and there is a coupon in the back to order even more! Most of these forms are written in complicated legalese that even most lawyers would find confusing. It is no wonder that most do-it-yourself legal forms invariably do not work.

Putting your property into your Loving Trust is easy only if you know what you are doing. Anyone who tells you differently doesn't have any idea of the legal problems and complexities that can arise if you don't do the job right.

If you have property in joint tenancy with right of survivorship, property in tenancy in common, life insurance, a retirement plan, a business, investments, or other types of property, you are talking about a potential nightmare if you attempt to transfer it into your Loving Trust without help. Good old Murphy and his Law will be knocking at your door for sure.

Let's put this into perspective. In probate, the court-appointed agent almost always retains a lawyer to do the work. Probate takes a great deal of time, but not always because some lawyer is dragging his or her feet. Many times the probate process is longer than it ought to be because of the difficulty in finding exactly what property is owned and where the title to the property is.

Think about what you own. You are lucky if you can find it, let alone its title. Imagine how hard it will be for someone else to do it when you are not able to help.

When you put property into your Loving Trust, you are, in effect, probating your own estate. It is a whole lot easier and cheaper to do your own probate while you are alive and well than it is to have someone else do it after you are disabled or dead. The trick to putting property into your Loving Trust is to get it done *quickly* and *correctly* at the lowest possible cost.

Make Someone Accountable

A Dacey or Stock trust may end up invalid because a do-it-yourselfer chose the wrong form, signed in the wrong spot, or made some other mistake. Sometimes, the do-it-yourself form is valid, but is incorrectly utilized. In either case, what was supposed to happen—avoiding probate—didn't, because Murphy took over.

Who suffers from all of these mistakes? Not the author of the do-it-yourself book. The author sold the book and is on to other projects. Not Murphy. He has triumphed once again and is stalking more victims. The only ones who suffer are the do-it-yourselfers and their loved ones. What recourse is there if do-it-yourselfers make a mistake that costs a lot of money? If they are alive but disabled, we suppose they could sue themselves, and if they are dead, their loved ones could sue the estate for that mistake.

Ridiculous? Of course it is. Since our do-it-yourselfer wanted to save a few dollars by practicing law using the "on the job training" method advocated by do-it-yourself authors, he or she could cost loved ones a great deal of heartache and money. Often those loved ones would be better off if the do-it-yourselfer had left a cheap will. Had an equally incompetent lawyer done the same bad job, the lawyer could be sued for malpractice and be held accountable.

We know of a lawyer who once was asked to do a favor for a neighbor. The neighbor owned a summer home in the mountains with two of his brothers-in-law. The neighbor liked one brother-in-law; the other "deadbeat" he disliked intensely.

The neighbor wanted to give his third of the summer home to the brother-in-law he liked. So what did the lawyer do? A deed was prepared, signed, and recorded giving the neighbor's third of the summer home to the deadbeat. Our story has a good ending: The lawyer and his malpractice insurance company straightened it out and compensated the neighbor for the lawyer's mistake.

The task the lawyer was given was simple and done as a favor, but the lawyer was held accountable and paid for his error.

The best way to put property into your Loving Trust is to use other people to do it for you. Use your advisers' expertise. Many of them will charge you little or nothing to put your property into your Loving Trust. Let them take the responsibility, the accountability, and the liability for putting your property into your Loving Trust. You do not have to work hard if you do this, *you just have to work smart.*

Work Smart, Not Hard

We have shown you how to design your own Loving Trust and how to get it prepared at the lowest possible cost. Our techniques for putting property in your Loving Trust will also keep your costs down. By working smart on the front end, you can let others do the hard work at little or no cost to you. Even if you have to pay to get some of the work done, it will be cheaper than trying to do it yourself or not doing it at all. Not putting your property into your Loving Trust, or not putting it in correctly, will cost you and your loved ones far more than paying a few dollars to get it done right.

Fill In My Personal Information Checklist

At the end of this book you will find *My Personal Information Checklist*. Be careful to list all your property as you fill it in. Do not worry about things that you own that are of little value. You can lump them together in the category we call "Other Personal Property." Concern yourself with your valuable property. Your residence(s), your business, investments, collections, jewelry, and other valuable property should be included in your checklist.

Locate the Titles to Your Property

Locate the titles to the property you have listed. For every type of property, there is a method of identifying who owns it. The word "title" is a sort of general, catchall term used to describe how property is owned. The term "evidence of title" is the actual document that shows title. For example, a car title is the piece of paper you look at to decide who owns a particular car. The document itself is the evidence of title. The name on the car title determines the car's ownership. Like a car title, there is some document or other evidence that identifies how most property is owned. If the document that evidences title cannot be found, neither you nor your lawyer will be able to determine ownership.

Cowboy movies show a great example of the use of title. Remember the ones where some outlaws steal a herd of steers and then try to sell them? Someone always says, "How do I know you own 'em?" The outlaws don't have their own brand or a bill of sale, of course, and the fight is on.

Ascertaining the title to your real estate, cars, and investments can be easy. If you have real estate, your deed is your title. Read the deed and you know whose name your real estate is in. For a car or other licensed vehicle, like a boat or a truck, look at your title. It works the same as a deed. Whoever's name is on the title is the owner. For stocks, your stock certificate is your title. For bonds, the bond itself is the title.

To locate the title to most of your property, you need only remember one thing:

> Your title to property is whatever document or documents you received when you bought the property and would need if you were to sell it.

If you made investments in partnerships, real estate trusts, or other more exotic property, you signed documents when you made your investment. These documents are your evidence of title. If you handle your investments through stockbrokers and they hold your investments, then your brokerage account is your evidence of title. Whatever you signed to set up the account is what you need to ascertain your ownership.

There are some types of property that are sold without legal documents passing hands. Let's use your bicycle as an example. When you sell it, you either get cash or a check. No one asks about title. If you buy a bike from a store, however, you are given a bill of sale, called a receipt. That is your title to your bike. If you later sell your bike, you really should give the buyer a bill of sale. Almost all personal property like bikes, clothes, and furniture are bought and sold using a bill of sale. That is what is used to transfer them from one person to another.

The same is true of collections, such as artwork or stamps, and most other forms of personal property. Sometimes you keep the bill of sale (receipt), sometimes you do not. If you do not, then your canceled check is your receipt and your proof of title to the property. If you pay cash, then "possession is nine-tenths of the law." The fact that you have the property in your possession means you probably own it.

To determine title to the property you possess, but for which you do not have a receipt or a canceled check, you need to look to who paid for it. If you paid for it out of your money, it is yours. If the money came from a joint account, then the property is owned jointly.

Bank accounts, savings accounts, certificates of deposit, and other cash investments are created by signing a signature card or other document establishing the account. Whatever you signed to set the account up is your evidence of title to that account.

Life insurance policies, disability policies, and retirement plans differ from most types of property when you are looking for the particulars of ownership. You will need to locate your life insurance policies and disability policies, along with the application you originally signed and any changes in the policies, called endorsements. It is on the application—not the policy—that you will find who owns it and who will receive the proceeds.

You must find the beneficiary designations for your insurance policies and your retirement plans. They are needed so that the proceeds can be directed into your Loving Trust.

To help you locate the title to your property, each category of property in *My Personal Information Checklist* explains what document is your evidence of title. For real estate, as an example, it is a deed. For a partnership, it is usually the partnership agreement. It has spaces for you to mark whose name your property is in. You will mark one of the following categories of ownership:

- Your Name Alone.
- Your Spouse's Name Alone.
- Joint Tenancy with Right of Survivorship (This includes Tenancy by the Entirety Property).
- Tenancy in Common.
- Community Property.
- Don't know.

By reading the various titles to your property, you should have little trouble figuring out who legally owns what. If you cannot, don't worry about it. Bring the documents that you think show title to your lawyer and get help. There is no reason for you to agonize over title. It takes three years of law school and a few years of experience for a lawyer to begin to understand title. Do not expect to be an instant expert. It takes a lot of training to understand the intricacies of property ownership. This is a major point that traditional do-it-yourself authors neglect to tell their unfortunate readers.

Your other advisers can be of great assistance in locating title to your property. If you cannot find the deed to your house or to your investment properties, contact the broker or lawyer who handled the purchase for you, the bank who provided the mortgage money, or the title company that helped close the sale. One or the other will likely have the deed or a copy of it. For stock or bond investments, contact the broker who sold them to you. For life insurance, contact your life insurance agent. For your group insurance, go to your personnel department or benefits office.

If you devote a little thought to how you acquired your property, you should be able to think of someone who can help you. Don't be shy in asking your advisers to do this. They will likely not mind doing it and will save you time and money. Please remember to work smart, not hard.

Know the Name of Your Loving Trust

Your Loving Trust will have its own "legal" name that will appear on the titles to property contained in it. The legal name of your Loving Trust must state the names of your trustees, your name as its maker, and the date the trust was signed. For example, a Loving Trust created by Franklin H. Cosbie, whose trustees are Franklin and his wife, Gretchen, would have as its name:

> Franklin H. Cosbie and Gretchen E. Cosbie, trustees, or their successors in trust, under the Franklin H. Cosbie Living Trust, and any amendments thereto, dated ——, 19—.

That's quite a name, and will take some getting used to. Like anything else, after you use it for a while, it won't seem so bad. Using the proper name of your Loving Trust is vital when you are putting property into your Loving Trust. Both you and your advisers must know your Loving Trust's legal name.

The proper name of your Loving Trust will appear in your Loving Trust itself if your lawyer uses our approach. If, for some reason, the name of your Loving Trust does not appear in your Loving Trust, ask your lawyer to write it down for you.

Property in Joint Tenancy with Your Spouse

As you locate your titles, you may find that you have property in joint tenancy with right of survivorship, or tenancy by the entirety, with your spouse. Joint tenancy, as we made clear earlier in this book, is not a good way to hold title to property.

Joint tenancy is a very complex method of owning property, even though it may not seem so on its face. You will be making a major mistake if you attempt to change your joint tenancy property to some other form of ownership by yourself. You should not make any attempt to transfer property held in joint tenancy without consulting with your lawyer.

Joint tenancy property offers special problems that can have far-reaching effects if improperly transferred to your Loving Trust. Before it is put into your Loving Trust, you must either put it into your name, your spouse's name, or in tenancy in common. Which of these alternatives is best for you is based on your age, your spouse's age, the nature of the property, and what it is worth. The quality of your marriage and other personal considerations also weigh heavily on how this property is to be titled.

A few minutes with a Loving Trust lawyer will go a long way in determining how your joint property should be transferred into your Loving Trust. Failure to correctly transfer this property can result in unfavorable tax results.

Community Property

In some community property states, you and your spouse will find it quite easy to create your own Loving Trusts and put your community property in them. However, in community property states like California, there are hidden traps for those who stumble along without proper advice. In California, use of a special joint Loving Trust for you and your spouse eliminates most of the problems that arise with regard to property transfers.

Willy-nilly transfers of community property can create havoc when funding a Loving Trust. A Loving Trust lawyer can quickly advise you how to properly transfer your community property to your Loving Trust.

If you live in a community property state and you have prop-

erty in joint tenancy with your spouse, there are some potentially devastating income tax results that can occur upon either
of your deaths. It is especially important for you to discuss with
your lawyer how title to this property should be changed, and
this is true whether or not you use a Loving Trust.

Joint Tenancy Among Nonspouses

Property held in joint tenancy between nonspouses definitely
needs to be examined by a lawyer. We have seldom, if ever,
seen a situation where nonspouses owned property in joint tenancy and it accomplished their objectives, or where its owners
fully understood the consequences. Once property is in joint
tenancy between nonspouses, transferring it out can create gift
taxes and other unexpected consequences. Worse yet, there
may be lingering gift tax problems from when the property was
originally put in joint tenancy! Real problems arise when nonspouses hold property in joint tenancy, and we strongly recommend that you ask your lawyer how he or she is going to
straighten them out.

Let Your Fingers Do the Walking

Once you know what you own and where the titles are, you
can decide which advisers will transfer what property into your
Loving Trust. You need only contact them and tell them what
you want done.

Rather than give you 550 pages of Dacey-like forms, we will
show you how all your property can easily, quickly, and inexpensively be put into your Loving Trust by professionals who
know what they are doing and *who will be accountable for their
actions.*

We have included sample letters for you to use that will put
the burden on your advisers and other people to transfer property into your Loving Trust. You should use these letters, or
ones like them, if you expect to get your property into your
Loving Trust and have a chance to hold the professional who
does it accountable. Always keep a copy of the letter you write
for your files. If you leave a good paper trail, you will not get
lost or ambushed by fast-talking professionals.

Your Lawyer

The professional with whom the transferring process begins is your lawyer. He or she will have the expertise to advise you on the best and most efficient methods of transferring your property to your Loving Trust.

Generally, the more property you have and the more valuable it is, the more you need to rely on your lawyer to help transfer it into your Loving Trust. If you have modest amounts of property, you will be able to rely more heavily on others for help. In either case, you should discuss the transferring process with your lawyer. Taking a little extra time with your lawyer to discuss any transferring pitfalls and opportunities will certainly save you time, money, and aggravation.

In most situations, there is no need to have your lawyer make every transfer of property into your Loving Trust. Lawyers are better and more efficient at transferring some types of property than others. They are particularly skilled at transferring real estate. For example, getting your residence, or any other real estate, out of joint tenancy and into your Loving Trust is a perfect use of a lawyer's talents.

Community property transfers should also be left to your lawyer, because of the income tax ramifications. Putting valuable personal property into your Loving Trust—jewelry, artwork, collections, and the like—is old hat to a lawyer. Closely held business interests, such as family corporations, partnerships, and sole proprietorships, should be transferred by your lawyer. In addition, copyrights, patents, and other rights to receive income, like accounts or notes receivable, are best transferred by your lawyer.

Your lawyer will also know about different devices used to transfer property into a Loving Trust. For example, some states have adopted a law called the Uniform Probate Code. The Uniform Probate Code is a liberal probate law that is intended to make probate easier and cheaper to do. Whether it has or not is very questionable, but among its by-products are some simple methods for putting property into a Loving Trust.

One such method for transferring property into a Loving Trust is a payable on death (POD) designation. It is a device that allows you to have a beneficiary designation for many kinds of property. Under a POD, the title can remain in your name. Upon your death, however, the property automatically passes to your Loving Trust. A POD is simple and effective. Ask your lawyer if your state allows you to use it.

A useful device for transferring real estate into a Loving Trust is called an unrecorded deed. Some states allow you to complete a deed that effectively transfers your real estate into your Loving Trust even though you do not record it. Your trustee can record it on your death or disability. The effect is to avoid probate and avoid the sometimes inconvenient process of actually recording the deed. If you have a substantial amount of real estate, an unrecorded deed can eliminate some of the hassles of putting real estate in a trust. This is a transfer method that you should ask your lawyer about.

There are many methods for transferring property into your Loving Trust. Your lawyer has the expertise to determine which is best for you. Ask your lawyer which property he or she should transfer and which property your other advisers can transfer.

Life and disability insurance proceeds, bank accounts, brokerage accounts, and retirement plan proceeds are some types of property that can be transferred into your Loving Trust by your other advisers. We will explain how this is done in the sections that follow. By working together as a team, you, your lawyer, and your other advisers can properly and quickly transfer your property into your Loving Trust at the lowest possible cost.

After you and your lawyer have an understanding of what property he or she will be transferring into your Loving Trust, ask your lawyer how much it will cost. Most lawyers will charge hourly for this work. This is a fair approach because there is no way, in most cases, for your lawyer to know in advance how long it will take to get the job done.

Your lawyer should be able to estimate how many hours it will take to transfer your property into your Loving Trust. Use his or her estimate as your cost benchmark, and tell your lawyer to contact you if it appears that this estimate will be exceeded.

If your lawyer has paralegals, the name given to highly trained nonlegal professionals who work for lawyers, then ask your lawyer if his or her paralegals can do the work. Legal secretaries can also be used to transfer property into a Loving Trust, and you should ask your lawyer if that is possible in your case. Ideally, you want secretaries or paralegals to do all the transfer work and your lawyer to review what they have done. This takes far less of your lawyer's expensive time, and uses your lawyer's skills in the most efficient manner. The billing rate of secretaries and paralegals is usually far less than your lawyer's.

When you retain your lawyer to transfer all or some of your property to your Loving Trust, you should confirm your understanding in writing.

[Date]
[Heading]

Dear [Lawyer's Name]:

In our meeting on [Date], we agreed that you would transfer property into my Loving Trust. We agreed that you would charge on an hourly basis and that you anticipate spending no more than ＿＿ hours. Should the time you need exceed this number of hours, you will contact me before proceeding. It is my understanding that you will use paralegals and secretaries as much as possible to make the transfers, and that you will be involved primarily in the supervision and review of the transfers.

The property that you will transfer to my Loving Trust will be all the property listed on *My Personal Information Checklist,* with which I furnished you, except the following property, which my other advisers will transfer for me:

_____

_____

_____

We both recognize that transfers to my Loving Trust should be accomplished as soon as possible to avoid

any problems should I become disabled or die; time
is of the essence.

Sincerely yours,

Much of your property can be transferred by other people.
Many of them will do so at no cost or at significantly less cost
than your lawyer.

Your Insurance Agent

One of the best, if not the best, of your inexpensive advisers
is your insurance agent. For the most part, insurance agents
work on a commission. While the amount of commissions varies,
depending on what you buy and how much you spend, insurance agents usually earn every dime that they get. Once you
buy a product through them, they will continue to service that
product free of charge.

You need to contact the insurance agent who sold you your
life or disability insurance policies. Tell your agent that you
want to change the beneficiary of your insurance to your Loving
Trust and that you want him or her to do it.

Your agent should furnish you with change of beneficiary
forms that he or she has already filled in. If they are blank, ask
your agent to complete them before signing.

Most insurance companies require that a primary beneficiary
and a contingent beneficiary be named on a beneficiary designation. The primary beneficiary will be your Loving Trust.
The contingent beneficiary can be anyone you want. Your contingent beneficiary will receive the insurance proceeds only if
you revoke or cancel your Loving Trust and forget to change
your primary beneficiary.

Here is a form letter that you can send to your insurance
agent.

[Date]
[Heading]

RE: Change of Beneficiary Designation for [Your
Name]

Dear [Your Insurance Agent's Name]:

Pursuant to our conversation of [Date], this letter is to confirm changing the beneficiary designation of the following [Life Insurance] [Disability] policies:

Insured   *Name of Company*   *Policy Number*

Please change the primary beneficiary of each of the policies to:

_____,
trustees, or their successors in trust, under the
_____ Living Trust, and any
amendments thereto, dated _____, 19__.

I am relying on you, as my agent, to perform all the appropriate steps to assure that my beneficiary designations are changed properly. Please notify me in writing when you have completed the changes.

Sincerely yours,

In most cases, your agent will be kind enough to change the beneficiary designation of all your policies, whether he or she sold them to you or not. However, if he or she declines to do so, you should seriously consider changing agents. If you do not have an insurance agent, contact the local representative of the insurance company who issued the policy and explain what you need done. You should confirm your conversation in writing.

[Date]
[Heading]

RE: Change of Beneficiary Designation for [Your Name]

Dear [Name of Person with Whom You Spoke]:

Pursuant to our conversation of [Date], I wish to change the beneficiary designations of the following policy(ies):

Insured   *Policy Number*

Please send me a Change of Beneficiary designation for each policy, as soon as possible, as I am doing personal planning for me and my family. Thank you for your prompt attention to this matter.

Sincerely,

If you have any questions about the beneficiary designations you receive from the insurance company, call and have them explained to you. Life insurance companies are in a people-oriented business, and it has been our experience that they go overboard to be courteous and kind. They will help you as best they can to solve any problems or answer any questions you may have concerning your beneficiary designations.

Some life insurance companies are very particular about how they allow a beneficiary designation naming a trust to read. They have determined their own rules and may reject your beneficiary designation. If this happens to you, take the path of least resistance and use their suggested language. The result will be the same and you will be spared the aggravation of taking on the company's red-tape bureaucracy.

You would be wise to have your lawyer quickly review these changes. This will assure you that the beneficiary forms have been completed correctly and that your lawyer will stand behind them in the event of an error.

For employer group policies, you will need to seek out the proper person in your company's personnel or benefits office. This person will have the proper forms for you to sign. If your company benefits representative is unsure about what to do, you should have him or her talk with either your life insurance agent or your lawyer. You can also request that your company's insurance agent contact you. You can be sure that he or she will know about what you want, and how to accomplish it.

Whether you use your company benefits representative or the company's insurance agent to change the beneficiary of your company insurance policies, confirm the change in writing. Here is a form letter that you can use to confirm your request:

[Date]
[Heading]

RE: Change of Beneficiary Designation for [Your Name]

Dear [Company Representative or Your Company's Insurance Agent]:

I wish to change the beneficiary designation of the following policy(ies) that I have as an employee of [Company Name]:

Type of Policy   *Policy Number*

Please change the primary beneficiary of each of the policies to:

_____,
trustees, or their successors in trust, under the _____ Living Trust, and any amendments thereto, dated _____, 19___.

Since I am doing Loving Trust planning, it is very important that these changes are made as quickly as possible. I am relying on you to do so. If you have any questions, please do not hesitate to contact me at your earliest convenience.

Thank you for your prompt attention to this matter.

Sincerely,

Avoid completing any change of beneficiary designation forms yourself. If all else fails, let your lawyer do them. If you provide your lawyer with the proper forms, he or she will have no difficulty in completing them for you. Your objective should always be to have a professional make the change so, if there is a mistake, you will have someone who is accountable to make you or your loved ones whole.

Your Stockbroker

Ask your stockbroker to change the name of your stocks and bonds into the name of your Loving Trust. For good customers, there will be no charge. If you're a light trader, or a nontrader, you will be charged a fee ranging from a few dollars to about twelve dollars for each certificate you have. This is far less than a lawyer would charge.

To change the name on your stocks, bonds, or other securities, your stockbroker will need your original certificates. Make certain you are given a written receipt for these certificates. Once endorsed by you, they may well be negotiable and easily stolen. To protect yourself and to hold your stockbroker accountable, do not leave any securities with your stockbroker without a written, signed receipt.

If you own stocks, bonds, mutual funds, money market funds, or any other investments through an account with a stock brokerage firm, changing the name of the account to the name of your Loving Trust will have the effect of putting everything in that account in the name of your Loving Trust. Accounts like this are called "Street Name" accounts. There is no charge that we know of for changing a street account name. It can be done with a few entries into the stockbroker's computer.

As always, confirm the change of account name or the change of the certificates themselves in writing. Make your stockbroker accountable exactly as you have your lawyer and your insurance agent. Here are two form letters for you to use. The first is for actual stock certificates or bonds. The second is for a change in the name of your account.

[Date]
[Heading]

RE: Name Change of Securities for [Your Name]

Dear [Name of Stockbroker]:

On [Date], I left certain securities with you so that you can transfer the ownership from me to the name of my Loving Trust. I have attached a copy of the receipt that you gave me, setting forth the securities that I left with you.

Please change the name on each of the certificates to: _____,
trustees, or their successors in trust, under the
_____ Living Trust, and any
amendments thereto, dated _____, 19___.

I am relying on you to make these transfers accurately and as soon as possible, as I am doing personal planning for me and my family. It is my understanding that you will charge me _____ for each certificate changed.

Please notify me in writing when you have completed the changes.

Sincerely yours,

For a change of account name only, use the following letter:

[Date]
[Heading]

RE: Change of Account Name for [Your Name]

Dear [Name of Stockbroker]:
On [Date], I requested you to change account number _____, which is currently in the name of [Current Account Name], to the name of my Loving Trust. The account name should now read:

_____,
trustees, or their successors in trust, under the
_____ Living Trust, and any
amendments thereto, dated _____, 19___.

I am relying on you to make this change in account name accurately and as soon as possible, as I am doing personal planning for me and my family. It is my understanding that there is no charge for this name change.

Please notify me in writing when you have completed the change.

Sincerely yours,

Tax shelters, limited partnerships, and other investments that you have made through your stockbroker can also be changed into the name of your Loving Trust by your stockbroker. Your stockbroker will either know how to do it or whom to contact to make the change. If you cannot locate the broker who sold you these investments, look at your investment information and write the promoter directly. You will be instructed by the promoter in how to accomplish a name change. Once again, you need to use a letter to assure that the proper change of name will be made.

[Date]
[Heading]

Re: [Name of Investment]

Dear [Name of Promoter]:

   On [Date], I telephoned you with regard to changing the name of my investment in [Name of Investment] to the name of my Loving Trust. Enclosed are copies of the documents I signed when I purchased the investment.

   The name of my Loving Trust is:

_____,
trustees, or their successors in trust, under the
_____ Living Trust, and any
amendments thereto, dated _____, 19___.

   Please change the name of my investment from me to the name of my Loving Trust and send me any documents that I must sign to make the transfer complete. I would appreciate your making this change as soon as possible, as I am doing personal planning for me and my family. Thank you for your prompt attention to this matter.

Sincerely yours,

If you have an IRA or Keogh plan with your stockbroker, or if you have purchased life insurance through your stockbroker, your broker can arrange to change your beneficiary designations. You should use the following letters to request and confirm that your stockbroker has the forms necessary to change your beneficiaries.

[Date]
[Heading]

RE: Change of Beneficiary Designation for [Your Name]

Dear [Name of Stockbroker]:
This letter is to confirm changing the beneficiary designation of the following life insurance policies:

Insured	*Name of Company*	*Policy Number*

Please contact the primary beneficiary of each of the policies to:

_____,
trustees, or their successors in trust, under the
_____ Living Trust, and any
amendments thereto, dated _____, 19____.
I am relying on you to take all appropriate steps to assure that my beneficiary designations are properly changed. Please notify me in writing when you have completed the changes.

Sincerely yours,

The form letter to use for changing the beneficiary for an IRA or Keogh plan:

[Date]
[Heading]

RE: Change of Beneficiary Designation for [Name of Retirement Plan and Account Number]

Dear [Name of Stockbroker]:
This letter is to confirm changing the beneficiary

designation for [Name of Retirement Plan and Account Number].

Please change the primary beneficiary to:

_____,

trustees, or their successors in trust, under the _____ Living Trust, and any amendments thereto, dated _____, 19___.

I am relying on you to take all appropriate steps to assure that my beneficiary designations are changed properly. Please notify me in writing when you have completed the changes.

Sincerely yours,

Stockbrokers are the most competent people in the world to transfer securities into your Loving Trust. When directed properly, they can do this work better, faster, and cheaper than either you or your lawyer could ever hope to.

Your Banker

You may bank at a bank, save at a savings and loan, or get credit at a credit union. No matter what kind of financial institution you use, there will be someone there who can help you transfer your accounts to your Loving Trust. Contact your customer service representative and explain that you would like to transfer all your accounts to your Loving Trust. The customer service representative can provide the proper forms to make the changes and can help you fill them in.

You can be of great help in this process by providing as much information as possible for each of your accounts, including the account number and the statement the bank or savings and loan sends you regarding the account's status. With this information, the service representative can determine the type of account you have and the best method for changing its name to that of your Loving Trust. The changes in the names of these accounts can be made quickly and without a lot of red tape.

A frequently asked question with regard to changing checking accounts to the name of a Loving Trust is whether or not the checks themselves have to have the name of the Loving

Trust on them. *They do not.* The checks can remain in the same name as you have now, regardless of whose name is on the signature card. No one has to know by reading your checks that you have a Loving Trust.

It is common for a relative or an older person to want to be able to sign checks on the older person's account. The solution used by most people is to put the account in joint tenancy. Since joint tenancy is a terrible way to own property, the alternative is to name the relative as a co-trustee with the older person. Each trustee can then be given the authority to sign checks. The older person still owns the account, which is now in the name of his or her Loving Trust. The relative and the older person can each sign checks on the account as trustees of the Loving Trust. When the older person dies or becomes disabled, the account is controlled by the Loving Trust. It does not pass to the relative by operation of law as it does with joint tenancy.

When you change the name of your accounts into the name of your Loving Trust, you should confirm the changes in writing. Here is a form letter for you to use:

[Date]
[Heading]

RE: Change of Name of Accounts for [Your Name]

Dear [Name of Customer Service Representative]:
     This letter is to confirm changing the name of the following accounts to the name of my Loving Trust:

Current Name on Account	*Type of Account*	*Account Number*

     Please change the name of each account to:

_____,
trustees, or their successors in trust, under the
_____ Living Trust, and any
amendments thereto, dated _____, 19___.
     I am relying on you to take all appropriate steps

to assure that my accounts are properly changed. Please notify me in writing when you have completed the changes.

Sincerely yours,

If you have an IRA or other retirement plan at your bank or other financial institution, then your customer service representative can also help you change the beneficiary designation of the plan to your Loving Trust. The service representative will provide the proper forms and will, in most cases, be happy to fill in the forms for you. To protect yourself and your loved ones in case of an error, again confirm in writing the change of beneficiary designation.

[Date]
[Heading]

RE: Change of Beneficiary Designation for [Name of Retirement Plan and Account Number]

Dear [Name of Customer Service Representative]:
This letter is to confirm changing the beneficiary designation for [Name of Retirement Plan and Account Number] to my Loving Trust.
Please change the primary beneficiary of my plans to: _____,
trustees, or their successors in trust, under the _____ Living Trust, and any amendments thereto, dated _____, 19___.
I am relying on you to take all appropriate steps to assure that my beneficiary designations are changed properly. Please notify me in writing when you have completed the changes.

Sincerely yours,

Your banker should be very familiar with Loving Trusts. Bankers work with trusts on a daily basis. If, for some reason, you have any problems with changing the name of your accounts and your financial institution has a trust department, ask to see a trust officer. A trust officer can intervene and help you to get the job done.

A Special Word About Retirement Plans

Some types of retirement plan beneficiary designations need special treatment if you want to name your Loving Trust as the beneficiary. Congress requires that for some retirement plans your spouse must approve changing your beneficiary designation. Each plan has its own kind of Spousal Consent Form to accomplish this.

If you have any doubt about the meaning of spousal consent, or if you do not understand it, the trustee of your retirement plan can explain it to you. If you are not completely satisfied with the trustee's explanation, ask your lawyer, accountant, or insurance agent; these people should have no problem explaining it to you.

When They Ask to See Your Loving Trust

Your Loving Trust is your private plan to provide for you and your loved ones. You can choose to show it to whom you want, and you can choose who will not see it. That is your choice.

Because trusts of all types are mysterious to many people, they tend to become cautious when dealing with a trustee. They have no idea why they should be cautious, but they are. They are comfortable dealing with an individual, a corporation, or a partnership, but they are seldom comfortable dealing with a trust through its trustees.

As you put property into your Loving Trust and work with it, people in the business world are going to ask, or even demand, to see a copy of your Loving Trust. Since your Loving Trust is private, and since it may be quite lengthy, it will not be very convenient to let others read or keep a copy of it. There are some excellent alternatives to showing your Loving Trust to every person who is nervous about doing business with it.

Some states allow an affidavit of trust. This is a one-page document that will satisfy everyone that your trust is "legal" without having to read it. You should check with your lawyer to see if your state provides for a trust affidavit.

In most instances, people doing business with your Loving Trust will be interested in seeing or knowing only a few things about it. They will want to know if it is really your Loving Trust, that you are one of its trustees, that you have the authority to act on its behalf, and that it is valid. By giving them copies of the following parts of your Loving Trust, you will satisfy their needs without giving them your Loving Trust:

- The title page, which shows your name as the maker and the names of your trustees.

- The signature pages, which show that your Loving Trust is valid.

- The Trustees Powers article of your Loving Trust, which describes the powers of the trustees.

This information should suffice for all purposes. There is no reason to show any other part of your Loving Trust to anybody. Your Loving Trust is a private document and should be kept that way.

There is a technique called a Nominee Partnership, which is a very effective device that is used to eliminate the need to tell anyone you even have a Loving Trust. It is a legal method to disguise your Loving Trust as a partnership, so nervous Nellies will not question you to death. We have written about how a nominee partnership works in *The Handbook of Estate Planning* and in our *A Loving Trust Compendium* for lawyers.

If you would like to keep your Loving Trust totally confidential, we strongly suggest that you discuss this technique with your lawyer.

Your Debts

Your Loving Trust has nothing to do with your creditors or what you owe them. You will still be liable for your debts whether you establish a Loving Trust or not. A Loving Trust is not used to avoid your creditors, either while you are alive or after you have died; it is used to avoid probate, provide for loved ones, and protect the property you leave to your loved ones from *their* creditors.

When you put your property into your Loving Trust, you do not have to put in your debts too. The law is very kind to your creditors, so transferring your property to your Loving Trust will not adversely affect their rights; you will still owe them whatever you owe them. In most cases, you do not have to notify your creditors that you are putting your property into your Loving Trust.

There is one instance where you may have to be somewhat careful. When you transfer mortgaged real estate to your Loving Trust, you should notify the mortgage holder. Sometimes they get upset when they see their collateral change hands, even if it is to a Loving Trust. Ask your lawyer before you make the transfer whether or not you should notify your mortgage holder. When in doubt, notify your lender. There is almost always no problem in making the transfer, and your notification can eliminate any misunderstandings that may arise.

What if You Do Not Put All Your Property into Your Loving Trust?

Some people are not very diligent about putting their property into their Loving Trusts. For some it is just too much of a hassle. Some people initially fund their Loving Trust and then neglect to keep it current by failing to put their new acquisitions into it. Other people just plain forget about putting some of their assets in it.

There are two methods to help insure that your Loving Trust will still control your property if you become disabled or die, even if you didn't manage to put all of your property into it. These "fail-safe" devices have helped many people throughout the years. You need both of them to protect you and your loved ones.

Durable Special Power of Attorney

Your lawyer should provide you with a Durable Special Power of Attorney as part of your Loving Trust package. A Durable Special Power of Attorney allows you to give others the power to transfer your property into your Loving Trust if you become disabled and are unable to do it yourself. This is where the "durable" comes from; the power survives your disability. For example, if you have a stroke that totally incapacitates you, and you have not transferred all your property into your Loving Trust, those people to whom you have given such a power can transfer your property into your Loving Trust for you. Durable Special Powers of Attorney are very effective and are valid almost everywhere.

Make sure that your Durable Special Power of Attorney is really "special." "Special" means that whoever you name can only transfer your property into your Loving Trust; they cannot sell, take, use, or give it to anyone. They can only put it in your trust, so that it can be administered pursuant to your Loving Trust instructions.

Some lawyers draft Durable Powers of Attorney that are general powers of attorney. *Do not sign one of these.* Limit the power of the people you name to one thing: the ability to transfer your property to your Loving Trust. Granting the holder any more power means you have lost control over your property. A general power of attorney, even if done in the guise of a Durable Power of Attorney, is dangerous and should be avoided.

Since Durable Special Powers of Attorney are limited to one function, you can give them to many people, although some states restrict them to relatives. Generally, the more you give out, the better chance there is that someone will always be available to transfer your property into your Loving Trust if you are disabled. Give one to your lawyer and one to your accountant. If you are close to your insurance agent, give one to him or her. Hand them out to relatives and to the trustees you name in your Loving Trust.

Durable Special Powers of Attorney, when limited to transferring your property into your Loving Trust, can only help you; they cannot hurt you. They are fail-safe devices to prevent probate on property you neglected to put in your Loving Trust.

Pour-Over Will

As much as we dislike wills, for every Loving Trust there must be a short, single-purpose, "fail-safe" will. For safety's sake, a special kind of will, called a "Pour-Over Will," must be signed so that property that you neglect to put in the name of your Loving Trust will end up in it after your death.

A Pour-Over Will simply says:

> I leave any property owned by me at my death, and not already in my Loving Trust, to my Loving Trust. Please have my executor put it in my Loving Trust.

Property in your name at your death is subject to probate. If you have not left a will leaving this property somewhere, it passes to your heirs as decided by the law of your state. Since you want your Loving Trust to control all your property after you die, you must provide that any property not in the name of your Loving Trust gets there through your Pour-Over Will. That's where it gets its name—any assets you forgot to put in your Loving Trust are poured over into it after your death.

Most states have a small-estate probate exemption. That means that if you do not put a small amount of property into your Loving Trust, this property will not have to go through the probate process. Say that you die with $10,000 worth of property that you forgot to transfer to your Loving Trust. In most states, this property can be transferred into your Loving Trust, if you have a Pour-Over Will, without a formal probate proceeding. Thus you can have the best of all worlds: the ability to forget a little bit of property and the opportunity to avoid probate. The amount of this small-estate exemption changes from state to state. Ask your lawyer what the amount is in your state.

It is always best to put all your property into your Loving Trust while you are alive and well. However, by using a Durable Special Power of Attorney and a Pour-Over Will, you can be doubly assured that you and your loved ones will still be able to take advantage of your Loving Trust instructions.

Your Loving Trust controls only the property that is in it. Putting your property into it may not be easy if you attempt to do so by yourself. By using our techniques, you can quickly and correctly get your property into your Loving Trust through utilizing the services of other people. By working smart, you can keep the time and dollar costs of doing so to an absolute minimum. You can also assure yourself that if mistakes are made, someone other than you or your loved ones will pay to correct them.

23

How to Get Your Advisers Involved to Save Your Time and Money

By properly using your advisers in the implementation of your Loving Trust, you should be able to save time and money and end up with a superior Loving Trust product.

We certainly advocate a "team" approach when designing a Loving Trust. Unfortunately, the public often views more than one professional as too many people on a single shovel. Sometimes this is true, but just as often it is not. Knowing how and when to use each of your advisers in the Loving Trust process is the key to saving time and money.

You May Want to Use Other Advisers

Reading this book will make you knowledgeable. It will not make you a certified Loving Trust specialist. It is very likely that you will have many questions that we have not raised or answered. We cannot anticipate and write about every conceivable method of designing and implementing your Loving Trust. We can only give you general principles, examples, and solutions.

If you have a relatively simple design for your Loving Trust and you understand its basics, you will only need a lawyer to answer a few of your questions, to draft your trust, and to help you put property into it. If you have a lot of questions, you may need to talk with your life insurance agent or accountant. You may also wish to talk with stockbrokers or financial planners, or you may want to seek the services of your bank's trust department before you meet with your lawyer. By receiving this "coaching" prior to meeting with your lawyer, you may be able to better communicate your Loving Trust desires.

Different advisers offer different planning perspectives. Professional advisers have a tendency to present a limited number of planning strategies to their clients. This is not done out of laziness or incompetence. It is the product of their education, experience, and background. By asking questions of all your advisers, you will elicit different opinions and get the benefit of many points of view. This will allow you to expand your horizons and give you greater insight into the Loving Trust alternatives that are best for you.

Lawyers do not have a monopoly on teaching trust law and estate planning. They are not your only source of information when it comes to designing your Loving Trust.

Professional advisers other than lawyers can often be profitably consulted in the design and implementation of your Loving Trust. In our experience, many nonlawyer advisers have a very strong working knowledge of trusts and are better at explaining and recommending trust-planning strategies than many lawyers.

Before we go on, we would like to emphasize that no matter how knowledgeable your nonlegal advisers may be, do not allow them to draft your Loving Trust. Only lawyers may draft Loving Trusts. Anyone else who does it, other than yourself, is breaking the law. Drafting legal documents without a license is a crime in every state. Doing it yourself is not a crime, it's just criminal.

Which Advisers to Involve

There are a number of professionals available to help you with the process of designing your Loving Trust. These are basically the same advisers who can help you put your property into your Loving Trust. They are your:

- Life insurance agents
- Trust officer
- Stockbroker
- Financial planner
- Accountant

They each have a specific professional function and perspective, and if properly utilized, can offer you much help in the design of your Loving Trust.

Your Life Insurance Agent

Loving Trusts work better when they have real-dollar fuel in them. Insurance proceeds represent that real-dollar Loving Trust fuel that will provide the cash it takes to support and care for your loved ones in the case of your untimely disability or death. It is the most inexpensive and most effective method of getting real-dollar fuel into your Loving Trust that we know of. It would be wise for you to involve your life insurance agent in designing your Loving Trust.

Many life insurance agents have had formal training in Loving Trusts, trusts in general, or estate planning. Life insurance companies have traditionally offered excellent training programs in these areas for years. In addition, national organizations, like the American College of Life Underwriters, offer extensive courses to life insurance professionals on all aspects of trust and estate planning. Those life insurance agents who have graduated from the American College are allowed to use the letters "CLU" (Chartered Life Underwriter) after their names, indicating that they have graduated from a thorough insurance and planning curriculum.

Many life insurance agents do not have a CLU designation yet have expertise in Loving Trust techniques. You should ask your agent what training he or she has had in the areas of Loving Trusts, trusts in general, and estate planning. You may be pleasantly surprised at just how much expertise your agent has.

A number of life insurance companies offer their agents a service known as advanced underwriting. Advanced underwriters are highly trained home-office employees whose sole function is to aid agents with clients having tough life insurance, tax, and other planning problems. If your agent does not know the answers to your questions, it may be that he or she represents a company with a strong advanced underwriting department that can be utilized to answer them and to help you design and implement your Loving Trust. Your agent should make these home-office experts available to you at no additional cost.

You should interview your life insurance agent much as you would your lawyer. It would be helpful if you could work with an agent who has some expertise in Loving Trusts or who has access to insurance company home-office experts who do. Your life insurance agent should be very much a part of your Loving Trust advisory team.

The more knowledgeable your life insurance agent is about Loving Trusts, the more likely it is that you will receive the correct answer to your questions and planning concerns for your loved ones. And the more likely it will be that your insurance portfolio will fit your family's needs.

Trying to be your own insurance agent is as dangerous as trying to be your own lawyer. In an effort to reduce the cost of life insurance, many life insurance companies have started to sell directly, through magazine and newspaper advertisements, to the consumer, without using a trained life insurance agent. Life insurance, like the law, is complicated. Because there are so many different types of policies and so many companies, it is almost impossible to know what policy and company is best for any given situation. Using an agent may mean you will pay slightly more for your life insurance, but the service and advice you get will more than make up for the extra cost. Life insurance agents are one of the better advisory bargains.

You should contact your agent early in the design stage of your Loving Trust. When you meet with your agent, tell him or her exactly what you are doing and that you would like him or her to help you design your Loving Trust.

It is likely that your life insurance agent will ask for some personal information. By giving him or her good information, you will make it easier for your agent to help you. Give him or her a copy of *My Personal Information Checklist*. If you are uncomfortable doing so, you should start searching for another agent.

Your agent should be able to explain how a Loving Trust works and how it can be used to provide for you and your loved ones. He or she should also have a working knowledge of the federal estate tax and how it may affect you and your family.

By far the most important input your life insurance agent

can give you—other than the amount and type of life insurance that you need—is his or her ideas on providing for loved ones. We have given seminars to many top life insurance agents all over the country. Their greatest strength, other than knowing their products, is their feeling for and knowledge of people. Life insurance agents are people-oriented.

Your life insurance agent should be familiar with the Loving Trust concept. It will help if the two of you are talking the same language. If you have to bring your agent up-to-speed, it will not delay your progress a great deal. Life insurance agents are used to studying; it will not take long for him or her to understand the concepts in this book.

We teach select members of the life insurance industry and have been impressed with their Loving Trust commitments. We encourage you to have a life insurance agent as one of your key advisers.

For the price of buying insurance protection, which you likely have or need anyway, you can enlist this knowledgeable adviser on your Loving Trust team. If you do not have an agent you are comfortable with, take the time to interview others. Find one you like who knows what he or she is doing. Together, you can design a Loving Trust that meets your needs and specifications and that has the proper amount of real-dollar fuel to make it work.

Your Trust Officer

Trust companies and banks with trust departments are wonderful sources of Loving Trust advice. Trust officers are well versed in trust law and in the day-to-day practicalities of how they work. They are competent to answer most all of your Loving Trust questions.

Trust officers offer a different design perspective. Where a life insurance agent will encourage planning for loved ones and will emphasize the love in your Loving Trust, trust officers will view your Loving Trust more from a business or operational perspective. They will be more concerned with complexity of administration, investment strategy, and liability issues. They will dwell on Loving Trust mechanics.

Many, if not most, trust officers are lawyers. If they are not lawyers, they will still have had considerable training in the creation and operation of trusts. Trust departments usually have large staffs that contain many trust specialist experts. If the person you talk to cannot answer your questions, he or she should be able to seek out fellow employees who will surely be able to.

Trust officers are in the business of operating and administering trusts. They want your business, which is why they will be more than willing to meet with you to discuss your Loving Trust thoughts without charge. Trust officers want you to name their institution as a trustee. You represent new business to the trust officer and his or her financial institution.

Trust departments and trust companies charge by taking a percentage of the value of the property they administer as their annual fee. This percentage is usually less than 2 percent, making them a real bargain in the marketplace. They would not charge this fee until your Loving Trust is activated on either your disability or death, or if you choose to have them be your trustee to manage your property now.

If you would like to discuss your situation with a trust officer, you should contact your bank or local trust company to set up an appointment. If your bank does not have a trust department, find the names of those that do. You do not have to bank at an institution in order to use their trust department's services. Institutional trustees offer a unique public service. They are staffed with professional people who will treat you both politely and kindly.

When you meet with a trust officer, please keep in mind that trust officers have many trusts to administer and that they have a limited amount of time. Prepare for the meeting by writing down the questions you wish to ask. Explain that you are in the process of designing a Loving Trust and that you are considering naming a financial institution as one of its trustees. Be sure to bring your copy of this book; again, you need to be talking the same language. The trust officer must be familiar with your Loving Trust goals to be an effective adviser.

A trust officer can be of service to you in several ways. He or she can help you understand how a Loving Trust works and what you can do to provide for loved ones. The trust officer can answer legal and nonlegal questions concerning trust law and your Loving Trust. He or she can offer invaluable experience in how a Loving Trust operates and how it can be administered. A trust officer can help you locate the Loving Trust lawyers in your community. Finally, a trust officer can help you transfer many types of property into your Loving Trust.

Traditionally, there is no fee for these implementation services. They are rendered as both a public service and as an inducement to you to name their bank as one of your trustees. When designing your Loving Trust, do not overlook the valuable services of a trust officer.

Your Financial Planner

There is a great deal of confusion as to what a financial planner is and what one does. We do not expect the confusion to dissipate until this relatively new breed of adviser is somehow licensed and controlled. Lack of licensing has made the selection and use of those who hold themselves out as financial planners somewhat risky.

Generally, financial planners analyze and make recommendations about almost every aspect of their clients' financial lives. Some of the services that they provide include family budgeting, choosing and managing investments, ways and means of building wealth, and estate planning. Financial planners come from all walks of life; they may be accountants, life insurance agents, lawyers, or even people who just believe they have expertise or experience in finances.

There are institutions that teach and offer certificates to people who desire to be financial planners. Once a financial planner has graduated from the American College, for example, he or she may use the designation ChFC (Chartered Financial Consultant). A financial planner may also belong to professional associations such as the International Association of Financial Planners.

You must be very careful in selecting a financial planner. Even those recommended by friends or other advisers should be subject to your most careful scrutiny. Make sure that anyone you are considering is certified or chartered and that he or she has the background and experience to assist you. Always ask for a resume and a list of references. Do not hire anyone until you have thoroughly checked his or her references.

Once you have gone through the preliminaries of establishing his or her credentials, you should immediatly inquire how that financial planner charges for his or her services.

Financial planners generally charge for their services in one of three ways. Some charge solely on a fee or hourly basis, much like a lawyer or an accountant. You should ask what the fee is and how it is determined. Your first consultation should be at no charge.

Other financial planners receive their compensation from commissions generated by the investment products they sell. These include life insurance, stocks, bonds, and investments of all types. These planners make money only if you buy, so they would like your business only if you are a buyer, not a looker. It is not uncommon for these types of financial planners to charge a minimal fee for the preparation of your master financial plan. This plan will have suggestions as to what investments you ought to make and sometimes even the amount of life insurance you need. The financial planner will then offer to sell you the products that your plan suggests you need.

Some financial planners charge both a fee and take commissions. Many of them will offset their fee by the commissions they earn, in effect giving you a fee rebate if you buy their products.

A financial planner who is well versed in Loving Trusts may very well save you money by being able to answer those nonlegal questions that you would otherwise ask your lawyer.

If you have a financial planner who is up-to-date on Loving Trusts, it will greatly facilitate your ability to quickly and successfully complete your Loving Trust planning. If you do not have a financial planner, there is no need to hire one just for Loving Trust planning.

Like an insurance agent, your financial planner can help you create and design a Loving Trust. Even though oriented to the financial side of planning, good financial planners are people-oriented. It is not by accident that some of the better financial planners are also members of the life insurance profession.

Your Stockbroker

Many brokerage firms offer free seminars concerning "Estate Planning." This topic encompasses wills and trusts, as well as related investment areas including life insurance. These seminars can prove to be the perfect opportunity to have many of your Loving Trust questions answered. Local lawyers are frequently the guest speakers at these seminars. They will offer their views on estate planning, trust planning, probate avoidance, and related planning areas. While not all the lawyers may understand the Loving Trust approach, you should be able to ask meaningful questions of them if you attend such a gathering. This will allow you to receive some "free" legal advice and facilitate your understanding.

The lawyers and other speakers who conduct these seminars are compensated by the sponsoring brokerage firm. They are free to you. They, just like the brokerage firm, hope to attract clients from the audience. These seminars may be a good place for you to find a lawyer.

Stockbrokers sometimes provide financial planning services for their clients. Their knowledge of Loving Trust planning goes well with their overall financial acumen. The larger brokerage firms sometimes have lawyers on their staffs who can assist the broker and his or her client with Loving Trust design.

The services offered by stockbrokers are usually not free unless you are a very good client. Fees vary. Sometimes they are hourly and sometimes they are set at a predetermined amount. Make sure you know in detail what services are provided by your stockbroker and how much they cost before agreeing to an engagement.

Unless you know your broker well, do not lean too heavily on him or her for guidance in the design of your Loving Trust. He or she has other things to do in order to make a living.

Your Accountant

If we could realistically do it, we would require that all our clients have an accountant. An accountant's objectivity, knowledge, and skills are very useful when confronting some of the financial problems that life has to offer. We have always encouraged our clients' accountants to get involved with us early in the Loving Trust process.

Accountants invariably charge by the hour, and their rates are usually very reasonable for the service they provide. The hourly rate charged by all but the most sophisticated accountants is usually well below that charged by lawyers.

Accountants understand the need for proper Loving Trust planning. They have been advocates of probate avoidance and providing for loved ones for many years. They have traditionally been major advocates of Loving Trust planning.

An accountant is invaluable in the Loving Trust process. This is because he or she usually knows more about his or her client than the clients know about themselves. If you have an accountant, you are far more likely to have more contact with him or her than with all your other advisers combined.

If you are single and you are worth in excess of $600,000 or if you and your spouse have property worth more than $600,000, we strongly suggest that you have an accountant as one of your Loving Trust advisers. Accountants are usually well versed in the federal estate tax aspects of Loving Trusts and can be very helpful in federal estate tax planning. We are confident that they are competent in this area because we wrote an American Institute of Certified Public Accountants' course on *Estate and Gift Taxation.* Having a professional to "run the numbers" will help you save time and money in the Loving Trust process.

Your accountant can help you and your lawyer transfer property to your Loving Trust. Many times we have had clients' accountants work with us in locating title to property and making sure it was transferred into our clients' Loving Trusts. Accountants are used to keeping good records, and they keep track of your transactions in great detail. They are invaluable when it comes to knowing the specifics of your financial life.

You do not need a team to design and implement your Loving Trust. You and your lawyer can do it very successfully together. We have found, however, that by using other advisers, you can make the process of designing and implementing your Loving Trust much more efficient—and a great deal more fun. By properly using your various advisers' talents, you can also keep your time and dollar outlays to an absolute minimum.

Authors' Note

We have shared our feelings and our Loving Trust knowledge with the hope that you can readily apply it in providing for your loved ones. We strongly believe that you can control your property and design the essence of your loving desires by using the techniques in this book.

We have tried hard to provide you with professional insights that will enable you to find and select the right lawyer for you. We have also shared our beliefs with respect to getting the best out of your other advisers. We believe strongly in professionalism and in the good that can come from working with professional men and women who care.

When we lecture, we often hand out a critique form to our audience, in effect asking them to tell us how we did. We would very much appreciate your taking the time to respond likewise. We care very much about the efficacy of the Loving Trust, and we want to improve upon our ability to share it with others.

If you would share your Loving Trust trek and your experiences—both good and bad—with us, we would be grateful. We care a great deal about how you fare in finding and selecting a lawyer. We would sincerely like to know if you ran into problems we did not forewarn you of. We would like to know: Did you get cooperation from your insurance agent or accountant? Was the bank trust officer what we said he or she would be? Was your lawyer's fee fair and his or her work to your satisfaction? Were you able to successfully design your trust consistent with your love? Above all else, WE CARE; please write and share your experiences with us. Address us at Viking Penguin Inc., 40 West 23rd Street, New York, N.Y. 10010.

We hope that you enjoy your Loving Trust walk and that your Loving Trust manifests your love as much as ours have for Liz, Karen, Rob, James, Andy, and Eric.

With loving trust,
Bob and Renno

My Personal Information Checklist

Date of Preparation ____ ____ ____

MY:

Full Legal Name _____

Nickname _____

Home Address _____

_____

_____

Home Phone (____) _____

Birth Date ____ ____ ____

Occupation/Title _____

Employer _____

Business Address _____

_____

_____

Business Phone (____) ____ ____

MY SPOUSE'S:

Full Legal Name _____

Nickname   _____

Birth Date   ____ ____ ____

Occupation/Title   _____

Employer   _____

Business Address   _____

                                   _____

                                   _____

Business Phone   (____) _____

MY CHILDREN:

Full Legal Name	Birth Date
_____	____ ____ ____
_____	____ ____ ____
_____	____ ____ ____
_____	____ ____ ____

MY SPOUSE'S CHILDREN:
(If different from mine)

Name	Birth Date
_____	____ ____ ____
_____	____ ____ ____
_____	____ ____ ____
_____	____ ____ ____

MY OTHER DEPENDENTS:
(Friends or relatives who depend on me for all or part of their support.)

Name   Relationship

_____   _____

_____   _____

_____   _____

_____   _____

QUESTIONS ABOUT YOU AND YOUR FAMILY:

You should fully brief your attorney on the following matters:

1. Do you have a child with a learning disability?
2. Do any of your children receive governmental support or benefits?
3. Do you have adopted children?
4. Do any of your children have special educational, medical, or physical needs?
5. Are any of your children institutionalized?
6. Are you or your spouse receiving social security or disability benefits?
7. Do you wish to disinherit any of your children, grandchildren, or other relatives?
8. Whom do you wish to be the primary guardians of your children?
9. Whom do you wish to be the contingent guardians?
10. Have you been divorced?
11. Are you making payments pursuant to a divorce or property settlement agreement?
12. Have you been widowed?
13. On what date were you married?
14. In what states have you lived while married to your current spouse? During what periods of time did you reside there?
15. Have you or your spouse ever filed federal gift tax returns?
16. Have you or your spouse completed previous will, trust, or estate planning?
17. Did you and your spouse ever sign a pre- or post-marriage contract?

HOW MY PROPERTY IS OWNED

This checklist is designed to help you list all the property you own and how it is titled. You may own more property than can be listed on this checklist. If so, use extra sheets of paper to list your additional property.

Immediately after the title heading for each kind of property is a brief explanation of what document or documents you will need as evidence of title to your property. Remember, having these documents is essential in transferring property to your Loving Trust. By collecting this documentation yourself, you will save substantial professional fees.

How you own your property is extremely important for purposes of properly designing and implementing your Loving Trust. For each property category, there is a column titled "How It's Owned." When filling in this column, use the following abbreviations:

For property owned in your name alone, use	MINE
For property in your spouse's name alone, use	SPOUSE
For property in joint tenancy with your spouse, use	JTS
For property in joint tenancy with someone other than your spouse, use	JTO
For property in tenancy in common with your spouse, use	TCS
For property in tenancy in common with someone other than your spouse, use	TCO
For community property, use	CP
If you can't determine how the property is owned, use	?

CASH ACCOUNTS
[Evidence of title: signature card or the document you signed to set up the account.]

How It's Owned

CHECKING ACCOUNT:

_____   _____

Institution where located

_____

Account Number

SAVINGS ACCOUNT:

_____   _____

Institution where located

_____

Account Number

CERTIFICATE OF DEPOSIT:

_____   _____

Institution where located

_____

Account Number

MONEY MARKET:

_____   _____

Institution where located

_____

Account Number

LIFE INSURANCE AND ANNUITIES
[Evidence of title: the policy itself, including all endorsements and amendments, and the original application you signed.]

How It's Owned

_____   _____

Name of Insured

_____

Company Issuing Policy

Type of Policy

(Is the policy whole life, universal life, single premium life, an endowment policy, an annuity, group term life, or some other type of policy? If you cannot tell, either call your insurance agent or bring the policy to your attorney for review.)

Policy Number

Primary Beneficiary

Contingent Beneficiary

DISABILITY INSURANCE

[Evidence of title: the policy itself and the application you signed.]

How It's Owned

Name of Insured

Company Issuing Policy

Policy Number

Beneficiary

(If you cannot find a beneficiary designation, either call your insurance representative or bring the policy to your attorney for review.)

RETIREMENT PLANS

[Evidence of title: summary plan description, documents you signed to set up the plan, account statement, beneficiary designation.]

How It's Owned

IRA:

Primary Beneficiary

Contingent Beneficiary

PROFIT-SHARING PLAN

_____   _____

Primary Beneficiary

_____

Contingent Beneficiary

PENSION PLAN

_____   _____

Primary Beneficiary

_____

Contingent Beneficiary

OTHER TYPES OF RETIREMENT PLANS

_____   _____

Type of Plan

_____

Primary Beneficiary

_____

Contingent Beneficiary

PUBLICLY TRADED STOCKS, BONDS, AND OTHER SECURITIES
[Evidence of title: Stock certificate, bond instrument, the documents you signed to set up a street account or a copy of the statement, documents you signed when purchasing the security.]

How It's Owned

STOCKS:

_____   _____

Name of Company

_____

Number of Shares

_____

Certificate Number

BONDS:

_____   _____

Name of Company

_____

Face Amount

_____

Identifying Number

OTHER SECURITIES:

_____   _____

Name of Company

_____

Amount

_____

Identifying Number

STREET NAME ACCOUNT:

_____   _____

Name of Brokerage Firm

_____

Account Number

NON–PUBLICLY TRADED INVESTMENTS, TAX SHELTERS*
[Evidence of title: documents you signed to purchase each investment or tax shelter.]

How It's Owned

_____   _____

Name of Investment

_____

Name of Broker or Promoter

_____

Type of Investment or Shelter

*Includes limited partnerships, REITs, and all other investments where you are not an active participant

NOTES, CONTRACTS, AND OTHER RECEIVABLES
[Evidence of title: promissory note, written contract, or other documents creating right to receive payment.]

How It's Owned

_____   _____

Person/Company Who Owes You

_____

Face Amount of Obligation

_____

Due Date

REAL ESTATE, INCLUDING YOUR RESIDENCE
[Evidence of title: deed or land contract (do not use mortgage or tax assessment).]

How It's Owned

_____   _____

Address or Description of Property

MY OWN BUSINESS
[Evidence of title: stock certificate, partnership agreement, or any other documents that you believe created your business entity.]

How It's Owned

CORPORATION:

_____   _____

Name of Corporation

_____

Type of Stock (Common or Preferred)

_____

Certificate Number

_____

Number of Shares

PARTNERSHIP:

_____   _____

Name of Partnership

_____

General or Limited Partnership

_____

Percentage Owned

SOLE PROPRIETORSHIP

(Since a sole proprietorship has no actual title to it, you must list all bank accounts and property owned in the name of the business for the purpose of determining title. If property used in the sole proprietorship is in your name, list it in this section rather than elsewhere.)

_____   _____

Name of Business

TANGIBLE PERSONAL PROPERTY*

[Evidence of title: Registration or title issued by your state, bill of sale, receipt, canceled check, or source of cash to purchase property, gift tax return, or inheritance tax return if you received property by gift or inheritance.]

How It's Owned

_____   _____

Description of Property

---

*Tangible personal property includes motor vehicles, boats, jewelry, collections, antiques, furs, and all other nonbusiness personal property.

OTHER PROPERTY*

[Evidence of title: documents you signed to purchase the property, documents you received when you received the property, or any other document you have that shows you own the property.]

How It's Owned

_____   _____

Brief description of property

---

*Other Property is any property that you have that does not fit into any listed category. For example, patents, royalties, and mineral interests, such as oil and gas could be listed here.

Index